# SPIRITUAL GEMS

D1521046

First Edition:  Kindle Direct Publishing          March 2017

Spiritual Gems

## Dedicated To

My Spiritual Parents: Revered Bauji (Jaswant Singh) &
Mataji (Charanjit Kaur)

And

My Parents: Major Balwant Singh and Surjit Kaur

## Table of Contents

## Introduction

SPIRITUAL GEMS are a collection of the sayings of the
Guru's Word (known as *Gurbani or Bani*) from the Sikh
Holy Scripture, "Guru Granth Sahib". "Granth" meaning, the
big holy book and "Sahib" implying high authority.

As I read the Holy Scripture, several verses or portions
deeply moved me.  A huge sigh escaped from me as I
realized that such a treasure is mostly unknown to my fellow,
Americans!  I began building note cards over a five-year
period and organized these in the form of "Spiritual Gems".
I then structured them under fifteen major headings
applicable to our daily lives.

To help you appreciate the Spiritual Gems, I am providing a
little history of the Indian Gurus and their journey in creating
the Sikh Holy Scripture Guru Granth Sahib.

The word "Guru" means the enlightened one or teacher who
removes darkness and ushers in light.  The word *"Sikh"
means disciple/student /learner.  In the Indian heritage, the
Guru/Student relationship is ingrained very deep; almost all
the Gods and Demi-Gods had their Gurus, including Lord
Krishna and Lord Rama.  Guru Nanak, the first Sikh Guru
(1469-1539) introduced the word "Gur' meaning "Guru" in
the Holy Scripture at the start meaning God Himself.  Hence
all references in the Scripture to the word Guru imply God or
the Wordless Word, mentioned as *Naam/Shabad.*

Guru Nanak, who kept his own writings in a diary called *"Pothi"* started the Holy Scripture compilation. He carried it with him on all his travels which were very extensive throughout India including Kashmir and, the Middle East, Mecca, Tibet, and parts of China. Guru Nanak's purpose was to disseminate the "Truth of Oneness of God", and move people away from Ritualism and Idol worship. During these travels, he also collected the holy writings of many famous saints of that time, including Baba Fareed, Kabir, Namdev, Ravidas and others, which are included in the Guru Granth Sahib. All this literature passed through the hands of the Second, Third, and Fourth Gurus each of them adding their own *"Bani"*, but still using the name Nanak. Finally, the Fifth Guru, Guru Arjan Dev also included his own *"Bani"* under the name Nanak and compiled it in the form of "Adi Granth", (Adi meaning first). He arranged all the literature in a meticulous order with a special numbering system so that no alterations in the future could be made.**

In 1604, the first reading of the "Adi Granth" was done at Harmadar Sahib, popularly known as the Golden Temple, the Sikh holy center like the Vatican. Here it was read in the presence of Guru Arjan Dev, with Baba Buddha a Sikh Saint presiding as the head priest.

In 1706, Guru Gobind Singh, the Tenth Guru dictated the entire Adi Granth to Bhai Mani Singh a Sikh Saint and included the Bani of Guru Teg Bahadur, the Ninth Guru. This 1432 Page Holy Scripture was titled "Guru Granth Sahib" to which Guru Gobind Singh bowed down in obedience and proclaimed," From now on the Guru Granth Sahib, the Wordless Word, Naam/Shabad/ as included in the Holy Scripture is The Guru and there shall be no other bodily Guru". From this point in time to the present, all Sikhs regard this as the "Eternal Living Guru".

The greatness of Guru Granth Sahib is in the fact that it is all poetry written in praise of God; most of the text is in 31 musical Raggaas. The holy versus if sung in the specified Raaga can facilitate the mind in becoming tuned to the underlying spiritual message. The Raggaas are of great significance in the Indian music system. Bhai Mardana (born muslim but considered to be the first Sikh) played Rabab (A type of guitar) and accompanied Guru Nanak on most of his travels. It is said that whenever Guru Nanak felt God's Word coming, he will say to Mardana, play the Rabab and the Guru will sing. Guru Nanak has mentioned in several versus "Anhad Dhuni", the Celestial Music as the binding force for all existence; human ears cannot hear it, but it can be heard within when you are connected to Your True Self.

The *Gurbani* (The versus of the Guru's Word) describes Love as the true religion and explains God's love for us, the humans, in human terms. It highlights that all human beings can have direct access to God without rituals or priests. God is addressed as the Beloved, Husband, Friend, Father, Mother, and many other adorations of Love. He is described to be within us, closer than hands, and everywhere outside. There is One and only One God and we are all His children; all pots made from the same clay. To emphasize the equality of all before God, the Holy Scripture includes writings of more than twenty Saints belonging to other religions and, of both lower and higher castes.

Ego is described to be the big barrier in our realizing the Truth. It can only be overcome by accepting the Divine Will in its totality which dawns on us upon achieving self-realization, called Anubhav in *Gurbani*.

The Guru Granth Sahib is fully treated by all Sikhs as the Living Guru. The scripture is respected by keeping in decorative wrappings, placed on a *palanquin* with overhead ceiling hung awning symbolizing the Infinite. The first words as read in the morning is called *hukamnama* and become "order of the day" for guidance. At the Golden Temple, singing praises of the Lord (*Keertan*) as included in the *Gurbani* is done almost 24 hours.

As you read the Spiritual Gems, I hope you will find the same understanding, joy and enlightenment that I have found. A step further, applying this great treasure even partially can lead to a much happier and rewarding life. Read and enjoy!

Humbly,
Shiv Singh

*The Sikhs' current worldwide population is approximately 30 million, 80 percent of which live in the State of Punjab, India; US Sikh population estimated to be slightly under one million. Development of the Sikh Faith occurred over a two-hundred fifty-year period starting with the advent of Guru Nanak, the first Guru 1469, and culminating in the installing of Guru Granth Sahib as the Guru by Guru Gobind Singh the Tenth Guru in 1708.

Conscious awareness of God, living a family life through honest work, and sharing your bread are the three cornerstones of a Sikh's life. The movement endured untold miseries including torturing of the Fifth Guru, Guru Arjun Dev to death by making him sit on a burning hot plate and pouring of hot sand on his head, beheading of the Ninth Guru, Guru Teg Bahadur (Guru Gobind Singh's father), killing of several Sikh Saints by equally or worse tortuous methods, killing of innocent women and children, etc. All this was done by the Mogul rulers who wanted to convert all of India by force to Islam, but the Sikh movement offered resistance.

Guru Gobind Singh, the Tenth Guru eventually formed the Khalsa (the Pure) in 1699 through baptizing the Sikhs (administering Ambrosial Nectar) and proclaimed that fighting in self-defense is also Godly. He prescribed the keeping of a sword, unshorn hair neatly tucked under a turban and having natural beard as dress codes for the saint soldiers. In addition, Sikh men shall have Singh (meaning lion) as the last name and women, Kaur (meaning princess) as the last name. This was done to instill a new spirit for the Sikhs to be able to stand up to the prevailing tyranny.

Subsequently the Khalsa was largely instrumental in removal of the tyrannous Mogul rulers and establishing the Sikh empire under

Maharaja Ranjit Singh, which included the territories of Punjab, Kashmir, Afghanistan, Tibet, and parts of China.

**The Sixth, Seventh, and Eighth Gurus in the Ten Gurus lineage did not write any *Bani*.  Guru Gobind Singh, the tenth Guru also wrote *Bani* extensively, which forms a separate scripture called the "Dasam Granth".

The Ten Gurus Lineage:

| First Guru: | Guru Nanak Dev | 1469-1539 |
|---|---|---|
| Second Guru: | Guru Angad Dev | 1539-1552 |
| Third Guru: | Guru Amar Das | 1552-1574 |
| Fourth Guru: | Guru Ram Das | 1574-1581 |
| Fifth Guru: | Guru Arjan Dev | 1581-1606 |
| Sixth Guru: | Guru Har Gobind | 1606-1644 |
| Seventh Guru: | Guru Har Rai | 1644-1661 |
| Eighth Guru: | Guru Har Krishan | 1661-1664 |
| Ninth Guru: | Guru Teg Bahadur | 1665-1675 |
| Tenth Guru: | Guru Gobind Singh | 1675-1708 |
| Eternal Guru: | Guru Granth Sahib | 1708-Onwards. |

## Forward

"Spiritual Gems" authored by Shiv Singh, whom I have intimately
known for over 25 years both as a person and colleague is a breath
of fresh air in the current environment, and reinforces our faith in
the omnipresence of God; a quote, "God has been from the
Beginning, is Now, and shall be Forever; The Infinite Lord is
never Born and never Dies". It says that we are all capable of
having a direct relationship with our Creator through inculcating
His awareness, being thankful to all His giving, and above all
loving Him, through His Grace. A quote, "One whose heart is
filled with Faith in God; the essence of spiritual wisdom is
revealed to him".

The message of love is common with that of Christ and possibly
other faiths, but many quotes in the Sikh Scripture are given in a
unique way to drive home the central theme of love and are
applicable to our daily lives. God is depicted as a loving entity like
a husband loves his wife, or a mother or father love their child; He
is always benevolent, forgiving, and caring, because we are all His
children. What He is hungry is of our love and that we abide by
His Will. The visible world is not the reality as everything in it
changes; He never changes and hence is the only Reality.

Our "ego" of the me, mine, is the biggest block in our path to
realizing Him. This does not mean that we do not aspire to
accomplish lofty goals and creativity in our lives; in fact, the living
of a family life truthfully, earning bread with honesty, and helping
others are described to be the cornerstones of the spiritual path. A
quote, "Truth is high but higher still is truthful living". The
emphasis is on our looking inwards and watch the workings of our

mind; it's the mind which pulls us away from the spiritual, a quote "win the mind and win the world".

On the other hand, we are reminded of the universal laws of "As you sow, so shall you reap" and that we are fully responsible for our own actions. An example of the contradictions, "one who plants acacia trees and wishes for grapes, or someone spinning wool but wishing to wear silk!"

True friends are quoted to be the ones in whose presence, God comes to mind. The same holds true of relationships, an example, "husband and wife are not who merely live under one roof, but only those who have two bodies but a single bond of the same eternal light"!

It is said that there is no difference between a Saint and God, a quote "O' Lord, you are me, and I am You; what kind of difference there is? Just the same as between gold and the gold bracelet, or as between water and the waves".

Examples of the ultimate stage of coming into God's presence, "upon coming Face to Face with Him, I lost all my senses and have been thrown upside down!" Another, "The Lord has shot me with His arrow and I fell to the ground with a hole in my heart!

You, being the company I have kept over the years and it has brought me closer to my faith and relationship with God.

This book is a highly-recommended reading for all those interested in pursuing a spiritual path or otherwise leading a fulfilling life.

David N. Hunt

## Chapter-1  Humility & Simplicity

O' my mother, by what virtues can I meet my Lord; I have none?  I am not pretty, am illiterate, devoid of any strength and have come from a faraway land (after going through many incarnations).  I have no wealth nor wisdom; O' God, I am an orphan, have mercy, please unite me with You. Searching and searching, I have gone insane, and am dying of the thirst to see You!

ਰਾਗੁ ਗਉੜੀ ਪੂਰਬੀ ਮਹਲਾ ੫
ਕਵਨ ਗੁਨ ਪ੍ਰਾਨਪਤਿ ਮਿਲਉ ਮੇਰੀ ਮਾਈ ॥੧॥ ਰਹਾਉ
ਰੂਪ ਹੀਨ ਬੁਧਿ ਬਲ ਹੀਨੀ ਮੋਹਿ ਪਰਦੇਸਨਿ ਦੂਰ ਤੇ ਆਈ ॥੧॥
ਨਾਹਿਨ ਦਰਬੁ ਨ ਜੋਬਨ ਮਾਤੀ ਮੋਹਿ ਅਨਾਥ ਕੀ ਕਰਹੁ ਸਮਾਈ ॥੨॥
ਖੋਜਤ ਖੋਜਤ ਭਈ ਬੈਰਾਗਨਿ ਪ੍ਰਭ ਦਰਸਨ ਕਉ ਹਉ ਫਿਰਤ ਤਿਸਾਈ ॥੩॥
Raag Gauri Poorbi Mahla 5: Kawan gun pranpat milon meri maii,(1)
Pause: Roop heen budh bal heeny mohey pardesan door the aaii;(1)
Nahin darab na joban maati mohe anath ki karo smaii;(2)
Khojat khojat bhai bairagan prabh darshan kao haun phirat tesaii;(3)   Page-204

One, who considers himself lowest to others is, actually, higher than everybody.  One, who deals with everybody most humbly, recognizes God's presence in everyone.

---

ਗਉੜੀ ਸੁਖਮਨੀ ਮਹਲਾ ੫ ॥
ਆਪਸ ਕਉ ਜੋ ਜਾਣੈ ਨੀਚਾ ॥ ਸੋਉ ਗਨੀਐ ਸਭ ਤੇ ਊਚਾ ॥
ਜਾ ਕਾ ਮਨੁ ਹੋਇ ਸਗਲ ਕੀ ਰੀਨਾ ॥ਹਰਿ ਹਰਿ ਨਾਮੁ ਤਿਨਿ ਘਟਿ ਘਟਿ ਚੀਨਾ ॥

Gourree Sukhamanee 5th Guru |
Aapas Ko Jo Jaanai Neechaa |Sooo Ganeeai Sabh Thae Oochaa |
Jaa Kaa Man Hoe Sagal Kee Reenaa |Har Har Naam Thin Ghatt Ghatt Cheenaa |    Page-266

The Simmel tree is straight as an arrow; it is very tall, and very thick.  But the birds which fly to it with hopes to find food, depart disappointed, as its fruits are tasteless, its flowers nauseating, and even the leaves are bitter. Sweetness and humility, O' Nanak, are the essence of virtue and goodness.  Everyone bows for selfish reasons; bowing is of the mind not the body.  When something is weighed on the balancing scale, the side that heavy is lower.

---

ਸਲੋਕੁ ਮਹਲਾ ੧ ॥
ਸਿੰਮਲ ਰੁਖੁ ਸਰਾਇਰਾ ਅਤਿ ਦੀਰਘ ਅਤਿ ਮੁਚੁ ॥ ਓਇ ਜਿ ਆਵਹਿ ਆਸ ਕਰਿ ਜਾਹਿ ਨਿਰਾਸੇ ਕਿਤੁ ॥
ਫਲ ਫਿਕੇ ਫੁਲ ਬਕਬਕੇ ਕੰਮਿ ਨ ਆਵਹਿ ਪਤ ॥ ਮਿਠਤੁ ਨੀਵੀ ਨਾਨਕਾ ਗੁਣ ਚੰਗਿਆਈਆ ਤਤੁ ॥
ਸਭੁ ਕੋ ਨਿਵੈ ਆਪ ਕਉ ਪਰ ਕਉ ਨਿਵੈ ਨ ਕੋਇ ॥ ਧਰਿ ਤਾਰਾਜੂ ਤੋਲੀਐ ਨਿਵੈ ਸੁ ਗਉਰਾ ਹੋਇ ॥
Salok First Guru |
Sinmal Rukh Saraaeiraa Ath Dheeragh Ath Much |
Oue J Aavehi Aas Kar Jaahi Niraasae Kith |
Fal Fikae Ful Bakabakae Kanm N Aavehi Path |
Mithath Neevee Naanakaa Gun Changiaaeeaa Thath |
Sabh Ko Nivai Aap Ko Par Ko Nivai N Koe |
Dhhar Thaaraajoo Tholeeai Nivai S Gouraa Hoe |    Page-470

O' Nanak, when a person humbly meditates on God with love and devotion, salvation is attained.

---

ਮਹਲਾ ੧ ॥
ਭਾਉ ਭਗਤਿ ਕਰਿ ਨੀਚੁ ਸਦਾਏ ॥ਤਉ ਨਾਨਕ ਮੋਖੰਤਰੁ ਪਾਏ ॥੨॥
1st Guru |
Bhaao Bhagath Kar Neech Sadhaaeae |Tho Naanak Mokhanthar Paaeae |2|    Page-470

---

O' my mind, become the lowest of the low, the very least of the tiny, and speak in utmost humility, so that God may then begin to like you.

---

ਦੇਵਗੰਧਾਰੀ ਮਹਲਾ ੫ ॥
ਮਨ ਜਿਉ ਅਪੁਨੇ ਪ੍ਰਭ ਭਾਵਉ ॥ ਨੀਚਹੁ ਨੀਚੁ ਨੀਚੁ ਅਤਿ ਨਾਨ੍ਹਾ ਹੋਇ ਗਰੀਬੁ ਬੁਲਾਵਉ ॥੧॥
Devgandhari 5th Guru ॥
Man, jion aapne prabh bhavo;
Neecho neech neech att nanah hoi greeb bulavo.(1)    Page-529

Those who are false within, but wear the image of goodness on the outside, may bathe at the sixty-eight sacred shrines of pilgrimage, but their filth can never be removed. On the other hand, who wear the silk of humility and love on the inside, but rags of detachment on the outside, are truly good. They are in love with God and are always thirsting to see God.

---

ਮਹਲਾ ੧ ॥
ਅੰਦਰਹੁ ਝੂਠੇ ਪੈਜ ਬਾਹਰਿ ਦੁਨੀਆ ਅੰਦਰਿ ਫੈਲੁ ॥ ਅਠਸਠਿ ਤੀਰਥ ਜੇ ਨਾਵਹਿ ਉਤਰੈ ਨਾਹੀ ਮੈਲੁ ॥
ਜਿਨ੍ਹ ਪਟੁ ਅੰਦਰਿ ਬਾਹਰਿ ਗੁਦੜੁ ਤੇ ਭਲੇ ਸੰਸਾਰਿ ॥ ਤਿਨ੍ਹ ਨੇਹੁ ਲਗਾ ਰਬ ਸੇਤੀ ਦੇਖਨ੍ਹੇ ਵੀਚਾਰਿ ॥
1st Guru |
Andharahu Jhoothae Paij Baahar Dhuneeaa Andhar Fail |
Athasath Theerathh Jae Naavehi Outharai Naahee Mail |
Jinh Patt Andhar Baahar Gudharr Thae Bhalae Sansaar |
Thinh Naehu Lagaa Rab Saethee Dhaekhanhae Veechaar |    Page-473

Make your mind work hard like a farmer, high character the tilling of land, good deeds the water, and your, body the farm. Then, sow the seed of God's Name, patience to cover the seed from desires, and simplicity the fence for its protection. In this manner with His Grace, the seed within you will sprout with Love and you will see how many other hearts have become rich with this wealth. O' my friend, the worldly wealth (Maya) does not go with anyone, still it has bewitched everybody. Only the very few understand the secret, that the real wealth that goes with you is God's Name.

---

ਸੋਰਠਿ ਮਹਲਾ ੧ ॥

ਮਨੁ ਹਾਲੀ ਕਿਰਸਾਣੀ ਕਰਣੀ ਸਰਮੁ ਪਾਣੀ ਤਨੁ ਖੇਤੁ ॥ਨਾਮੁ ਬੀਜੁ ਸੰਤੋਖੁ ਸੁਹਾਗਾ ਰਖੁ ਗਰੀਬੀ ਵੇਸੁ ॥

ਭਾਉ ਕਰਮ ਕਰਿ ਜੰਮਸੀ ਸੇ ਘਰ ਭਾਗਠ ਦੇਖੁ ॥੧॥

ਬਾਬਾ ਮਾਇਆ ਸਾਥਿ ਨ ਹੋਇ ॥ਇਨਿ ਮਾਇਆ ਜਗੁ ਮੋਹਿਆ ਵਿਰਲਾ ਬੂਝੈ ਕੋਇ ॥ ਰਹਾਉ ॥

Sorath 1st Guru |

Man Haalee Kirasaanee Karanee Saram Paanee Than Khaeth |

Naam Beej Santhokh Suhaagaa Rakh Gareebee Vaes |

Bhaao Karam Kar Janmasee Sae Ghar Bhaagath Dhaekh |1|

Baabaa Maaeiaa Saathh N Hoe |

Ein Maaeiaa Jag Mohiaa Viralaa Boojhai Koe |Pause|    Page-595

O' God, I cannot survive by being shy of asking you; if You do not give, I will beg. If I am hungry, I cannot meditate; here take away Your string of beads (used to make the mind still). Please give me two pounds of flour, a quarter pound of butter, some salt, and a pound of lentils; these will be enough for me to eat two times daily. I also need a cot, mattress, a pillow, and a quilt to cover myself; to becoming carefree of the body's needs. I can then concentrate in meditating on You. Says Kabeer, I have not shown any greed in asking for these basics; though in truth I am in Love with You and only then I have come to Know You.

---

ਰਾਗੁ ਸੋਰਠਿ ਬਾਣੀ ਭਗਤ ਕਬੀਰ ਜੀ ਕੀ ॥

ਭੂਖੇ ਭਗਤਿ ਨ ਕੀਜੈ ॥ ਯਹ ਮਾਲਾ ਅਪਨੀ ਲੀਜੈ ॥

ਮਾਧੋ ਕੈਸੀ ਬਨੈ ਤੁਮ ਸੰਗੋ ॥ ਆਪਿ ਨ ਦੇਹੁ ਤ ਲੇਵਉ ਮੰਗੋ ॥ ਰਹਾਉ ॥

ਦੁਇ ਸੇਰ ਮਾਂਗਉ ਚੂਨਾ ॥ ਪਾਉ ਘੀਉ ਸੰਗਿ ਲੂਨਾ ॥ਅਧ ਸੇਰ ਮਾਂਗਉ ਦਾਲੇ ॥

ਮੋ ਕਉ ਦੋਨਉ ਵਖਤ ਜਿਵਾਲੇ ॥੨॥ ਖਾਟ ਮਾਂਗਉ ਚਉਪਾਈ ॥ ਸਿਰਹਾਨਾ ਅਵਰ ਤੁਲਾਈ ॥

ਊਪਰ ਕਉ ਮਾਂਗਉ ਖੀਂਧਾ ॥ ਤੇਰੀ ਭਗਤਿ ਕਰੈ ਜਨੁ ਥੀ.ਧਾ ॥੩॥ਮੈ ਨਾਹੀ ਕੀਤਾ ਲਭੋ ॥

ਇਕੁ ਨਾਉ ਤੇਰਾ ਮੈ ਫਬੋ ॥ਕਹਿ ਕਬੀਰ ਮਨੁ ਮਾਨਿਆ ॥ ਮਨੁ ਮਾਨਿਆ ਤਉ ਹਰਿ ਜਾਨਿਆ ॥੪॥੧੧॥

Raag Sorath, Bani Bhagat Kabir JI Ki:

Bhukhey bhagat na keejay. Yeah mala apni leejay. Madho kaisi baney tum sangay. Aap na deho tan levao mangey(2). Pause.

Duey ser mangon chuna. Pao ghio sang loona.

Adh ser mangon daley. Mo kau dono waqhat jiwaley.(2)

Khat mango chaupai. Sihrana awar tulai.

Upar kao mangon khidha. Teri bhagat karey jan beedha.(3)

Mai nahin keeta labbo. Ikk nao tera mai phabo.

Kahey Kabir man manya. Man manya tau har janiya.(4;11) Page-654/56

# Humility and Simplicity

Some say, God is very near to us, others say that He is far away; but to reach a conclusion with just discussions, is like a fish trying to climb a palm tree. O' brother, why are you trying to show off your intellectual knowledge of religious writings, etc. He, who has found God, keeps quiet about it, and does not try to invite attention to gain any recognition.

ਟੇਢੀ ਬਾਣੀ ਭਗਤਾਂ ਕੀ ਨਾਮਦੇਉ ॥
ਕੋਈ ਬੋਲੈ ਨਿਰਵਾ ਕੋਈ ਬੋਲੈ ਦੂਰਿ ॥ਜਲ ਕੀ ਮਾਛੁਲੀ ਚਰੈ ਖਜੂਰਿ ॥੧॥
ਕਾਂਇ ਰੇ ਬਕਬਾਦੁ ਲਾਇਓ ॥ਜਿਨਿ ਹਰਿ ਪਾਇਓ ਤਿਨਹਿ ਛਪਾਇਓ ॥੧॥ ਰਹਾਉ ॥
Ttoddee Baanee Bhagathaan Kee Naamadhaeo |
Koee Bolai Niravaa Koee Bolai Dhoor |
Jal Kee Maashhulee Charai Khajoor |1|
Kaane Rae Bakabaadh Laaeiou |
Jin Har Paaeiou Thinehi Shhapaaeiou |1|Pause |    Page-718

Blessed is the straw hut in which God's praises are sung; but the palace in which God is forgotten is worthless. In the Company of the Holy (*Saadh Sangat*), even poverty is a bliss, because in that aura God Consciousness prevails. The worldly glory in which man is engulfed by Illusion (*Maya*) may as well perish. In poverty, grinding corn and wearing a coarse blanket; one can find bliss as the mind is at peace. On the other hand, silk and satin may be worthless, if they lead to greed.

---

ਰਾਗੁ ਸੂਹੀ ਮਹਲਾ ੫ ॥
ਭਲੀ ਸੁਹਾਵੀ ਛਾਪਰੀ ਜਾ ਮਹਿ ਗੁਨ ਗਾਏ ॥ ਕਿਤ ਹੀ ਕਾਮਿ ਨ ਧਉਲਹਰ ਜਿਤੁ ਹਰਿ ਬਿਸਰਾਏ ॥੧॥ ਰਹਾਉ ॥
ਅਨਦੁ ਗਰੀਬੀ ਸਾਧਸੰਗਿ ਜਿਤੁ ਪ੍ਰਭ ਚਿਤਿ ਆਏ ॥ ਜਲਿ ਜਾਉ ਏਹੁ ਬਡਪਨਾ ਮਾਇਆ ਲਪਟਾਏ ॥੧॥
ਪੀਸਨੁ ਪੀਸਿ ਓਢਿ ਕਾਮਰੀ ਸੁਖੁ ਮਨੁ ਸੰਤੋਖਾਏ ॥ਪਾਟ ਪਟੰਬਰ ਬਿਰਥਿਆ ਜਿਹ ਰਚਿ ਲੋਭਾਏ ॥੩॥
Raag Soohee 5th Guru |
Bhalee Suhaavee Shhaaparee Jaa Mehi Gun Gaaeae |
Kith Hee Kaam N Dhhoulehar Jith Har Bisaraaeae |1| Pause |
Anadh Gareebee Saadhhasang Jith Prabh Chith Aaeae |
Jal Jaao Eaehu Baddapanaa Maaeiaa Lapattaaeae |1|
Peesan Pees Oudt Kaamaree Sukh Man Santhokhaaeae |
Paatt Pattanbar Birathhiaa Jih Rach Lobhaaeae |3|   Page-745

O' God, some have the false support of another and yet another; but mine, the meek and humble, You, are the only One. Until You abide in my heart, why should I not die crying? O' Lord, I am lowly as a worm, how can I sing Your glories and great praises? You are beyond our reach, but full of Mercy and Yourself unite us with You at Your own pleasure.

---

ਸਲੋਕ ਮਹਲਾ ੨ ॥
ਕਿਸ ਹੀ ਕੋਈ ਕੋਇ ਮੰਞੁ ਨਿਮਾਣੀ ਇਕੁ ਤੂ ॥
ਕਿਉ ਨ ਮਰੀਜੈ ਰੋਇ ਜਾ ਲਗੁ ਚਿਤਿ ਨ ਆਵਹੀ ॥੧॥
ਪਉੜੀ ॥ਹਉ ਕਿਆ ਸਾਲਾਹੀ ਕਿਰਮ ਜੰਤੁ ਵਡੀ ਤੇਰੀ ਵਡਿਆਈ ॥
ਤੂ ਅਗਮ ਦਇਆਲੁ ਅਗੰਮੁ ਹੈ ਆਪਿ ਲੈਹਿ ਮਿਲਾਈ ॥
Salok 2nd Guru |
Kis Hee Koee Koe Mannj Nimaanee Eik Thoo |
Kio N Mareejai Roe Jaa Lag Chith N Aavehee |1|
Pourree | Ho Kiaa Saalaahee Kiram Janth Vaddee Thaeree Vaddiaaee |
Thoo Agam Dhaeiaal Aganm Hai Aap Laihi Milaaee |   Page-791

O' Lord of the Universe, my Guru, You, are the all- powerful Cause and Creator. Please cover my faults, I am a sinner and have come to seek the Sanctuary of Your Feet. We, the frail humans are naturally inclined to make mistakes, but Mercy is Your ingrained virtue to save the forgetful ones.

---

ਬਿਲਾਵਲੁ ਮਹਲਾ ੫ ॥

ਤੁਮ੍ਹ ਸਮਰਥਾ ਕਾਰਨ ਕਰਨ ॥

ਢਾਕਨ ਢਾਕਿ ਗੋਬਿਦ ਗੁਰ ਮੇਰੇ ਮੋਹਿ ਅਪਰਾਧੀ ਸਰਨ ਚਰਨ ॥੧॥ ਰਹਾਉ ॥

ਹਮਰੇ ਸਹਾਉ ਸਦਾ ਸਦ ਭੂਲਨ ਤੁਮ੍ਹਰੋ ਬਿਰਦੁ ਪਤਿਤ ਉਧਰਨ ॥

Bilawal 5th Guru

Tumh samarath kaaran karan;

dhakan dhakgobind gur merey mohey apradhi saran charan. (1)  Pause.

hamro suhao sada sad bhulan tumor birdh patit udharan.   Page-828

O' Lord, save me! I never learnt how to walk the righteous path in my life. Never inculcated good habits, nor took responsibility for my own actions, and neither practiced humility or devotional worship. I have been egoistic and full of pride, and clung on to unrighteous ways. Believing this body to be immortal, I pampered it, but it turned out to be fragile and a claylike perishable vessel. Forgetting the Lord who formed, fashioned and embellished me, I became attached to Maya, the world of illusion.

---

ਬਿਲਾਵਲੁ ਬਾਣੀ ਭਗਤਾ ਕੀ ॥ ਕਬੀਰ ਜੀਉ ਕੀ ॥
ਰਾਖਿ ਲੇਹੁ ਹਮ ਤੇ ਬਿਗਰੀ ॥ਸੀਲੁ ਧਰਮੁ ਜਪੁ ਭਗਤਿ ਨ ਕੀਨੀ ਹਉ ਅਭਿਮਾਨ ਟੇਢ ਪਗਰੀ ॥੧॥ ਰਹਾਉ ॥
ਅਮਰ ਜਾਨਿ ਸੰਚੀ ਇਹ ਕਾਇਆ ਇਹ ਮਿਥਿਆ ਕਾਚੀ ਗਗਰੀ ॥
ਜਿਨਹਿ ਨਿਵਾਜਿ ਸਾਜਿ ਹਮ ਕੀਏ ਤਿਸਹਿ ਬਿਸਾਰਿ ਅਵਰ ਲਗਰੀ ॥੧॥
Bilaaval Baanee Bhagathaa Kee | Kabeer Jeeo Kee |
Raakh Laehu Ham Thae Bigaree |
Seel Dhharam Jap Bhagath N Keenee Ho Abhimaan Ttaedt Pagaree |1| Pause |
Amar Jaan Sanchee Eih Kaaeiaa Eih Mithhiaa Kaachee Gagaree |
Jinehi Nivaaj Saaj Ham Keeeae Thisehi Bisaar Avar Lagaree |1|    Page-856

Prays Nanak, "my Friend-Lord, I have come to seek Your
Sanctuary, have Mercy so that I may ever be the dust of Your
Feet and see you always with me in body and spirit". O'
Father, unfortunately I have always been acquiring the false
worldly things and hence, my doubt deluded mind could
never acquire Your Name. What separation could be worse
than separation from the Lord? For those who are united with
Him, what other union can there be? Praise the Lord and
Master forever, who, having created this worldly drama
beholds and takes care of it.

---

ਰਾਗੁ ਮਾਰੂ ਮਹਲਾ ੧ ਸਲੋਕੁ ॥
ਸਾਜਨ ਤੇਰੇ ਚਰਨ ਕੀ ਹੋਇ ਰਹਾ ਸਦ ਧੂਰਿ ॥ ਨਾਨਕ ਸਰਣਿ ਤੁਹਾਰੀਆ ਪੇਖਉ ਸਦਾ ਹਜੂਰਿ ॥੧॥
ਬਾਬਾ ਮੈ ਕਰਮਹੀਣ ਕੁੜਿਆਰ ॥ ਨਾਮੁ ਨ ਪਾਇਆ ਤੇਰਾ ਅੰਧਾ ਭਰਮਿ ਭੂਲਾ ਮਨੁ ਮੇਰਾ ॥੧॥ ਰਹਾਉ ॥
ਵਿਛੁੜਿਆ ਕਾ ਕਿਆ ਵੀਛੁੜੈ ਮਿਲਿਆ ਕਾ ਕਿਆ ਮੇਲੁ ॥
ਸਾਹਿਬੁ ਸੋ ਸਾਲਾਹੀਐ ਜਿਨਿ ਕਰਿ ਦੇਖਿਆ ਖੇਲੁ ॥੩॥
Raag Maaroo 1st Guru Salok |
Saajan Thaerae Charan Kee Hoe Rehaa Sadh Dhhoor |
Naanak Saran Thuhaareeaa Paekho Sadhaa Hajoor |1|
Baabaa Mai Karameheen Koorriaar |
Naam N Paaeiaa Thaeraa Andhhaa Bharam Bhoolaa Man Maeraa |1| Pause |
Vishhurriaa Kaa Kiaa Veeshhurrai Miliaa Kaa Kiaa Mael |
Saahib So Saalaaheeai Jin Kar Dhaekhiaa Khael |3|  Page-989

Says Kabeer upon realizing God's Name, the ego has vanished and I feel, "I am the worst, and everybody else is better than me". Furthermore, anyone else, who feels likewise, is truly my friend.

ਸਲੋਕ ਭਗਤ ਕਬੀਰ ਜੀਉ ਕੇ ॥
ਕਬੀਰ ਸਭ ਤੇ ਹਮ ਬੁਰੇ ਹਮ ਤਜਿ ਭਲੇ ਸਭੁ ਕੋਇ ॥ਜਿਨਿ ਐਸਾ ਕਰਿ ਬੁਝਿਆ ਮੀਤੁ ਹਮਾਰਾ ਸੋਇ ॥੭॥
Salok Bhagath Kabeer Jeeo Kae
Kabeer Sabh Thae Ham Burae Ham Thaj Bhalo Sabh Koe |
Jin Aisaa Kar Boojhiaa Meeth Hamaaraa Soe |7|   Page-1364 |

The Lord's Name is like sugar, which is scattered in the sand (world); the elephant cannot pick it. Says Kabeer, the Guru has given me the sublime understanding, that a man becoming tiny like an ant (humble) can pick and eat it.

ਸਲੋਕ ਭਗਤ ਕਬੀਰ ਜੀਉ ਕੇ ॥
ਹਰਿ ਹੈ ਖਾਂਡੁ ਰੇਤੁ ਮਹਿ ਬਿਖਰੀ ਹਾਥੀ ਚੁਨੀ ਨ ਜਾਇ ॥
ਕਹਿ ਕਬੀਰ ਗੁਰਿ ਭਲੀ ਬੁਝਾਈ ਕੀਟੀ ਹੋਇ ਕੈ ਖਾਇ ॥੨੩੮॥
Salok Bhagath Kabeer Jeeo Kae |
Har Hai Khaandd Raeth Mehi Bikharee Haathhee Chunee N Jaae |
Kehi Kabeer Gur Bhalee Bujhaaee Keettee Hoe Kai Khaae |238|   Page-1377

O' Fareed, if you are of sound wisdom, then do not try to dwell on the misdeeds of other people; instead bend your head down and look underneath your own collar.
O' Fareed, if someone hits and hurts you, do not turn around and hit back in revenge; instead kiss his feet and return to your own home to enjoy complete bliss and peace of mind.

---

ਸਲੋਕ ਸੇਖ ਫਰੀਦ ਕੇ ॥
ਫਰੀਦਾ ਜੇ ਤੂ ਅਕਲਿ ਲਤੀਫੁ ਕਾਲੇ ਲਿਖੁ ਨ ਲੇਖ ॥ਆਪਨੜੇ ਗਿਰੀਵਾਨ ਮਹਿ ਸਿਰੁ ਨੀਵਾਂ ਕਰਿ ਦੇਖੁ ॥੬॥
ਫਰੀਦਾ ਜੋ ਤੈ ਮਾਰਨਿ ਮੁਕੀਆਂ ਤਿਨ੍ਹਾ ਨ ਮਾਰੇ ਘੁੰਮਿ ॥ਆਪਨੜੈ ਘਰਿ ਜਾਈਐ ਪੈਰ ਤਿਨ੍ਹਾ ਦੇ ਚੁੰਮਿ ॥੭॥
Salok Saekh Fareedh Kae |
Fareedhaa Jae Thoo Akal Latheef Kaalae Likh N Laekh |
Aapanarrae Gireevaan Mehi Sir Nanaeevaan Kar Dhaekh |6|
Fareedhaa Jo Thai Maaran Mukeeaaan Thinhaa N Maarae Ghunm |
Aapanarrai Ghar Jaaeeai Pair Thinhaa Dhae Chunm |7|  Page-1378

O' Fareed, I eat my dry bread baked through hard earned living, and with it use hunger as my sauce. But, those who eat buttered bread through dishonesty will eventually suffer terrible pain.

O' Fareed, eat your simple dry bread, and drink cold water, but live honestly. Do not envy others, when you see those eating lavish meals.

ਸਲੋਕ ਸੇਖ ਫਰੀਦ ਕੇ ॥
ਫਰੀਦਾ ਰੋਟੀ ਮੇਰੀ ਕਾਠ ਕੀ ਲਾਵਣੁ ਮੇਰੀ ਭੁਖ ॥ਜਿਨਾ ਖਾਧੀ ਚੋਪੜੀ ਘਣੇ ਸਹਨਿਗੇ ਦੁਖ ॥੨੮॥
ਰੁਖੀ ਸੁਖੀ ਖਾਇ ਕੈ ਠੰਢਾ ਪਾਣੀ ਪੀਓ ॥ਫਰੀਦਾ ਦੇਖਿ ਪਰਾਈ ਚੋਪੜੀ ਨਾ ਤਰਸਾਏ ਜੀਉ ॥੨੯॥
Salok Saekh Fareedh Kae |
Fareedhaa Rottee Maeree Kaath Kee Laavan Maeree Bhukh |
Jinaa Khaadhhee Choparree Ghanae Sehanigae Dhukh |28|
Rukhee Sukhee Khaae Kai Thandtaa Paanee Peeo |
Fareedhaa Dhaekh Paraaee Choparree Naa Tharasaaeae Jeeo |29|    Page-1378

Says Fareed, I am wearing black clothes and a black outfit; hence people call me saint. But I am wandering around full of sins!

O' Fareed, to the evil doer, answer with goodness; do not let anger come to your mind. This way, your body shall not suffer from any disease, and all your goodness shall flourish within you.

---

ਸਲੋਕ ਸੇਖ ਫਰੀਦ ਕੇ ॥
ਫਰੀਦਾ ਕਾਲੇ ਮੈਡੇ ਕਪੜੇ ਕਾਲਾ ਮੈਡਾ ਵੇਸੁ ॥ਗੁਨਹੀ ਭਰਿਆ ਮੈ ਫਿਰਾ ਲੋਕੁ ਕਹੈ ਦਰਵੇਸੁ ॥੬੧॥
ਫਰੀਦਾ ਬੁਰੇ ਦਾ ਭਲਾ ਕਰਿ ਗੁਸਾ ਮਨਿ ਨ ਹਢਾਇ ॥ਦੇਹੀ ਰੋਗੁ ਨ ਲਗਈ ਪਲੈ ਸਭੁ ਕਿਛੁ ਪਾਇ ॥੭੮॥
Salok Saekh Fareedh Kae |
Fareedhaa Kaalae Maiddae Kaparrae Kaalaa Maiddaa Vaes |
Gunehee Bhariaa Mai Firaa Lok Kehai Dharavaes |61|
Fareedhaa Burae Dhaa Bhalaa Kar Gusaa Man N Hadtaae |
Dhaehee Rog N Lagee Palai Sabh Kishh Paae |78|  Page-1381/82

O' sister, what is that word, what is that virtue, what is that magic mantra? What should I wear to captivate my Husband Lord?
O' sister, humility is the word, forgiveness is the virtue, and sweet talk is the word. Wear these three robes and you will captivate your Husband Lord!

---

ਸਲੋਕ ਸੇਖ ਫਰੀਦ ਕੇ
ਕਵਣੁ ਸੁ ਅਖਰੁ ਕਵਣੁ ਗੁਣੁ ਕਵਣੁ ਸੁ ਮਣੀਆ ਮੰਤੁ ॥
ਕਵਣੁ ਸੁ ਵੇਸੋ ਹਉ ਕਰੀ ਜਿਤੁ ਵਸਿ ਆਵੈ ਕੰਤੁ ॥੧੨੬॥
ਨਿਵਣੁ ਸੁ ਅਖਰੁ ਖਵਣੁ ਗੁਣੁ ਜਿਹਬਾ ਮਣੀਆ ਮੰਤੁ ॥
ਏ ਤ੍ਰੈ ਭੈਣੇ ਵੇਸ ਕਰਿ ਤਾਂ ਵਸਿ ਆਵੀ ਕੰਤੁ ॥੧੨੭॥
Salok Saekh Fareedh Kae
Kavan S Akhar Kavan Gun Kavan S Maneeaa Manth ||
Kavan S Vaeso Ho Karee Jith Vas Aavai Kanth ||126||
Nivan S Akhar Khavan Gun Jihabaa Maneeaa Manth ||
Eae Thrai Bhainae Vaes Kar Thaan Vas Aavee Kanth ||127||   Page-1384

O' God, we humans keep making so many mistakes; there is no end or limit to these. O' Lord, please be merciful and forgive; I am a sinner, a great offender. Dear Lord, if You kept an account of my mistakes, my turn to be forgiven would never, ever come. It is only through Your Ingrained Nature of Mercy, that You may unite me with Yourself.

---

ਸਲੋਕ ਮਹਲਾ ੩ ॥

ਅਸੀ ਖਤੇ ਬਹੁਤੁ ਕਮਾਵਦੇ ਅੰਤੁ ਨ ਪਾਰਾਵਾਰੁ ॥

ਹਰਿ ਕਿਰਪਾ ਕਰਿ ਕੈ ਬਖਸਿ ਲੈਹੁ ਹਉ ਪਾਪੀ ਵਡ ਗੁਨਹਗਾਰੁ ॥

ਹਰਿ ਜੀਉ ਲੇਖੈ ਵਾਰ ਨ ਆਵਈ ਤੂੰ ਬਖਸਿ ਮਿਲਾਵਣਹਾਰੁ ॥

Salok 3rd Guru |

Asee Khathae Bahuth Kamaavadhae Anth N Paaraavaar |

Har Kirapaa Kar Kai Bakhas Laihu Ho Paapee Vadd Gunehagaar |

Har Jeeo Laekhai Vaar N Aavee Thoon Bakhas Milaavanehaar |    Page-1416

## Chapter-2   Materialism & Illusion (Maya)

If salvation can be obtained by bathing in water (of a river considered holy), then what about the frog, which is always bathing in water?  As is the case with the frog, so is true of the mortal; without God's Name, he suffers reincarnations, again and again.

ਆਸਾ ਸ੍ਰੀ ਕਬੀਰ ਜੀਉ ॥
ਜਲ ਕੈ ਮਜਨਿ ਜੇ ਗਤਿ ਹੋਵੈ ਨਿਤ ਨਿਤ ਮੇਂਡੁਕ ਨਾਵਹਿ ॥
ਜੈਸੇ ਮੇਂਡੁਕ ਤੈਸੇ ਓਇ ਨਰ ਫਿਰਿ ਫਿਰਿ ਜੋਨੀ ਆਵਹਿ ॥੨॥
Aasaa Sree Kabeer Jeeo |
Jal Kai Majan Jae Gath Hovai Nith Nith Maenadduk Naavehi |
Jaisae Maenadduk Thaisae Oue Nar Fir Fir Jonee Aavehi |2|   Page-484

Engulfed by love of the Maya (Illusion), look how the puppet of clay (human) is dancing; going astray. He looks for, listens, hears, speaks, and runs around only for Maya. When he acquires wealth, he is inflated with ego; but when the wealth is gone, he cries and bewails. Says Ravi Daas, O'brother, the world is just a drama. Instead of Maya, I have enshrined love for the Lord, who is the magician of this magic show.

ਆਸਾ ਬਾਣੀ ਸ੍ਰੀ ਰਵਿਦਾਸ ਜੀਉ ਕੀ ॥
ਮਾਟੀ ਕੋ ਪੁਤਰਾ ਕੈਸੇ ਨਚਤੁ ਹੈ ॥ਦੇਖੈ ਦੇਖੈ ਸੁਨੈ ਬੋਲੈ ਦਉਰਿਓ ਫਿਰਤੁ ਹੈ ॥੧॥ ਰਹਾਉ ॥
ਜਬ ਕਛੁ ਪਾਵੈ ਤਬ ਗਰਬੁ ਕਰਤੁ ਹੈ ॥ਮਾਇਆ ਗਈ ਤਬ ਰੋਵਨੁ ਲਗਤੁ ਹੈ ॥੧॥
ਕਹਿ ਰਵਿਦਾਸ ਬਾਜੀ ਜਗੁ ਭਾਈ ॥ਬਾਜੀਗਰ ਸਉ ਮੋਹਿ ਪ੍ਰੀਤਿ ਬਨਿ ਆਈ ॥੩॥੬॥
Aasaa Baanee Sree Ravidhaas Jeeo Kee |
Maattee Ko Putharaa Kaisae Nachath Hai |
Dhaekhai Dhaekhai Sunai Bolai Dhouriou Firath Hai |1|Pause |
Jab Kashh Paavai Thab Garab Karath Hai |
Maaeiaa Gee Thab Rovan Lagath Hai |1|
Kehi Ravidhaas Baajee Jag Bhaaee |
Baajeegar So Muohi Preeth Ban Aaee |3|6|    Page-486/87

21

Maya is like a serpent, clinging to the entire world. Whosoever serves her, is ultimately devoured by her. Only a rare God Oriented one knows the treatment for her venom; he throws her down and tramples her under his feet. Says Nanak, only those have escaped this Maya serpent, who remain lovingly absorbed in the True Lord.

---

ਮਹਲਾ ੩ ॥
ਮਾਇਆ ਹੋਈ ਨਾਗਨੀ ਜਗਤਿ ਰਹੀ ਲਪਟਾਇ ॥ ਇਸ ਕੀ ਸੇਵਾ ਜੋ ਕਰੇ ਤਿਸ ਹੀ ਕਉ ਫਿਰਿ ਖਾਇ ॥
ਗੁਰਮੁਖਿ ਕੋਈ ਗਾਰੜੂ ਤਿਨਿ ਮਲਿ ਦਲਿ ਲਾਈ ਪਾਇ ॥
ਨਾਨਕ ਸੇਈ ਉਬਰੇ ਜਿ ਸਚਿ ਰਹੇ ਲਿਵ ਲਾਇ ॥੨॥

3rd Guru |
Maaeiaa Hoee Naaganee Jagath Rehee Lapattaae |
Eis Kee Saevaa Jo Karae This Hee Ko Fir Khaae |
Guramukh Koee Gaararroo Thin Mal Dhal Laaee Paae |
Naanak Saeee Oubarae J Sach Rehae Liv Laae |2|    Page-510

O' dear friend, know this truth in your mind; the entire world is entangled in its own pleasures; no one is there for anyone else. In good times, many come and sit around you; but through hard times they all leave, and no one comes to your rescue. Even your wife, whom you loved so much, and who remained ever attached to you, runs away crying, "Ghost, Ghost" as soon as the swan-soul leaves the body. This is how the world that you love so much actually is. Says Nanak, in the end no one is of any help except the Dear Lord.

---

ਸੋਰਠਿ ਮਹਲਾ ੯ ॥
ਪ੍ਰੀਤਮ ਜਾਨਿ ਲੇਹੁ ਮਨ ਮਾਹੀ ॥ ਅਪਨੇ ਸੁਖ ਸਿਉ ਹੀ ਜਗੁ ਫਾਂਧਿਓ ਕੋ ਕਾਹੂ ਕੋ ਨਾਹੀ ॥੧॥ ਰਹਾਉ ॥
ਸੁਖ ਮੈ ਆਨਿ ਬਹੁਤੁ ਮਿਲਿ ਬੈਠਤ ਰਹਤ ਚਹੂ ਦਿਸਿ ਘੇਰੈ ॥
ਬਿਪਤਿ ਪਰੀ ਸਭ ਹੀ ਸੰਗੁ ਛਾਡਿਤ ਕੋਊ ਨ ਆਵਤ ਨੇਰੈ ॥੧॥
ਘਰ ਕੀ ਨਾਰਿ ਬਹੁਤੁ ਹਿਤੁ ਜਾ ਸਿਉ ਸਦਾ ਰਹਤ ਸੰਗ ਲਾਗੀ ॥
ਜਬ ਹੀ ਹੰਸ ਤਜੀ ਇਹ ਕਾਂਇਆ ਪ੍ਰੇਤ ਪ੍ਰੇਤ ਕਰਿ ਭਾਗੀ ॥੨॥
ਇਹ ਬਿਧਿ ਕੋ ਬਿਉਹਾਰੁ ਬਨਿਓ ਹੈ ਜਾ ਸਿਉ ਨੇਹੁ ਲਗਾਇਓ ॥
ਅੰਤ ਬਾਰ ਨਾਨਕ ਬਿਨੁ ਹਰਿ ਜੀ ਕੋਊ ਕਾਮਿ ਨ ਆਇਓ ॥੩॥੧੨॥੧੩੯॥
Sorath Mehalaa 9 |
Preetham Jaan Laehu Man Maahee |
Apanae Sukh Sio Hee Jag Faandhhiou Ko Kaahoo Ko Naahee |1| Pause |
Sukh Mai Aan Bahuth Mil Baithath Rehath Chehoo Dhis Ghaerai |
Bipath Paree Sabh Hee Sang Shhaaddith Kooo N Aavath Naerai |1|
Ghar Kee Naar Bahuth Hith Jaa Sio Sadhaa Rehath Sang Laagee |
Jab Hee Hans Thajee Eih Kaaneiaa Praeth Praeth Kar Bhaagee |2|
Eih Bidhh Ko Biouhaar Baniou Hai Jaa Sio Naehu Lagaaeiou |
Anth Baar Naanak Bin Har Jee Kooo Kaam N Aaeiou |3|12|139|   Page-634

The feeling of "my wealth" is enticing; without any teeth Maya has eaten up the world! The egoistic self-willed are eaten away, while the God Oriented are saved as they focus their consciousness on the True Lord. Without God's Name, the world is running around insane. Says Nanak, only those receive God's Name in whose heart, God has placed it through His Mercy.

---

ਸਲੋਕੁ ਮਹਲਾ ੩ ॥

ਮਾਇਆ ਮਮਤਾ ਮੋਹਣੀ ਜਿਨਿ ਵਿਣੁ ਦੰਤਾ ਜਗੁ ਖਾਇਆ ॥
ਮਨਮੁਖ ਖਾਧੇ ਗੁਰਮੁਖਿ ਉਬਰੇ ਜਿਨੀ ਸਚਿ ਨਾਮਿ ਚਿਤੁ ਲਾਇਆ ॥
ਬਿਨੁ ਨਾਵੈ ਜਗੁ ਕਮਲਾ ਫਿਰੈ ਗੁਰਮੁਖਿ ਨਦਰੀ ਆਇਆ ॥
ਨਾਨਕ ਨਾਮੁ ਤਿਨਾ ਕਉ ਮਿਲਿਆ ਜਿਨ ਕਉ ਧੁਰਿ ਲਿਖਿ ਪਾਇਆ ॥੧॥

Salok 3rd Guru |

Maaeiaa Mamathaa Mohanee Jin Vin Dhanthaa Jag Khaaeiaa |
Manamukh Khaadhhae Guramukh Oubarae Jinee Sach Naam Chith Laaeiaa |
Bin Naavai Jag Kamalaa Firai Guramukh Nadharee Aaeiaa |
Naanak Naam Thinaa Ko Miliaa Jin Ko Dhhur Likh Paaeiaa |1|    Page-643

The Hindus waste their time in idol worship and the Muslims bowing to the Mecca, thinking God only lives there. They burn or bury their dead and argue about it, but none understand the Truth (God). The body if burnt becomes ashes and if buried is eaten away by insects. The unbaked clay pitcher dissolves, when water is poured into it; this is also the nature of the human body. Why, O' brother why are you showing off all puffed up with pride? Like the bee which collects honey, the fool miserly gathers and collects wealth, but in the end, it belongs to someone else.

---

ਰਾਗੁ ਸੋਰਠਿ ਬਾਣੀ ਭਗਤ ਕਬੀਰ ਜੀ ਕੀ ॥
ਬੁਤ ਪੂਜਿ ਪੂਜਿ ਹਿੰਦੂ ਮੂਏ ਤੁਰਕ ਮੂਏ ਸਿਰੁ ਨਾਈ ॥ ਓਇ ਲੇ ਜਾਰੇ ਓਇ ਲੇ ਗਾਡੇ ਤੇਰੀ ਗਤਿ ਦੁਹੂ ਨ ਪਾਈ ॥੧॥
ਜਬ ਜਰੀਐ ਤਬ ਹੋਇ ਭਸਮ ਤਨੁ ਰਹੈ ਕਿਰਮ ਦਲ ਖਾਈ ॥
ਕਾਚੀ ਗਾਗਰਿ ਨੀਰੁ ਪਰਤੁ ਹੈ ਇਆ ਤਨ ਕੀ ਇਹੈ ਬਡਾਈ ॥੧॥ਕਾਹੇ ਭਈਆ ਫਿਰਤੌ ਫੂਲਿਆ ਫੂਲਿਆ ॥
ਜਿਉ ਮਧੁ ਮਾਖੀ ਤਿਉ ਸਠੋਰਿ ਰਸੁ ਜੋਰਿ ਜੋਰਿ ਧਨੁ ਕੀਆ ॥
Raag Sorath Baanee Bhagath Kabeer Jee Kee |
Buth Pooj Pooj Hindhoo Mooeae Thurak Mooeae Sir Naaee |
Oue Lae Jaarae Oue Lae Gaaddae Thaeree Gath Dhuhoo N Paaee |1|
Jab Jareeai Thab Hoe Bhasam Than Rehai Kiram Dhal Khaaee |
Kaachee Gaagar Neer Parath Hai Eiaa Than Kee Eihai Baddaaee |1|
Kaahae Bheeaa Firatha Fooliaa Fooliaa |
Jio Madhh Maakhee Thio Sathor Ras Jor Jor Dhhan Keeaa |    Page-654

O' brother why do you go searching for God in the forests?
He, who lives in everyone, but is always unattached from
Maya, dwells within you and is your companion. Like the
fragrance in the flower and the reflection in the mirror, the
Lord is deep within you; search for Him in your own heart.
The Guru has imparted to me the wisdom that the One Lord
is everywhere, both within and outside. Says Nanak, that
without self-realization, the fungus of doubt can never be
removed.

---

ਧਨਾਸਰੀ ਮਹਲਾ ੯ ॥
ਕਾਹੇ ਰੇ ਬਨ ਖੋਜਨ ਜਾਈ ॥ ਸਰਬ ਨਿਵਾਸੀ ਸਦਾ ਅਲੇਪਾ ਤੋਹੀ ਸੰਗਿ ਸਮਾਈ ॥੧॥ ਰਹਾਉ ॥
ਪੁਹਪ ਮਧਿ ਜਿਉ ਬਾਸੁ ਬਸਤੁ ਹੈ ਮੁਕਰ ਮਾਹਿ ਜੈਸੇ ਛਾਈ ॥
ਤੈਸੇ ਹੀ ਹਰਿ ਬਸੇ ਨਿਰੰਤਰਿ ਘਟ ਹੀ ਖੋਜਹੁ ਭਾਈ ॥੧॥
ਬਾਹਰਿ ਭੀਤਰਿ ਏਕੋ ਜਾਨਹੁ ਇਹੁ ਗੁਰ ਗਿਆਨੁ ਬਤਾਈ ॥
ਜਨ ਨਾਨਕ ਬਿਨੁ ਆਪਾ ਚੀਨੈ ਮਿਟੈ ਨ ਭ੍ਰਮ ਕੀ ਕਾਈ ॥੨॥੧॥
Dhhanaasaree Mehalaa 9 |
Kaahae Rae Ban Khojan Jaaee |
Sarab Nivaasee Sadhaa Alaepaa Thohee Sang Samaaee |1| Pause |
Puhap Madhh Jio Baas Basath Hai Mukar Maahi Jaisae Shhaaee |
Thaisae Hee Har Basae Niranthar Ghatt Hee Khojahu Bhaaee |1|
Baahar Bheethar Eaeko Jaanahu Eihu Gur Giaan Bathaaee |
Jan Naanak Bin Aapaa Cheenai Mittai N Bhram Kee Kaaee |2|1|   Page-684

Cursed is the life, in which one only eats and make his belly big. O Nanak, without awareness of the True Name, all the worldly hungers, due to their obviously harmful results, become your enemy.

ਮਹਲਾ ੧ ॥
ਫਿਟੁ ਇਵੇਹਾ ਜੀਵਿਆ ਜਿਤੁ ਖਾਇ ਵਧਾਇਆ ਪੇਟੁ ॥ਨਾਨਕ ਸਚੇ ਨਾਮ ਵਿਣੁ ਸਭੇ ਦੁਸਮਨ ਹੇਤੁ ॥੨॥
1$^{st}$ Guru |
Fitt Eivaehaa Jeeviaa Jith Khaae Vadhhaaeiaa Paett |
Naanak Sachae Naam Vin Sabho Dhusaman Haeth |2|    Page-790

O' Lord, Master of the Universe, this worldly illusion (Maya) has made me forget your Benevolent Presence. Not even a bit of love for You wells up in Your humble servant; what can Your poor helpless servants do?

ਬਿਲਾਵਲੁ ਬਾਣੀ ਭਗਤਾ ਕੀ ॥ ਕਬੀਰ ਜੀਉ ॥
ਇਨਿ੍ਹ ਮਾਇਆ ਜਗਦੀਸ ਗੁਸਾਈ ਤੁਮ੍ਹਰੇ ਚਰਨ ਬਿਸਾਰੇ ॥
ਕਿੰਚਤ ਪ੍ਰੀਤਿ ਨ ਉਪਜੈ ਜਨ ਕਉ ਜਨ ਕਹਾ ਕਰਹਿ ਬੇਚਾਰੇ ॥੧॥ ਰਹਾਉ ॥
Bilaaval Baanee Bhagathaa Kee || Kabeer Jeeo ||
Einih Maaeiaa Jagadhees Gusaaee Thumharae Charan Bisaarae |
Kinchath Preeth N Oupajai Jan Ko Jan Kehaa Karehi Baechaarae |1| Pause |    Page-857

27

O' foolish person, give up your envy of others, as your sojourn in this world is like a night's stay. Intoxicated with Maya illusion, you will soon depart, but do not realize that you are involved in a dream. After several incarnations, you have obtained this precious human body, but without God's Name it will be reduced to dust. Worse than a beast, a demon or an idiot, is he, who does not become aware of the One Lord, who created him.

---

ਰਾਮਕਲੀ ਮਹਲਾ ੫ ॥
ਛਾਡਿ ਵਿਡਾਣੀ ਤਾਤਿ ਮੂੜੇ ॥ਈਹਾ ਬਸਨਾ ਰਾਤਿ ਮੂੜੇ ॥
ਮਾਇਆ ਕੇ ਮਾਤੇ ਤੈ ਉਠਿ ਚਲਨਾ ॥ਰਾਚਿ ਰਹਿਓ ਤੂ ਸੰਗਿ ਸੁਪਨਾ ॥੧॥ ਰਹਾਉ ॥
ਚਿਰੰਕਾਲ ਪਾਈ ਦੂਲਭ ਦੇਹ ॥ਨਾਮ ਬਿਹੂਣੀ ਹੋਈ ਖੇਹ ॥
ਪਸੂ ਪਰੇਤ ਮੁਗਧ ਤੇ ਬੁਰੀ ॥ਤਿਸਹਿ ਨ ਬੂਝੈ ਜਿਨਿ ਏਹ ਸਿਰੀ ॥੩॥
Raamakalee 5th Guru|
Shhaadd Viddaanee Thaath Moorrae |Eehaa Basanaa Raath Moorrae |
Maaeiaa Kae Maathae Thai Outh Chalanaa |
Raach Rehiou Thoo Sang Supanaa |1|Pause |
Chirankaal Paaee Dhraalabh Dhaeh |Naam Bihoonee Hoee Khaeh |
Pasoo Paraeth Mugadhh Thae Buree |Thisehi N Boojhai Jin Eaeh Siree |3|    Page-889

28

O' my mind, how can you forget the Lord's Name? When the body perishes, you shall have to deal with the Messenger of Death. This world is just a mountain of smoke, which can be blown away by a gust of wind. O' my mind on what basis you think that it is real and everlasting?

---

ਬਸੰਤੁ ਮਹਲਾ ੯ ॥
ਮਨ ਕਹਾ ਬਿਸਾਰਿਓ ਰਾਮ ਨਾਮੁ ॥ ਤਨੁ ਬਿਨਸੈ ਜਮ ਸਿਉ ਪਰੈ ਕਾਮੁ ॥੧॥ ਰਹਾਉ ॥
ਇਹੁ ਜਗੁ ਧੂਏ ਕਾ ਪਹਾਰ ॥ ਤੈ ਸਾਚਾ ਮਾਨਿਆ ਕਿਹ ਬਿਚਾਰਿ ॥੧॥

Basanth 9<sup>th</sup> Guru |
Man Kehaa Bisaariou Raam Naam |
Than Binasai Jam Sio Parai Kaam |1| Pause|
Eihu Jag Dhhooeae Kaa Pehaar | Thai Saachaa Maaniaa Kih Bichaar |1|   Page-1186

Just engulfed in eating, drinking, laughing and sleeping, the mortal forgets about dying. Forgetting the Husband Lord, the mortal is involved in tasks that ruin his life and he is cursed. When our stay here is a temporary phenomenon, then why not make it a Truthful experience. O' mortal, meditate on the One Lord and gain His awareness. You shall then go to your true home with honor (find a place at the Lord's Feet).

---

ਰਾਗੁ ਮਲਾਰ ਚਉਪਦੇ ਮਹਲਾ ੧
ਖਾਣਾ ਪੀਣਾ ਹਸਣਾ ਸਉਣਾ ਵਿਸਰਿ ਗਇਆ ਹੈ ਮਰਣਾ ॥
ਖਸਮੁ ਵਿਸਾਰਿ ਖੁਆਰੀ ਕੀਨੀ ਧ੍ਰਿਗੁ ਜੀਵਣੁ ਨਹੀ ਰਹਣਾ ॥੧॥
ਪ੍ਰਾਣੀ ਏਕੋ ਨਾਮੁ ਧਿਆਵਹੁ ॥ ਅਪਨੀ ਪਤਿ ਸੇਤੀ ਘਰਿ ਜਾਵਹੁ ॥੧॥ ਰਹਾਉ ॥

Raag Malaar Choupadhae Mehalaa 1Guru |
Khaanaa Peenaa Hasanaa Sounaa Visar Gaeiaa Hai Maranaa |
Khasam Visaar Khuaaree Keenee Dhhrig Jeevan Nehee Rehanaa |1|
Praanee Eaeko Naam Dhhiaavahu |
Apanee Path Saethee Ghar Jaavahu |1| Pause |   Page-

## Chapter-3   Reality & Ritualism (Pakhand)

The woman gardener tears off leaves to present to the stone idol, which is lifeless, but in each, and every leaf there is life. The mistaken gardener forgets the reality that the True Guru (God) is the living deity.

ਆਸਾ ਸ੍ਰੀ ਕਬੀਰ ਜੀਉ ਕੇ ॥

ਪਾਤੀ ਤੋਰੈ ਮਾਲਿਨੀ ਪਾਤੀ ਪਾਤੀ ਜੀਉ ॥ ਜਿਸੁ ਪਾਹਨ ਕਉ ਪਾਤੀ ਤੋਰੈ ਸੋ ਪਾਹਨ ਨਿਰਜੀਉ ॥੧॥

ਭੂਲੀ ਮਾਲਨੀ ਹੈ ਏਉ ॥ ਸਤਿਗੁਰੁ ਜਾਗਤਾ ਹੈ ਦੇਉ ॥੧॥ ਰਹਾਉ ॥

Aasaa Sree Kabeer Jeeo Kae |

Paathee Thorai Maalinee Paathee Paathee Jeeo |Jis Paahan Ko Paathee Thorai So Paahan Nirajeeo |1|Bhoolee Maalanee Hai Eaeo |Sathigur Jaagathaa Hai Dhaeo |1|Pause |   Page-479

O' ignorant stupid people, how can you cross the world ocean by worshipping the stone idols, which themselves sink.

ਮਹਲਾ ੧ ॥

ਪਾਥਰੁ ਲੇ ਪੂਜਹਿ ਮੁਗਧ ਗਵਾਰ ॥ ਓਹਿ ਜਾ ਆਪਿ ਡੁਬੇ ਤੁਮ ਕਹਾ ਤਰਣਹਾਰੁ ॥੨॥

1st Guru |

Paathhar Lae Poojehi Mugadhh Gavaar |

Ouhi Jaa Aap Ddubae Thum Kehaa Tharanehaar |2|   Page-556

In this world, God is the only Husband; all other are His brides.   The Husband Lord is operating in all, yet He remains detached, is invisible and cannot be described.

---

ਮਹਲਾ ੩ ॥
ਇਸੁ ਜਗ ਮਹਿ ਪੁਰਖੁ ਏਕੁ ਹੈ ਹੋਰ ਸਗਲੀ ਨਾਰਿ ਸਬਾਈ ॥
ਸਭਿ ਘਟ ਭੋਗਵੈ ਅਲਿਪਤੁ ਰਹੈ ਅਲਖੁ ਨ ਲਖਣਾ ਜਾਈ ॥
3rd Guru |
Eis Jag Mehi Purakh Eaek Hai Hor Sagalee Naar Sabaaee |
Sabh Ghatt Bhogavai Alipath Rehai Alakh N Lakhanaa Jaaee |   Page-591

---

Like the child, innocently makes thousands of mistakes; yet his father gives him advice, scolds him so many times, but still, hugs him close to his heart.   Likewise, the Father God, forgets the human's past sins and puts them on the righteous path for the future.

---

ਸੋਰਠਿ ਮਹਲਾ ੫ ॥
ਜੈਸਾ ਬਾਲਕੁ ਭਾਇ ਸੁਭਾਈ ਲਖ ਅਪਰਾਧ ਕਮਾਵੈ ॥
ਕਰਿ ਉਪਦੇਸੁ ਝਿੜਕੇ ਬਹੁ ਭਾਤੀ ਬਹੁਰਿ ਪਿਤਾ ਗਲਿ ਲਾਵੈ ॥
ਪਿਛਲੇ ਅਉਗੁਣ ਬਖਸਿ ਲਏ ਪ੍ਰਭੁ ਆਗੈ ਮਾਰਗਿ ਪਾਵੈ ॥੨॥
Sorath 5th Guru |
Jaisaa Baalak Bhaae Subhaaee Lakh Aparaadhh Kamaavai |
Kar Oupadhaes Jhirrakae Bahu Bhaathee Bahurr Pithaa Gal Laavai |
Pishhalae Aougun Bakhas Leae Prabh Aagai Maarag Paavai |2|   Page-624

The religious rites, rituals, and hypocrisies which are commonly practiced, are plundered by the Messenger of Death, like the tax collector. That is why, sing the Creator's Praises. Contemplating on Him, even for an instant, one is saved. O Saints, singing the Lord's praises with Guru's Grace, one can overcome the worldly illusion and see Reality.

---

ਸੂਹੀ ਮਹਲਾ ੫ ॥

ਕਰਮ ਧਰਮ ਪਾਖੰਡ ਜੋ ਦੀਸਹਿ ਤਿਨ ਜਮੁ ਜਾਗਾਤੀ ਲੂਟੈ ॥

ਨਿਰਬਾਣ ਕੀਰਤਨੁ ਗਾਵਹੁ ਕਰਤੇ ਕਾ ਨਿਮਖ ਸਿਮਰਤ ਜਿਤੁ ਛੂਟੈ ॥੧॥

ਸੰਤਹੁ ਸਾਗਰੁ ਪਾਰਿ ਉਤਰੀਐ ॥ਜੇ ਕੋ ਬਚਨੁ ਕਮਾਵੈ ਸੰਤਨ ਕਾ ਸੋ ਗੁਰ ਪਰਸਾਦੀ ਤਰੀਐ ॥੧॥ ਰਹਾਉ ॥

Soohee 5t Guru |

Karam Dhharam Paakhandd Jo Dheesehi Thin Jam Jaagaathee Loottai |

Nirabaan Keerathan Gaavahu Karathae Kaa Nimakh Simarath Jith Shhoottai |1|

Santhahu Saagar Paar Outhareeai |

Jae Ko Bachan Kamaavai Santhan Kaa So Gur Parasaadhee Thareeai |1|Rehaao |   Page-747

The Lord God has initiated the wedding ceremony and He has come to marry the God oriented one. She, by His Mercy, has attained Him through righteous path, and became the fond wife that He begins to Love. The saints have gotten together to sing His praises, as God Himself has embellished His devotee. The angels and mortal beings, the heavenly heralds and celestial singers, have come together and formed a wondrous wedding party. Says Nanak, I have found my True Husband Lord, who never dies, and is never born.

(Note: The Guru's this writing is typically used to perform a wedding ceremony in the Sikh religion.)

---

ਰਾਗੁ ਸੂਹੀ ਛੰਤ ਮਹਲਾ ੪ ॥

ਹਰਿ ਪ੍ਰਭਿ ਕਾਜੁ ਰਚਾਇਆ ॥ਗੁਰਮੁਖਿ ਵੀਆਹਣਿ ਆਇਆ ॥

ਵੀਆਹਣਿ ਆਇਆ ਗੁਰਮੁਖਿ ਹਰਿ ਪਾਇਆ ਸਾ ਧਨ ਕੰਤ ਪਿਆਰੀ ॥

ਸੰਤ ਜਨਾ ਮਿਲਿ ਮੰਗਲ ਗਾਏ ਹਰਿ ਜੀਉ ਆਪਿ ਸਵਾਰੀ ॥

ਸੁਰਿ ਨਰ ਗਣ ਗੰਧਰਬ ਮਿਲਿ ਆਏ ਅਪੂਰਬ ਜੰਞ ਬਣਾਈ ॥

ਨਾਨਕ ਪ੍ਰਭੁ ਪਾਇਆ ਮੈ ਸਾਚਾ ਨਾ ਕਦੇ ਮਰੈ ਨ ਜਾਈ ॥੪॥੧॥੩॥

Raag Soohee Shhanth Mehalaa 4 |

Har Prabh Kaaj Rachaaeiaa | Guramukh Veeaahan Aaeiaa |

Veeaahan Aaeiaa Guramukh Har Paaeiaa Saa Dhhan Kanth Piaaree |

Santh Janaa Mil Mangal Gaaeae Har Jeeo Aap Savaaree |

Sur Nar Gan Gandhharab Mil Aaeae Apoorab Jannj Banaaee |

Naanak Prabh Paaeiaa Mai Saachaa Naa Kadhae Marai N Jaaee |4|1|3|   Page-775

O my Lord; You are the Master of all and unattached, yet there are countless maidens like me, ready to serve You. You are the Ocean, the Source of riches; but, I never realized Your value. You are the Priceless Jewel, Infinitely Deep, Serene and Calm; You are my Husband and I am your Bride. You are the greatest of the great, exalted and lofty, but I am a lowly little servant. With Your blessing, I have become invaluable and of tremendous weight, and the doors to the path of liberation and Truth, have flung open. Says Nanak, ever since the Lord has become my shield and shelter, I have become fearless.

---

ਰਾਗੁ ਸੂਹੀ ਛੰਤ ਮਹਲਾ ੫ ॥
ਤੂ ਠਾਕੁਰੋ ਬੈਰਾਗਰੋ ਮੈ ਜੇਹੀ ਘਣ ਚੇਰੀ ਰਾਮ ॥ਤੂੰ ਸਾਗਰੋ ਰਤਨਾਗਰੋ ਹਉ ਸਾਰ ਨ ਜਾਣਾ ਤੇਰੀ ਰਾਮ ॥
ਤੁਮ੍ਹ ਗਉਹਰ ਅਤਿ ਗਹਿਰ ਗੰਭੀਰਾ ਤੁਮ ਪਿਰ ਹਮ ਬਹੁਰੀਆ ਰਾਮ ॥
ਤੁਮ ਵਡੇ ਵਡੇ ਵਡ ਊਚੇ ਹਉ ਇਤਨੀਕ ਲਹੁਰੀਆ ਰਾਮ ॥
ਭਈ ਅਮੋਲੀ ਭਾਰਾ ਤੋਲੀ ਮੁਕਤਿ ਜੁਗਤਿ ਦਰੁ ਖੋਲ੍ਹਾ ॥
ਕਹੁ ਨਾਨਕ ਹਉ ਨਿਰਭਉ ਹੋਈ ਸੋ ਪ੍ਰਭੁ ਮੇਰਾ ਓਲ੍ਹਾ ॥੪॥੧॥੪॥
Raag Soohee Shhanth 5th Guru |
Thoo Thaakuro Bairaagaro Mai Jaehee Ghan Chaeree Raam |
Thoon Saagaro Rathanaagaro Ho Saar N Jaanaa Thaeree Raam |
Thumh Gouhar Ath Gehir Ganbheeraa Thum Pir Ham Bahureeaa Raam |
Thum Vaddae Vaddae Vadd Oochae Ho Eithaneek Lahureeaa Raam |
Bhee Amolee Bhaaraa Tholee Mukath Jugath Dhar Kholhaa |
Kahu Naanak Ho Nirabho Hoee So Prabh Maeraa Oulhaa |4|1|4|  Page-779

My Dear Lord and Master is my Friend and always speaks so sweetly. I have grown weary of testing Him, but still, He never ever speaks harshly. He does not know any bitter words; the Perfect Lord God does not even consider my faults and demerits. It is the Lord's natural way to purify sinners; He does not overlook even an iota of service to Him. He dwells in each and every heart, pervading everywhere; He is the nearest of the near. Servant Nanak seeks His Sanctuary forever; the Lord is my Ambrosial Friend.

ਰਾਗੁ ਸੂਹੀ ਮਹਲਾ ੫ ॥
ਮਿਠ ਬੋਲੜਾ ਜੀ ਹਰਿ ਸਜਣੁ ਸੁਆਮੀ ਮੋਰਾ ॥ਹਉ ਸੰਮਲਿ ਥਕੀ ਜੀ ਓਹੁ ਕਦੇ ਨ ਬੋਲੈ ਕਉਰਾ ॥
ਕਉੜਾ ਬੋਲਿ ਨ ਜਾਨੈ ਪੂਰਨ ਭਗਵਾਨੈ ਅਉਗਣੁ ਕੋ ਨ ਚਿਤਾਰੇ ॥
ਪਤਿਤ ਪਾਵਨੁ ਹਰਿ ਬਿਰਦੁ ਸਦਾਏ ਇਕੁ ਤਿਲੁ ਨਹੀ ਭੰਨੈ ਘਾਲੇ ॥
ਘਟ ਘਟ ਵਾਸੀ ਸਰਬ ਨਿਵਾਸੀ ਨੇਰੈ ਹੀ ਤੇ ਨੇਰਾ ॥
ਨਾਨਕ ਦਾਸੁ ਸਦਾ ਸਰਣਾਗਤਿ ਹਰਿ ਅੰਮ੍ਰਿਤ ਸਜਣੁ ਮੇਰਾ ॥੧॥
Raag Soohee Mehalaa 5 |
Mith Bolarraa Jee Har Sajan Suaamee Moraa |
Ho Sanmal Thhakee Jee Ouhu Kadhae N Bolai Kouraa |
Kourraa Bol N Jaanai Pooran Bhagavaanai Aougan Ko N Chithaarae |
Pathith Paavan Har Biradh Sadhaaeae Eik Thil Nehee Bhannai Ghaalae |
Ghatt Ghatt Vaasee Sarab Nivaasee Naerai Hee Thae Naeraa |
Naanak Dhaas Sadhaa Saranaagath Har Anmrith Sajan Maeraa |1|   Page-784

Without the Guru's Word, no one can escape dying from the Spiritual Self. Practicing hypocrisy and ritualism, one can never attain Liberation. Like the black crow can never become white, the one engulfed in the worldly illusion, never finds honor and respect, here and thereafter.

---

ਬਿਲਾਵਲੁ ਮਹਲਾ ੧ ॥

ਬਿਨੁ ਗੁਰ ਸਬਦ ਨ ਛੂਟਸਿ ਕੋਇ ॥ ਪਾਖੰਡਿ ਕੀਨ੍ਹੈ ਮੁਕਤਿ ਨ ਹੋਇ ॥੨॥

ਝੂਠੇ ਕਉ ਨਾਹੀ ਪਤਿ ਨਾਉ ॥ ਕਬਹੂ ਨ ਸੂਚਾ ਕਾਲਾ ਕਾਉ ॥

Bilaaval 1st Guru |

Bin Gur Sabadh N Shhoottas Koe | Paakhandd Keenhai Mukath N Hoe |2|

Jhoothae Ko Naahee Path Naao |Kabahu N Soochaa Kaalaa Kaao |    Page-838

What is the purpose of life, and what teachings have to be learnt in this human lifetime? Who is your Guru and whose Disciple are you?

Life Force (God) Himself is the beginning and this human birth is the time of learning the True Guru's (God's) teachings. Says Nanak, the Wordless Word is my Guru and focusing my consciousness on the Word is the Disciple.

(Note: A group of Siddhas' (yogis of the highest order) and Guru Nanak had a lengthy discourse, in which the Guru emphasized the importance of direct relationship with God, while living a normal life, through the Wordless Word; in lieu of renunciation and yoga.)

---

ਰਾਮਕਲੀ ਮਹਲਾ ੧ ਸਿਧ ਗੋਸਟਿ ॥
ਕਵਣ ਮੂਲੁ ਕਵਣ ਮਤਿ ਵੇਲਾ ॥ਤੇਰਾ ਕਵਣੁ ਗੁਰੂ ਜਿਸ ਕਾ ਤੂ ਚੇਲਾ ॥
ਪਵਨ ਅਰੰਭੁ ਸਤਿਗੁਰ ਮਤਿ ਵੇਲਾ ॥ਸਬਦੁ ਗੁਰੂ ਸੁਰਤਿ ਧੁਨਿ ਚੇਲਾ ॥
Raamakalee Mehalaa 1 Sidhh Gosatti |
Kavan Mool Kavan Math Vaelaa |Thaeraa Kavan Guroo Jis Kaa Thoo Chaelaa |
Pavan Aranbh Sathigur Math Vaelaa |Sabadh Guroo Surath Dhhun Chaelaa | Page-942

Like the lotus flower rises above water and is untouched, the God conscious person, can live in his own home and family environment, but stay unattached.

ਮਾਰੂ ਮਹਲਾ 8 ॥
ਵਿਚੇ ਗ੍ਰਿਹ ਸਦਾ ਰਹੈ ਉਦਾਸੀ ਜਿਉ ਕਮਲੁ ਰਹੈ ਵਿਚਿ ਪਾਣੀ ਹੇ ॥੧੦॥
Maaroo 4th Guru |
Vichae Grih Sadhaa Rehai Oudhaasee Jio Kamal Rehai Vich Paanee Hae |10|
Page-1070

People apply ceremonial marks to their foreheads, hold a string of beads in their hands, and wear religious robes to show off as God's devotees. These people think, the Lord is a toy and can get His attention by such ritualism. If you truly love the Lord, only then you may come into His Presence. Says Kabeer, whosoever has found God, it has been through searching within oneself.

ਭੈਰਉ ਬਾਣੀ ਭਗਤਾ ਕੀ ॥ਕਬੀਰ ਜੀਉ ॥
ਮਾਥੇ ਤਿਲਕੁ ਹਥਿ ਮਾਲਾ ਬਾਨਾਂ ॥ਲੋਗਨ ਰਾਮੁ ਖਿਲਉਨਾ ਜਾਨਾਂ ॥੧॥
ਰਿਦੈ ਇਖਲਾਸੁ ਨਿਰਖਿ ਲੇ ਮੀਰਾ ॥ਆਪੁ ਖੋਜਿ ਖੋਜਿ ਮਿਲੇ ਕਬੀਰਾ ॥੪॥੭॥
Bhairo Baanee Bhagathaa Kee |Kabeer Jeeo |
Maathhae Thilak Hathh Maalaa Baanaan | Logan Raam Khilounaa Jaanaan |1|
Ridhai Eikhalaas Nirakh Lae Meeraa | Aap Khoj Khoj Milae Kabeeraa |4|7|    Page-1158

The mind of the poor child is innocent; he tries to play with a snake and even touch fire. However, his mother and father hug him close in their embrace, and so he plays carefree in joy and bliss. What hunger can the child ever have, O my Lord and Master, when You are his Father? The supreme treasure of the Wordless Word and all other treasures are in Your celestial household. You fulfill the desires of Your children as they wish in their minds.

---

ਮਲਾਰ ਮਹਲਾ ੫ ॥

ਚੰਚਲ ਮਤਿ ਬਾਰਿਕ ਬਪੁਰੇ ਕੀ ਸਰਪ ਅਗਨਿ ਕਰ ਮੇਲੈ ॥

ਮਾਤਾ ਪਿਤਾ ਕੰਠਿ ਲਾਇ ਰਾਖੈ ਅਨਦ ਸਹਜਿ ਤਬ ਖੇਲੈ ॥੨॥

ਜਿਸ ਕਾ ਪਿਤਾ ਤੂ ਹੈ ਮੇਰੇ ਸੁਆਮੀ ਤਿਸੁ ਬਾਰਿਕ ਭੂਖ ਕੈਸੀ ॥

ਨਵ ਨਿਧਿ ਨਾਮੁ ਨਿਧਾਨੁ ਗ੍ਰਿਹਿ ਤੇਰੈ ਮਨਿ ਬਾਂਛੈ ਸੋ ਲੈਸੀ ॥੩॥

Malaar 5th Guru |

Chanchal Math Baarik Bapurae Kee Sarap Agan Kar Maelai |

Maathaa Pithaa Kanth Laae Raakhai Anadh Sehaj Thab Khaelai |2|

Jis Kaa Pithaa Thoo Hai Maerae Suaamee This Baarik Bhookh Kaisee |

Nav Nidhh Naam Nidhhaan Grihi Thaerai Man Baanshhai So Laisee |3|    Page-1266

Kabeer, the mortal loses his faith, for the sake of pleasing the world, but in the end, the world never stands by him. It is akin to carelessly striking the axe on your own foot; hence suffering due to your own actions.

---

ਸਲੋਕ ਭਗਤ ਕਬੀਰ ਜੀਉ ਕੇ ॥
ਕਬੀਰ ਦੀਨੁ ਗਵਾਇਆ ਦੁਨੀ ਸਿਉ ਦੁਨੀ ਨ ਚਾਲੀ ਸਾਥਿ ॥
ਪਾਇ ਕੁਹਾੜਾ ਮਾਰਿਆ ਗਾਫਲਿ ਅਪੁਨੈ ਹਾਥਿ ॥੧੩॥
Salok Bhagath Kabeer Jeeo Kae |
Kabeer Dheen Gavaaeiaa Dhunee Sio Dhunee N Chaalee Saathh |
Paae Kuhaarraa Maariaa Gaafal Apunai Haathh |13|   Page-1365

---

Says Kabeer, being born as a human being comes with great difficulty and it is wasting the opportunity by forgetting the Lord; as it does not happen over, and over again. It is like the ripe fruit on the tree; when it falls to the ground, it can never be re-attached to the branch again.

---

ਸਲੋਕ ਭਗਤ ਕਬੀਰ ਜੀਉ ਕੇ ॥
ਕਬੀਰ ਮਾਨਸ ਜਨਮੁ ਦੁਲੰਭੁ ਹੈ ਹੋਇ ਨ ਬਾਰੈ ਬਾਰ ॥
ਜਿਉ ਬਨ ਫਲ ਪਾਕੇ ਭੁਇ ਗਿਰਹਿ ਬਹੁਰਿ ਨ ਲਾਗਹਿ ਡਾਰ ॥੩੦॥
Salok Bhagath Kabeer Jeeo Kae |
Kabeer Maanas Janam Dhulanbh Hai Hoe N Baarai Baar |
Jio Ban Fal Paakae Bhue Girehi Bahur N Laagehi Ddaar |30|   Page-1366

---

Says Kabeer, if by good fortune, you have obtained the Treasure of the Lord's Name, do not go about opening the knot of this bundle in front of everyone. In the world, generally, there is no market, no buyers, and no one willing to pay the price of this Treasure by giving up the worldly attachments.

---

ਸਲੋਕ ਭਗਤ ਕਬੀਰ ਜੀਉ ਕੇ
ਰਾਮ ਪਦਾਰਥੁ ਪਾਇ ਕੈ ਕਬੀਰਾ ਗਾਂਠਿ ਨ ਖੋਲ੍ਹ ॥
ਨਹੀ ਪਟਣੁ ਨਹੀ ਪਾਰਖੁ ਨਹੀ ਗਾਹਕੁ ਨਹੀ ਮੋਲੁ ॥੨੩॥
Salok Bhagath Kabeer Jeeo Kae |
Raam Padhaarathh Paae Kai Kabeeraa Gaanth N Kholh |
Nehee Pattan Nehee Paarakhoo Nehee Gaahak Nehee Mol |23|   Page-1365

---

God's virtues are like pearls that are scattered in the path of the life of human beings. But here the ignorant blind man without the Light of the Lord of the Universe, just tramples them under his feet.

---

ਸਲੋਕ ਭਗਤ ਕਬੀਰ ਜੀਉ ਕੇ
ਮਾਰਗਿ ਮੋਤੀ ਬੀਥਰੇ ਅੰਧਾ ਨਿਕਸਿਓ ਆਇ ॥
ਜੋਤਿ ਬਿਨਾ ਜਗਦੀਸ ਕੀ ਜਗਤੁ ਉਲੰਘੇ ਜਾਇ ॥੧੧੪॥
Salok Bhagath Kabeer Jeeo Kae |
Maarag Mothee Beethharae Andhhaa Nikasiou Aae |
Joth Binaa Jagadhees Kee Jagath Oulanghae Jaae ||114||   Page-1370

Kabeer, if a person goes to a religious place every day for prayers and then practices dishonesty and actions harmful to others; he is knowingly committing these sinful acts. God's service is like a lit-up lamp which shows the way in the darkness of life. What good is a lamp in one's hand, if even with its light he falls into a well?

---

ਸਲੋਕ ਭਗਤ ਕਬੀਰ ਜੀਉ ਕੇ
ਕਬੀਰ ਮਨੁ ਜਾਨੈ ਸਭ ਬਾਤ ਜਾਨਤ ਹੀ ਅਉਗਨੁ ਕਰੈ ॥
ਕਾਹੇ ਕੀ ਕੁਸਲਾਤ ਹਾਥਿ ਦੀਪੁ ਕੂਏ ਪਰੈ ॥੨੧੬॥
Salok Bhagath Kabeer Jeeo Kae |
Kabeer Man Jaanai Sabh Baath Jaanath Hee Aougan Karai |
Kaahae Kee Kusalaath Haathh Dheep Kooeae Parai |216|  Page-1376

---

O' Fareed, at first due to my mind's utter confusion, I thought, I am the only one having pain, but actually the entire world is suffering. When rising above my pain's threshold I looked all around; I saw that this fire is lit up in every household.

---

ਸਲੋਕ ਸੇਖ ਫਰੀਦ ਕੇ ॥
ਫਰੀਦਾ ਮੈ ਜਾਨਿਆ ਦੁਖੁ ਮੁਝ ਕੂ ਦੁਖੁ ਸਬਾਇਐ ਜਗਿ ॥
ਉਚੇ ਚੜਿ ਕੈ ਦੇਖਿਆ ਤਾਂ ਘਰਿ ਘਰਿ ਏਹਾ ਅਗਿ ॥੮੧॥
Salok Saekh Fareedh Kae |
Fareedhaa Mai Jaaniaa Dhukh Mujh Koo Dhukh Sabaaeiai Jag |
Oochae Charr Kai Dhaekhiaa Thaan Ghar Ghar Eaehaa Ag |81|  Page-1382

Says Fareed, the faces of those who forget the Lord's Name look dreadful, no matter how rich and powerful they may be. So long as they live, they suffer many pains and hereafter also find no place of rest or refuge.

O' Fareed, if you do not wake up in the early hours before dawn (the time for Ambrosial Nectar) to remember the Lord, you are like the dead living an unbecoming life. Although you have forgotten God, God has not forgotten you as He is always watching.

---

ਸਲੋਕ ਸੇਖ ਫਰੀਦ ਕੇ |
ਫਰੀਦਾ ਤਿਨਾ ਮੁਖ ਡਰਾਵਣੇ ਜਿਨਾ ਵਿਸਾਰਿਓਨੁ ਨਾਉ ॥ਐਥੈ ਦੁਖ ਘਣੇਰਿਆ ਅਗੈ ਠਉਰ ਨ ਠਾਉ ॥੧੦੬॥
ਫਰੀਦਾ ਪਿਛਲ ਰਾਤਿ ਨ ਜਾਗਿਓਹਿ ਜੀਵਦੜੋ ਮੁਇਓਹਿ ॥
ਜੇ ਤੈ ਰਬੁ ਵਿਸਾਰਿਆ ਤ ਰਬਿ ਨ ਵਿਸਰਿਓਹਿ ॥੧੦੭॥
Salok Saekh Fareedh Kae |
Fareedhaa Thinaa Mukh Ddaraavanae Jinaa Visaarioun Naao |
Aithhai Dhukh Ghanaeriaa Agai Thour N Thaao |106|
Fareedhaa Pishhal Raath N Jaagiouhi Jeevadharro Mueiouhi |
Jae Thai Rab Visaariaa Th Rab N Visariouhi |107|   Page-1383

O' Nanak, like you dream while asleep and in that dream, see several things, so is this world. Without God's Name, nothing in this world is the Truth.

Says Nanak, listen my friend; as the bubbles in the water well up and disappear soon; in the same way God, has created the Creation.

Says Nanak, whatever has come into existence in this world will surely perish. Everyone will have to leave today or tomorrow; hence sing the Lord's praises and free yourself of the worldly entanglements.

---

ਸਲੋਕ ਮਹਲਾ ੯ ॥

ਜਿਉ ਸੁਪਨਾ ਅਰੁ ਪੇਖਨਾ ਐਸੇ ਜਗ ਕਉ ਜਾਨਿ ॥ਇਨ ਮੈ ਕਛੁ ਸਾਚੋ ਨਹੀ ਨਾਨਕ ਬਿਨੁ ਭਗਵਾਨ ॥੨੩॥
ਜੈਸੇ ਜਲ ਤੇ ਬੁਦਬੁਦਾ ਉਪਜੈ ਬਿਨਸੈ ਨੀਤ ॥ਜਗ ਰਚਨਾ ਤੈਸੇ ਰਚੀ ਕਹੁ ਨਾਨਕ ਸੁਨਿ ਮੀਤ ॥੨੫॥
ਜੋ ਉਪਜਿਓ ਸੋ ਬਿਨਸਿ ਹੈ ਪਰੋ ਆਜੁ ਕੈ ਕਾਲਿ ॥ਨਾਨਕ ਹਰਿ ਗੁਨ ਗਾਇ ਲੇ ਛਾਡਿ ਸਗਲ ਜੰਜਾਲ ॥੫੨॥

Salok 9th Guru|
Jio Supanaa Ar Paekhanaa Aisae Jag Ko Jaan |
Ein Mai Kashh Saacho Nehee Naanak Bin Bhagavaan |23|
Jaisae Jal Thae Budhabudhaa Oupajai Binasai Neeth |
Jag Rachanaa Thaisae Rachee Kahu Naanak Sun Meeth |25|
Jo Oupajiou So Binas Hai Paro Aaj Kai Kaal |
Naanak Har Gun Gaae Lae Shhaadd Sagal Janjaal |52|     Page-1426 & 1429

## Chapter-4 As You Sow, So Shall You Reap

O' the nomads, people of temporary abode in this world, carefully trade on God's Name, and take care of this precious merchandise. It will bear with you in the long run and the All-knowing Merchant Lord will ultimately take charge. O' dear brother, utter and contemplate on God's Name with single minded consciousness. Carry the Merchandise of the Lord's Praises with you; the Husband Lord shall fully satisfy Himself and then accept.

ਸਿਰੀਰਾਗੁ ਮਹਲਾ ੧ ॥
ਵਣਜੁ ਕਰਹੁ ਵਣਜਾਰਿਹੋ ਵਖਰੁ ਲੇਹੁ ਸਮਾਲਿ ॥ ਤੈਸੀ ਵਸਤੁ ਵਿਸਾਹੀਐ ਜੈਸੀ ਨਿਬਹੈ ਨਾਲਿ ॥
ਅਗੈ ਸਾਹੁ ਸੁਜਾਣੁ ਹੈ ਲੈਸੀ ਵਸਤੁ ਸਮਾਲਿ ॥੧॥
ਭਾਈ ਰੇ ਰਾਮੁ ਕਹਹੁ ਚਿਤੁ ਲਾਇ ॥ ਹਰਿ ਜਸੁ ਵਖਰੁ ਲੈ ਚਲਹੁ ਸਹੁ ਦੇਖੈ ਪਤੀਆਇ ॥੧॥ ਰਹਾਉ ॥
Sireeraag Mehalaa 1 |
Vanaj Karahu Vanajaariho Vakhar Samaal |1|
Bhaaee Rae Raam Kehahu Chith Laae |
Har Jas Vakhar Lai Chalahu Sahu Dhaekhai Patheeaae |1| Pause |   Page-22

When a person dies, all the relatives that he was so attached to, abandon him in an instant. Upon seeing death's vision, he becomes repentant, wringing his hands, the body shivers in pain, and its colors change as he is bewildered. As you sow so shall you reap; such is the field of karma. Nanak seeks God's Refuge; God has given him the Sanctuary at His Feet.

---

ਬਾਰਹ ਮਾਹਾ ਮਾਂਝ ਮਹਲਾ ੫

ਛਡਿ ਖੜੋਤੇ ਖਿਨੈ ਮਾਹਿ ਜਿਨ ਸਿਉ ਲਗਾ ਹੇਤੁ ॥ ਹਥ ਮਰੋੜੈ ਤਨੁ ਕਪੇ ਸਿਆਹਹੁ ਹੋਆ ਸੇਤੁ ॥
ਜੇਹਾ ਬੀਜੈ ਸੋ ਲੁਣੈ ਕਰਮਾ ਸੰਦੜਾ ਖੇਤੁ ॥ ਨਾਨਕ ਪ੍ਰਭ ਸਰਣਾਗਤੀ ਚਰਣ ਬੋਹਿਥ ਪ੍ਰਭ ਦੇਤੁ ॥

Baareh Maahaa Maanjh Mehalaa 5|
Shhadd Kharrothae Khinai Maahi Jin Sio Lagaa Haeth |
Hathh Marorrai Than Kapae Siaahahu Hoaa Saeth |
Jaehaa Beejai So Lunai Karamaa Sandharraa Khaeth |
Naanak Prabh Saranaagathee Charan Bohithh Prabh Dhaeth |   Page-134

The great and powerful people that you see are the most afflicted with the disease of anxiety. For example, the landlord is caught in concerns over his land each day, but his desire for ownership is never satisfied; although he will leave it behind in the end. Says Nanak upon deep contemplation, that without remembering God' Name, one is never liberated from the worldly attachments.

---

ਗਉੜੀ ਮਹਲਾ ੫ ॥

ਵਡੇ ਵਡੇ ਜੋ ਦੀਸਹਿ ਲੋਗ ॥ ਤਿਨ ਕਉ ਬਿਆਪੈ ਚਿੰਤਾ ਰੋਗ ॥੧॥

ਭੂਮੀਆ ਭੂਮਿ ਉਪਰਿ ਨਿਤ ਲੁਝੈ ॥ ਛੋਡਿ ਚਲੈ ਤ੍ਰਿਸਨਾ ਨਹੀ ਬੁਝੈ ॥੨॥

ਕਹੁ ਨਾਨਕ ਇਹੁ ਤਤੁ ਬੀਚਾਰਾ ॥ ਬਿਨੁ ਹਰਿ ਭਜਨ ਨਾਹੀ ਛੁਟਕਾਰਾ ॥੩॥੪੪॥੧੧੩॥

Gourree Mehalaa 5|

Those who seem to be great and powerful |Thin ko biaapai chinthaa rog |1|

Bhoomeeaa bhoom oopar nith lujhai |Shhodd chalai thrisanaa nehee bujhai |2|

Kahu Naanak eihu Thath beechaaraa | Bin Har bhajan naahee shhuttakaaraa |3|

Page-188

One whose heart is filled with Faith in God; the essence of
spiritual wisdom is revealed to him!

ਗਉੜੀ ਸੁਖਮਨੀ ਮਹਲਾ ੫ ॥
ਜਾ ਕੈ ਰਿਦੈ ਬਿਸ੍ਵਾਸੁ ਪ੍ਰਭ ਆਇਆ ॥ਤਤੁ ਗਿਆਨੁ ਤਿਸੁ ਮਨਿ ਪ੍ਰਗਟਾਇਆ ॥
Gourree Sukhamanee Fifth Guru |
Jaa Kai Ridhai Bisvaas Prabh Aaeiaa |Thath Giaan This Man Pragattaaeiaa |
Page-285

O' my crazy mind, now stop wavering! The woman who
takes vermillion coated coconut in her hand (symbol of
challenge to death) must burn to die on her husbands' pyre to
attain" Sati" (a tradition earlier practiced by the Hindu faith).
Now that you have taken God's sanctuary, you must die
within from ego, to reach the Truth.

ਗਉੜੀ ਕਬੀਰ ਜੀ ॥
ਡਗਮਗ ਛਾਡਿ ਰੇ ਮਨ ਬਉਰਾ ॥ ਅਬ ਤਉ ਜਰੇ ਮਰੇ ਸਿਧਿ ਪਾਈਐ ਲੀਨੋ ਹਾਥਿ ਸੰਧਉਰਾ ॥੧॥ ਰਹਾਉ ॥
Gourree Kabeer Jee |
Ddagamag Shhaadd Rae Man Bouraa |Ab Tho Jarae Marae Sidhh Paaeeai Leeno
Haathh Sandhhouraa |1|Pause |   Page-338

Dadda (a Punjabi script word used to make a point): Do not blame others for your suffering; take full responsibility and blame instead your own actions. Whatever I did myself, I have borne its fruit; I must not blame anyone else.

ਰਾਗੁ ਆਸਾ ਮਹਲਾ ੧
ਦਦੈ ਦੋਸੁ ਨ ਦੇਊ ਕਿਸੈ ਦੋਸੁ ਕਰੰਮਾ ਆਪਣਿਆ ॥ ਜੋ ਮੈ ਕੀਆ ਸੋ ਮੈ ਪਾਇਆ ਦੋਸੁ ਨ ਦੀਜੈ ਅਵਰ ਜਨਾ ॥
Raag Aasaa Mehalaa 1 |
Dhadhai Dhos N Dhaeoo Kisai Dhos Karanmaa Aapaniaa |
Jo Mai Keeaa So Mai Paaeiaa Dhos N Dheejai Avar Janaa |21|   Page-433

The world is full of pain; seeing this, my inner self is shivering with fear and I do not know whom to beg for help other than God.   Hence, I have stopped looking in all other directions and contemplate on the Lord's Name. He is forever the Giver and is everyday New, forever and forever He Gives.

ਧਨਾਸਰੀ ਮਹਲਾ ੧ ॥
ਜੀਉ ਡਰਤੁ ਹੈ ਆਪਣਾ ਕੈ ਸਿਉ ਕਰੀ ਪੁਕਾਰ ॥ ਦੂਖ ਵਿਸਾਰਣੁ ਸੇਵਿਆ ਸਦਾ ਸਦਾ ਦਾਤਾਰੁ ॥੧॥
ਸਾਹਿਬੁ ਮੇਰਾ ਨੀਤ ਨਵਾ ਸਦਾ ਸਦਾ ਦਾਤਾਰੁ ॥੧॥ ਰਹਾਉ ॥
Dhhanaasaree First Guru |
Jeeo Ddarath Hai Aapanaa Kai Sio Karee Pukaar |
Dhookh Visaaran Saeviaa Sadhaa Sadhaa Dhaathaar |1|
Saahib Maeraa Neeth Navaa Sadhaa Sadhaa Dhaathaar |1|Pause |   Page-660

The body beautiful, pretty clothes, etc., will be left behind in this world. You must reap the fruit of your own good and bad deeds. One may be commanding others as he wishes, but for any injustice he must bear the consequences. Such a person is shown the bad deeds committed, sees his dreadful appearance, and is thrown into hell. He then regrets upon his sins.

---

ਸਲੋਕੁ ਮਹਲਾ ੧ ॥

ਕਪੜੁ ਰੂਪੁ ਸੁਹਾਵਣਾ ਛਡਿ ਦੁਨੀਆ ਅੰਦਰਿ ਜਾਵਣਾ ॥ ਮੰਦਾ ਚੰਗਾ ਆਪਣਾ ਆਪੇ ਹੀ ਕੀਤਾ ਪਾਵਣਾ ॥ ਹੁਕਮ ਕੀਏ ਮਨਿ ਭਾਵਦੇ ਰਾਹਿ ਭੀੜੈ ਅਗੈ ਜਾਵਣਾ ॥ ਨੰਗਾ ਦੋਜਕਿ ਚਾਲਿਆ ਤਾ ਦਿਸੈ ਖਰਾ ਡਰਾਵਣਾ ॥ ਕਰਿ ਅਉਗਣ ਪਛੋਤਾਵਣਾ ॥੧੪॥

Salok First Guru|
Kaparr Roop Suhaavanaa Shhadd Dhuneeaa Andhar Jaavanaa |
Mandhaa Changaa Aapanaa Aapae Hee Keethaa Paavanaa |
Hukam Keeeae Man Bhaavadhae Raahi Bheerrai Agai Jaavanaa |
Nangaa Dhojak Chaaliaa Thaa Dhisai Kharaa Ddaraavanaa |
Kar Aougan Pashhothaavanaa |14|    Page-470

O' God, You Yourself Created the Creation and have Yourself, infused the Power into it. You behold Your Own Creation and having brought to life good and bad people, watch and nourish them. Whosoever has come into this world shall depart by his/or own turn, then why should we forget from our mind the Lord Master who owns our soul, and very breath of life? Hence, so long as we live we must set right our life, ourselves, by contemplating on Him.

---

ਸਲੋਕੁ ਮਹਲਾ ੧ ॥
ਪਉੜੀ ॥
ਆਪੇ ਹੀ ਕਰਣਾ ਕੀਓ ਕਲ ਆਪੇ ਹੀ ਤੈ ਧਾਰੀਐ ॥ ਦੇਖਹਿ ਕੀਤਾ ਆਪਣਾ ਧਰਿ ਕਚੀ ਪਕੀ ਸਾਰੀਐ ॥
ਜੋ ਆਇਆ ਸੋ ਚਲਸੀ ਸਭੁ ਕੋਈ ਆਈ ਵਾਰੀਐ ॥
ਜਿਸ ਕੇ ਜੀਅ ਪਰਾਣ ਹਹਿ ਕਿਉ ਸਾਹਿਬੁ ਮਨਹੁ ਵਿਸਾਰੀਐ ॥
ਆਪਣ ਹਥੀ ਆਪਣਾ ਆਪੇ ਹੀ ਕਾਜੁ ਸਵਾਰੀਐ ॥੨੦॥
Salok First Guru| Pauree:
Aapae Hee Karanaa Keeou Kal Aapae Hee Thai Dhhaareeai |
Dhaekhehi Keethaa Aapanaa Dhhar Kachee Pakee Saareeai |
Jo Aaeiaa So Chalasee Sabh Koee Aaee Vaareeai |
Jis Kae Jeea Paraan Hehi Kio Saahib Manahu Visaareeai |
Aapan Hathhee Aapanaa Aapae Hee Kaaj Savaareeai |20|   Page-474

O' Kabeer, the gate of liberation is narrow, less than one-tenth of a mustard seed, but the mind with ego has become as big as an elephant.   How can it then pass through this gate? O' Nanak, the gate of liberation is very narrow; only the very meek and humble can pass through. Meeting the True Guru, egotism departs, and one is filled with the Divine Light. Then, this conscience is liberated forever, and it remains absorbed in celestial bliss.

---

ਸਲੋਕੁ ॥ ਕਬੀਰ ਮੁਕਤਿ ਦੁਆਰਾ ਸੰਕੁੜਾ ਰਾਈ ਦਸਵੈ ਭਾਇ ॥
ਮਨੁ ਤਉ ਮੈਗਲੁ ਹੋਇ ਰਹਾ ਨਿਕਸਿਆ ਕਿਉ ਕਰਿ ਜਾਇ ॥
ਮਹਲਾ ੩ ॥ਨਾਨਕ ਮੁਕਤਿ ਦੁਆਰਾ ਅਤਿ ਨੀਕਾ ਨਾਨੑਾ ਹੋਇ ਸੁ ਜਾਇ ॥
ਸਤਿਗੁਰ ਮਿਲਿਐ ਹਉਮੈ ਗਈ ਜੋਤਿ ਰਹੀ ਸਭ ਆਇ ॥
ਇਹੁ ਜੀਉ ਸਦਾ ਮੁਕਤੁ ਹੈ ਸਹਜੇ ਰਹਿਆ ਸਮਾਇ ॥੨॥

Salok |Kabeer Mukath Dhuaaraa Sankurraa Raaee Dhasavai Bhaae |
Man Tho Maigal Hoe Rehaa Nikasiaa Kio Kar Jaae |
Third Guru |Naanak Mukath Dhuaaraa Ath Neekaa Naanhaa Hoe S Jaae |
Sathigur Miliai Houmai Gee Joth Rehee Sabh Aae |
Eihu Jeeo Sadhaa Mukath Hai Sehajae Rehiaa Samaae |2|    Page-509

Now, what efforts should I make, by which I may dispel the anxieties of my mind and cross the terrifying world-ocean? Obtaining this human incarnation, I have done no good deeds; this makes me very fearful! In thought, word and deed, I have not sung the Lord's Praises; this worries my mind. I listened to the Guru's Teachings, but spiritual wisdom did not well up within me instead, like a beast, I stuff my belly. Says Nanak, O God, me the sinner can only be saved when You conform to Your Basic Nature of Mercy and Forgiveness.

ਧਨਾਸਰੀ ਮਹਲਾ ੯ ॥
ਅਬ ਮੈ ਕਉਨੁ ਉਪਾਉ ਕਰਉ ॥ ਜਿਹ ਬਿਧਿ ਮਨ ਕੋ ਸੰਸਾ ਚੂਕੈ ਭਉ ਨਿਧਿ ਪਾਰਿ ਪਰਉ ॥੧॥ ਰਹਾਉ ॥
ਜਨਮੁ ਪਾਇ ਕਛੁ ਭਲੋ ਨ ਕੀਨੋ ਤਾ ਤੇ ਅਧਿਕ ਡਰਉ ॥ ਮਨ ਬਚ ਕ੍ਰਮ ਹਰਿ ਗੁਨ ਨਹੀ ਗਾਏ ਯਹ ਜੀਅ ਸੋਚ ਧਰਉ ॥੧॥ ਗੁਰਮਤਿ ਸੁਨਿ ਕਛੁ ਗਿਆਨੁ ਨ ਉਪਜਿਓ ਪਸੁ ਜਿਉ ਉਦਰੁ ਭਰਉ ॥
ਕਹੁ ਨਾਨਕ ਪ੍ਰਭ ਬਿਰਦੁ ਪਛਾਨਉ ਤਬ ਹਉ ਪਤਿਤ ਤਰਉ ॥੨॥੪॥੯॥੯॥੧੩॥੫੮॥੪॥੯੩॥
Dhhanaasaree Ninth Guru |
Ab Mai Koun Oupaao Karo | Jih Bidhh Man Ko Sansaa Chookai Bho Nidhh Paar Paro |1| Pause |Janam Paae Kashh Bhalo N Keeno Thaa Thae Adhhik Ddaro | Man Bach Kram Har Gun Nehee Gaaeae Yeh Jeea Soch Dhharo |1|Guramath Sun Kashh Giaan N Oupajiou Pas Jio Oudhar Bharo |Kahu Naanak Prabh Biradh Pashhaano Thab Ho Pathith Tharo | Page-685

They dig deep foundations, and build lofty palaces. Can anyone live longer than Markanda, (name of a sage who had a very long life), who passed his days with only a handful of straw upon his head (straw hut)? The Creator Lord is our True Love; man, why are you so full of pride and arrogance? This body is only temporary and shall pass away.

---

ਧਨਾਸਰੀ ਬਾਣੀ ਭਗਤ ਨਾਮਦੇਵ ਜੀ ਕੀ ॥
ਗਹਰੀ ਕਰਿ ਕੈ ਨੀਵ ਖੁਦਾਈ ਉਪਰਿ ਮੰਡਪ ਛਾਏ ॥
ਮਾਰਕੰਡੇ ਤੇ ਕੋ ਅਧਿਕਾਈ ਜਿਨਿ ਤ੍ਰਿਣ ਧਰਿ ਮੂੰਡ ਬਲਾਏ ॥੧॥
ਹਮਰੋ ਕਰਤਾ ਰਾਮੁ ਸਨੇਹੀ ॥ ਕਾਹੇ ਰੇ ਨਰ ਗਰਬੁ ਕਰਤ ਹਹੁ ਬਿਨਸਿ ਜਾਇ ਝੂਠੀ ਦੇਹੀ ॥੧॥ ਰਹਾਉ ॥
Dhhanaasaree Baanee Bhagath Naamadhaev Jee Kee
Geharee Kar Kai Neev Khudhaaee Oopar Manddap Shhaaeae |
Maarakanddae Thae Ko Adhhikaaee Jin Thrin Dhhar Moondd Balaaeae |1|
Hamaro Karathaa Raam Sanaehee | Kaahae Rae Nar Garab Karath Hahu Binas Jaae Jhoothee Dhaehee |1| Pause | Page-693

Merciful, the Lord Master is Merciful. My Lord Master is
Merciful. He gives His gifts of everything to all beings.
Why do you waver, O mortal being? The Creator Lord
Himself shall protect you. He who gave you this life, will
also provide all the necessities.

---

ਤਿਲੰਗ ਮਹਲਾ ੫ ॥
ਮਿਹਰਵਾਨੁ ਸਾਹਿਬੁ ਮਿਹਰਵਾਨੁ ॥ ਸਾਹਿਬੁ ਮੇਰਾ ਮਿਹਰਵਾਨੁ ॥ ਜੀਅ ਸਗਲ ਕਉ ਦੇਇ ਦਾਨੁ ॥ ਰਹਾਉ ॥
ਤੂ ਕਾਹੇ ਡੋਲਹਿ ਪ੍ਰਾਣੀਆ ਤੁਧੁ ਰਾਖੈਗਾ ਸਿਰਜਣਹਾਰੁ ॥ ਜਿਨਿ ਪੈਦਾਇਸਿ ਤੂ ਕੀਆ ਸੋਈ ਦੇਇ ਆਧਾਰੁ ॥੧॥
Thilang Mehalaa 5 |
Miharavaan Saahib Miharavaan |Saahib Maeraa Miharavaan | Jeea Sagal Ko
Dhaee Dhaan | Pause |
Thoo Kaahae Ddolehi Praaneeaa Thudhh Raakhaigaa Sirajanehaar |
Jin Paidhaaeis Thoo Keeaa Soee Dhaee Aadhhaar |1| Page-724

A beautiful dagger hangs by your waist, and you ride such a beautiful horse. But don't be too proud; O Nanak, you may fall head first to the ground any moment.

---

ਮਹਲਾ ੧ ॥
ਕਮਰਿ ਕਟਾਰਾ ਬੰਕੁੜਾ ਬੰਕੇ ਕਾ ਅਸਵਾਰੁ ॥ ਗਰਬੁ ਨ ਕੀਜੈ ਨਾਨਕਾ ਮਤੁ ਸਿਰਿ ਆਵੈ ਭਾਰੁ ॥੩॥
First Guru |
Kamar Kattaaraa Bankurraa Bankae Kaa Asavaar |Garab N Keejai Naanakaa Math Sir Aavai Bhaar |3|   Page-956

---

Fareed, (a man without prayer) is like the farmer who plants acacia trees, and wishes for grapes, or someone spinning wool all his life, but wishing to wear silk.

---

ਸਲੋਕ ਸੇਖ ਫਰੀਦ ਕੇ ॥
ਫਰੀਦਾ ਲੋੜੈ ਦਾਖ ਬਿਜਉਰੀਆਂ ਕਿਕਰਿ ਬੀਜੈ ਜਟੁ ॥ਹੰਢੈ ਉਂਨ ਕਤਾਇਦਾ ਪੈਧਾ ਲੋੜੈ ਪਟੁ ॥੨੩॥
Fareedhaa Lorrai Dhaakh Bijoureeaaan Kikar Beejai Jatt |Handtai Ounan Kathaaeidhaa Paidhhaa Lorrai Patt |23|   Page-137

## Chapter-5  Mind

A mind filled with the filth of ego cannot inculcate God
Consciousness and abide His Name in his heart.  The self-
oriented always have polluted minds, remain spiritually dead,
and depart in disgrace.  By the Guru's Grace, when the
Wordless Word lives in one's mind, the ego vanishes and he
gains Lord's awareness.  Like, when a lamp is lit, darkness
goes away; the Lord's awareness dispels darkness of the ego
intellect.

ਸਿਰੀਰਾਗੁ ਮਹਲਾ ੩ ॥
ਮਨਿ ਮੈਲੈ ਭਗਤਿ ਨ ਹੋਵਈ ਨਾਮੁ ਨ ਪਾਇਆ ਜਾਇ ॥
ਮਨਮੁਖ ਮੈਲੇ ਮੈਲੇ ਮੁਏ ਜਾਸਨਿ ਪਤਿ ਗਵਾਇ ॥
ਗੁਰ ਪਰਸਾਦੀ ਮਨਿ ਵਸੈ ਮਲੁ ਹਉਮੈ ਜਾਇ ਸਮਾਇ ॥
ਜਿਉ ਅੰਧੇਰੈ ਦੀਪਕੁ ਬਾਲੀਐ ਤਿਉ ਗੁਰ ਗਿਆਨਿ ਅਗਿਆਨੁ ਤਜਾਇ ॥੨॥
Sireeraag Mehalaa 3 |
Mana Mailai Bhagath N Hovee Naam N Paaeiaa Jaae |
Manamukh Mailae Mailae Mueae Jaasan Path Gavaae |
Gur Parasaadhee Man Vasai Mal Houmai Jaae Samaae |
Jio Andhhaerai Dheepak Baaleeai Thio Gur Giaan Agiaan Thajaae |2|   Page-39

# Mind

O' my mind, take the support of God's Name, nothing of this world will harm you, not even a whiff of hot air will touch you.  Like a boat saves from drowning in a stormy ocean, the lamp gives light in darkness; meditating on the Lord's Name, the mind enjoys bliss.

---

ਗਉੜੀ ਗੁਆਰੇਰੀ ਮਹਲਾ ੫ ॥
ਮਨ ਮੇਰੇ ਗਹੁ ਹਰਿ ਨਾਮ ਕਾ ਓਲਾ ॥ ਤੁਝੈ ਨ ਲਾਗੈ ਤਾਤਾ ਝੋਲਾ ॥੧॥ ਰਹਾਉ ॥
ਜਿਉ ਬੋਹਿਥੁ ਭੈ ਸਾਗਰ ਮਾਹਿ ॥ ਅੰਧਕਾਰ ਦੀਪਕ ਦੀਪਾਹਿ ॥
ਅਗਨਿ ਸੀਤ ਕਾ ਲਾਹਸਿ ਦੂਖ ॥ ਨਾਮੁ ਜਪਤ ਮਨਿ ਹੋਵਤ ਸੂਖ ॥੨॥
Gourree Guaaraeree 5th Guru |
Mana Maerae Gahu Har Naam Kaa Oulaa |
Thujhai N Laagai Thaathaa Jholaa |1| Pause |
Jio Bohithh Bhai Saagar Maahi | Andhhakaar Dheepak Dheepaahi |
Agan Seeth Kaa Laahas Dhookh | Naam Japath Man Hovath Sookh |2|    Page-179

# Mind

O' brother, somebody should search the mind to learn;" when it is separated from the body, where does it go?" There is One Soul and it pervades all bodies. Kabeer only Contemplates on this Mind!

---

ਰਾਗੁ ਗਉੜੀ ਗੁਆਰੇਰੀ ਅਸਟਪਦੀ ਕਬੀਰ ਜੀ ॥
ਇਸੁ ਮਨ ਕਉ ਕੋਈ ਖੋਜਹੁ ਭਾਈ ॥ ਤਨ ਛੂਟੇ ਮਨੁ ਕਹਾ ਸਮਾਈ ॥੪॥
ਜੀਉ ਏਕੁ ਅਰੁ ਸਗਲ ਸਰੀਰਾ ॥ ਇਸੁ ਮਨ ਕਉ ਰਵਿ ਰਹੇ ਕਬੀਰਾ ॥੯॥੧॥੩੬॥

Raag Gourree Guaaraeree Asattapadhee Kabeer Jee Kee |
Eis Man Ko Koee Khojahu Bhaaee |Than Shhoottae Man Kehaa Samaaee |4|
Jeeo Eaek Ar Sagal Sareeraa |Eis Man Ko Rav Rehae Kabeeraa |9|1|36|   Page-330

Mind

O' respected elder, my mind is intoxicated with the Lord's Name, drinking its Nectar. It is completely at peace and remains absorbed in God's Love, night and day enjoying the celestial music of the Wordless Word.

ਆਸਾ ਮਹਲਾ ੧ ॥
ਬਾਬਾ ਮਨੁ ਮਤਵਾਰੋ ਨਾਮ ਰਸੁ ਪੀਵੈ ਸਹਜ ਰੰਗ ਰਚਿ ਰਹਿਆ ॥
ਅਹਿਨਿਸਿ ਬਨੀ ਪ੍ਰੇਮ ਲਿਵ ਲਾਗੀ ਸਬਦੁ ਅਨਾਹਦ ਗਹਿਆ ॥੧॥ ਰਹਾਉ ॥
Aasaa 1st Guru |
Baabaa Man Mathavaaro Naam Ras Peevai Sehaj Rang Rach Rehiaa |
Ahinis Banee Praem Liv Laagee Sabadh Anaahadh Gehiaa |1| Pause |   Page-360

O' brother, who should I tell about such a bad state of the human mind? Engrossed in greed, running around in all directions, and ever busy in the desire to accumulate wealth!

ਰਾਗੁ ਆਸਾ ਮਹਲਾ ੯ ॥
ਬਿਰਥਾ ਕਹਉ ਕਉਨ ਸਿਉ ਮਨ ਕੀ ॥
ਲੋਭਿ ਗ੍ਰਸਿਓ ਦਸ ਹੂ ਦਿਸ ਧਾਵਤ ਆਸਾ ਲਾਗਿਓ ਧਨ ਕੀ ॥੧॥ ਰਹਾਉ ॥
Raag Aasaa 9th Guru |
Birathhaa Keho Koun Sio Man Kee |
Lobh Grasiou Dhas Hoo Dhis Dhhaavath Aasaa Laagiou Dhhan Kee |1|Pause |   Page-411

# Mind

O' my mind, you are the embodiment of Divine Light - recognize your own origin. The Dear Lord is always with you; through the Guru's Teachings, enjoy His Love.
O' my mind, you are so full of ego; you shall depart loaded with pride. You are lured by love of the worldly illusion; this results in your going through the birth and death cycle ever and ever again.

---

ਆਸਾ ਮਹਲਾ ੩ ॥
ਮਨ ਤੂੰ ਜੋਤਿ ਸਰੂਪੁ ਹੈ ਆਪਣਾ ਮੂਲੁ ਪਛਾਣੁ ॥ ਮਨ ਹਰਿ ਜੀ ਤੇਰੈ ਨਾਲਿ ਹੈ ਗੁਰਮਤੀ ਰੰਗੁ ਮਾਣੁ ॥
ਮਨ ਤੂੰ ਗਾਰਬਿ ਅਟਿਆ ਗਾਰਬਿ ਲਦਿਆ ਜਾਹਿ ॥ ਮਾਇਆ ਮੋਹਣੀ ਮੋਹਿਆ ਫਿਰਿ ਫਿਰਿ ਜੂਨੀ ਭਵਾਹਿ ॥
Aasaa 3<sup>rd</sup> Guru |
Mana Thoon Joth Saroop Hai Aapanaa Mool Pashhaan |
Mana Har Jee Thaerai Naal Hai Guramathee Rang Maan |
Mana Thoon Gaarab Attiaa Gaarab Ladhiaa Jaahi |
Maaeiaa Mohanee Mohiaa Fir Fir Joonee Bhavaahi |    Page-441

# Mind

O' my dear mind, gone astray from your own Center, come Home! O' dear beloved, come into the Guru's Presence and you will realize, the Lord abides within you.

My beloved mind, revel in His love, as the Lord showers His Mercy. Says Nanak, the one to whom the Lord-Guru is Merciful, are united with the Lord.

---

ਆਸਾ ਮਹਲਾ 8 ॥

ਮੇਰੇ ਮਨ ਪਰਦੇਸੀ ਵੇ ਪਿਆਰੇ ਆਉ ਘਰੇ ॥ਹਰਿ ਗੁਰੂ ਮਿਲਾਵਹੁ ਮੇਰੇ ਪਿਆਰੇ ਘਰਿ ਵਸੈ ਹਰੇ ॥

ਰੰਗਿ ਰਲੀਆ ਮਾਣਹੁ ਮੇਰੇ ਪਿਆਰੇ ਹਰਿ ਕਿਰਪਾ ਕਰੇ ॥ਗੁਰੁ ਨਾਨਕੁ ਤੁਠਾ ਮੇਰੇ ਪਿਆਰੇ ਮੇਲੇ ਹਰੇ ॥੧॥

Aasaa 4<sup>th</sup> Guru |

Maerae Man Paradhaesee Vae Piaarae Aao Gharae |

Har Guroo Milaavahu Maerae Piaarae Ghar Vasai Harae |

Rang Raleeaa Maanahu Maerae Piaarae Har Kirapaa Karae |

Gur Naanak Thuthaa Maerae Piaarae Maelae Harae |1|   Page-451

# Mind

The snake sheds its skin, but does not lose its venom. Standing in water, the crane appears to be meditating, but it is deception (like a hypocrite with saintly outerwear closing eyes and pretending meditation). Similarly, why do you practice meditation and repeat the Lord's Name, when your mind is not pure?

ਆਸਾ ਬਾਣੀ ਸ੍ਰੀ ਨਾਮਦੇਉ ਜੀ ਕੀ ॥
ਸਾਪੁ ਕੁੰਚ ਛੋਡੈ ਬਿਖੁ ਨਹੀ ਛਾਡੈ ॥ ਉਦਕ ਮਾਹਿ ਜੈਸੇ ਬਗੁ ਧਿਆਨੁ ਮਾਡੈ ॥੧॥
ਕਾਹੇ ਕਉ ਕੀਜੈ ਧਿਆਨੁ ਜਪੰਨਾ ॥ ਜਬ ਤੇ ਸੁਧੁ ਨਾਹੀ ਮਨੁ ਅਪਨਾ ॥੧॥ ਰਹਾਉ ॥
Aasaa Baanee Sree Naamadhaeo Jee Kee |
Saap Kunch Shhoddai Bikh Nehee Shhaaddai |
Oudhak Maahi Jaisae Bag Dhhiaan Maaddai |1|
Kaahae Ko Keejai Dhhiaan Japannaa |
Jab Thae Sudhh Naahee Man Apanaa |1|Pause |    Page-485

# Mind

O my mind, remain steady within, where the Lord abides; do not wander away looking for Him outside.
By searching Him on the outside, you shall suffer great pain; the Ambrosial Nectar is found within the Home of your Own Being!

ਸੋਰਠਿ ਮਹਲਾ ੧ ॥
ਮਨ ਰੇ ਥਿਰੁ ਰਹੁ ਮਤੁ ਕਤ ਜਾਹੀ ਜੀਉ ॥
ਬਾਹਰਿ ਢੂਢਤ ਬਹੁਤੁ ਦੁਖੁ ਪਾਵਹਿ ਘਰਿ ਅੰਮ੍ਰਿਤੁ ਘਟ ਮਾਹੀ ਜੀਉ ॥ ਰਹਾਉ ॥
Sorath 1<sup>st</sup> Guru |
Mana Rae Thhir Rahu Math Kath Jaahee Jeeo |
Baahar Dtoodtath Bahuth Dhukh Paavehi Ghar Anmrith Ghatt Maahee Jeeo |Paus|
Page-598

# Mind

O' mother, my mind is not under control. Night and day, it runs around acquiring worldly riches; how can I restrain it? He listens to the holy books and teachings, but does not enshrine them in his heart, even for an instant. Engrossed in the wealth and women of others, his life is wasted away. He has gone insane with the wine of worldly illusion, and does not understand even a bit of spiritual wisdom. Deep within his heart, the Immaculate Lord dwells, but he does not know this secret.

---

ਸੋਰਠਿ ਮਹਲਾ ੯

ਮਾਈ ਮਨੁ ਮੇਰੋ ਬਸਿ ਨਾਹਿ ॥ ਨਿਸ ਬਾਸੁਰ ਬਿਖਿਅਨ ਕਉ ਧਾਵਤ ਕਿਹਿ ਬਿਧਿ ਰੋਕਉ ਤਾਹਿ ॥੧॥ ਰਹਾਉ ॥
ਬੇਦ ਪੁਰਾਨ ਸਿਮ੍ਰਿਤਿ ਕੇ ਮਤ ਸੁਨਿ ਨਿਮਖ ਨ ਹੀਏ ਬਸਾਵੈ ॥
ਪਰ ਧਨ ਪਰ ਦਾਰਾ ਸਿਉ ਰਚਿਓ ਬਿਰਥਾ ਜਨਮੁ ਸਿਰਾਵੈ ॥੧॥
ਮਦਿ ਮਾਇਆ ਕੈ ਭਇਓ ਬਾਵਰੋ ਸੂਝਤ ਨਹ ਕਛੁ ਗਿਆਨਾ ॥
ਘਟ ਹੀ ਭੀਤਰਿ ਬਸਤ ਨਿਰੰਜਨੁ ਤਾ ਕੋ ਮਰਮੁ ਨ ਜਾਨਾ ॥੨॥

Sorath 9th Guru |
Maaee Man Maero Bas Naahi |
Nis Baasur Bikhian Ko Dhhaavath Kihi Bidhh Roko Thaahi |1| Pause |
Baedh Puraan Simrith Kae Math Sun Nimakh N Heeeae Basaavai |
Par Dhhan Par Dhaaraa Sio Rachiou Birathhaa Janam Siraavai |1|
Madh Maaeiaa Kai Bhaeiou Baavaro Soojhath Neh Kashh Giaanaa |
Ghatt Hee Bheethar Basath Niranjan Thaa Ko Maram N Jaanaa |2|   Page-632

# Mind

The filth of countless incarnations sticks to this mind; it has become pitch black. The oily rag cannot be cleaned by merely washing it, even if it is washed a hundred times.

(Note: the referenced oily rag was used to clean oil from the indigenous mill while extracting it from cotton seed).

---

ਸਲੋਕੁ ਮਹਲਾ ੩ ॥
ਜਨਮ ਜਨਮ ਕੀ ਇਸੁ ਮਨ ਕਉ ਮਲੁ ਲਾਗੀ ਕਾਲਾ ਹੋਆ ਸਿਆਹੁ ॥
ਖੰਨਲੀ ਧੋਤੀ ਉਜਲੀ ਨ ਹੋਵਈ ਜੇ ਸਉ ਧੋਵਣਿ ਪਾਹੁ ॥
Salok 3<sup>rd</sup> Guru |
Janam Janam Kee Eis Man Ko Mal Laagee Kaalaa Hoaa Siaahu |
Khannalee Dhhothee Oujalee N Hovee Jae So Dhhovan Paahu |    Page-651

---

O' brother, keep searching your mind; watching the mind's movements in different directions, you find the Lord' Name, which is the nine treasures (ultimate treasure).

---

ਭੈਰਉ ਮਹਲਾ ੩ ॥
ਇਸੁ ਮਨ ਕਉ ਕੋਈ ਖੋਜਹੁ ਭਾਈ ॥ ਮਨੁ ਖੋਜਤ ਨਾਮੁ ਨਉ ਨਿਧਿ ਪਾਈ ॥੧॥ ਰਹਾਉ
Bhairo 3<sup>rd</sup> Guru |
Eis Man Ko Koee Khojahu Bhaaee |
Mana Khojath Naam No Nidhh Paaee |1| Rehaao |    Page-1128

# Mind

Practicing hypocrisy, he acquires the wealth of others; returning home, he squanders it on his wife and children. O' my mind, to make a living do not practice deception, even inadvertently. In the end, your own soul shall have to answer for its deeds. And, every moment old age is eating up your body; later no one will even pour water into your begging hands to quench thirst. Says Kabeer, none belongs to you; then why not meditate on the Lord's Name in your heart, when you are still young?

---

ਰਾਗੁ ਸੋਰਠਿ ਬਾਣੀ ਭਗਤ ਕਬੀਰ ਜੀ॥
ਬਹੁ ਪਰਪੰਚ ਕਰਿ ਪਰ ਧਨੁ ਲਿਆਵੈ ॥ ਸੁਤ ਦਾਰਾ ਪਹਿ ਆਨਿ ਲੁਟਾਵੈ ॥੧॥
ਮਨ ਮੇਰੇ ਭੂਲੇ ਕਪਟੁ ਨ ਕੀਜੈ ॥ ਅੰਤਿ ਨਿਬੇਰਾ ਤੇਰੇ ਜੀਅ ਪਹਿ ਲੀਜੈ ॥੧॥ ਰਹਾਉ ॥
ਛਿਨੁ ਛਿਨੁ ਤਨੁ ਛੀਜੈ ਜਰਾ ਜਨਾਵੈ ॥ ਤਬ ਤੇਰੀ ਓਕ ਕੋਈ ਪਾਨੀਓ ਨ ਪਾਵੈ ॥੨॥
ਕਹਤੁ ਕਬੀਰੁ ਕੋਈ ਨਹੀ ਤੇਰਾ ॥ ਹਿਰਦੈ ਰਾਮੁ ਕੀ ਨ ਜਪਹਿ ਸਵੇਰਾ ॥੩॥੯॥

Raag Sorath Baanee Bhagath Kabeer Jee |
Bahu Parapanch Kar Par Dhhan Liaavai | Suth Dhaaraa Pehi Aan Luttaavai |1|
Mana Maerae Bhoolae Kapatt N Keejai |
Anth Nibaeraa Thaerae Jeea Pehi Leejai |1|Rehaao |
Shhin Shhin Than Shheejai Jaraa Janaavai |
Thab Thaeree Ouk Koee Paaneeou N Paavai |2|
Kehath Kabeer Koee Nehee Thaeraa |
Hiradhai Raam Kee N Japehi Savaeraa |3|9| Page-656

# Mind

If one's mind becomes a stranger to God, the entire world appears to him a separate entity. Separated from God, everyone is full of pain and suffering, then to whom should I open the pack of my suffering and pain? Those gone astray from the Lord's Name, are caught in the never ending dreadful life and birth/death cycles. If a man's mind is estranged from God, the ego of "mine and your" abides in him.

---

ਸੂਹੀ ਮਹਲਾ ੧ ॥
ਮਨੁ ਪਰਦੇਸੀ ਜੇ ਥੀਐ ਸਭੁ ਦੇਸੁ ਪਰਾਇਆ ॥ਕਿਸੁ ਪਹਿ ਖੋਲ੍ਹਉ ਗੰਠੜੀ ਦੂਖੀ ਭਰਿ ਆਇਆ ॥
ਆਵਟੇ ਜਾਵਟੇ ਖਰੇ ਡਰਾਵਟੇ ਤੋਟਿ ਨ ਆਵੈ ਫੇਰੀਆ ॥
ਮਨੁ ਪਰਦੇਸੀ ਜੇ ਥੀਐ ਸਭੁ ਦੇਸੁ ਪਰਾਇਆ ॥੭॥

Soohee 1<sup>st</sup> Guru |
Mana Paradhaesee Jae Thheeai Sabh Dhaes Paraaeiaa |
Kis Pehi Kholho Gantharree Dhookhee Bhar Aaeiaa |
Aavanae Jaavanae Kharae Ddaraavanae Thott N Aavai Faereeaa |
Mana Paradhaesee Jae Thheeai Sabh Dhaes Paraaeiaa |7|   Page-767

# Mind

O' my mother, I have gathered the wealth of Lord's Name.
My mind has stopped its wanderings of seeking worldly
pleasures and now, it has become still in the treasure of
Lord's Name.
Ever since with His Mercy, I have found the crown jewel of
His Name, the fear and anxiety of countless life times has
been eradicated. My mind has become free of all desires and
I stay in bliss, which is ever within me.

---

ਬਸੰਤੁ ਮਹਲਾ ੯ ॥
ਮਾਈ ਮੈ ਧਨੁ ਪਾਇਓ ਹਰਿ ਨਾਮੁ ॥ ਮਨੁ ਮੇਰੋ ਧਾਵਨ ਤੇ ਛੂਟਿਓ ਕਰਿ ਬੈਠੋ ਬਿਸਰਾਮੁ ॥੧॥ ਰਹਾਉ ॥
ਜਨਮ ਜਨਮ ਕਾ ਸੰਸਾ ਚੂਕਾ ਰਤਨੁ ਨਾਮੁ ਜਬ ਪਾਇਆ ॥
ਤ੍ਰਿਸਨਾ ਸਕਲ ਬਿਨਾਸੀ ਮਨ ਤੇ ਨਿਜ ਸੁਖ ਮਾਹਿ ਸਮਾਇਆ ॥੨॥

Basanth 9<sup>th</sup> Guru |
Maaee Mai Dhhan Paaeiou Har Naam |
Mana Maero Dhhaavan Thae Shhoottiou Kar Baitho Bisaraam |1| Pause |
Janam Janam Kaa Sansaa Chookaa Rathan Naam Jab Paaeiaa |
Thrisanaa Sakal Binaasee Man Thae Nij Sukh Maahi Samaaeiaa |2|   Page-1186

# Mind

Other than God, who can be the Help and Support of the mind? Attachments to mother, father, spouse, children and sibling, are all an illusion. So, build a raft of the Lord's Name to go across; what reliance can you place on the worldly wealth? How can you rely on the fragile vessel (body) which can wither away with the slightest stroke? O' saints, whenever you have a desire, desire the dust of the God Oriented ones' feet. Says Kabeer, the mind is like a bird flying in the forest; seek Company of the Holy (*Saadh Sangat*) for it to come to rest.

---

ਸਾਰੰਗ ਕਬੀਰ ਜੀਉ ॥

ਹਰਿ ਬਿਨੁ ਕਉਨੁ ਸਹਾਈ ਮਨ ਕਾ ॥ ਮਾਤ ਪਿਤਾ ਭਾਈ ਸੁਤ ਬਨਿਤਾ ਹਿਤੁ ਲਾਗੋ ਸਭ ਫਨ ਕਾ ॥੧॥ ਰਹਾਉ ॥

ਆਗੇ ਕਉ ਕਿਛੁ ਤੁਲਹਾ ਬਾਂਧਹੁ ਕਿਆ ਭਰਵਾਸਾ ਧਨ ਕਾ ॥

ਕਹਾ ਬਿਸਾਸਾ ਇਸ ਭਾਂਡੇ ਕਾ ਇਤਨਕੁ ਲਾਗੈ ਠਨਕਾ ॥੧॥

ਸਗਲ ਧਰਮ ਪੁੰਨ ਫਲ ਪਾਵਹੁ ਧੂਰਿ ਬਾਂਛਹੁ ਸਭ ਜਨ ਕਾ ॥

ਕਹੈ ਕਬੀਰੁ ਸੁਨਹੁ ਰੇ ਸੰਤਹੁ ਇਹੁ ਮਨੁ ਉਡਨ ਪੰਖੇਰੂ ਬਨ ਕਾ ॥੨॥੧॥੯॥

Saarang Kabeer Jeeo |

Har Bin Koun Sehaaee Man Kaa |

Maath Pithaa Bhaaee Suth Banithaa Hith Laago Sabh Fan Kaa |1|Pause |

Aagae Ko Kishh Thulehaa Baandhhahu Kiaa Bharavaasaa Dhhan Kaa |

Kehaa Bisaasaa Eis Bhaanddae Kaa Eithanak Laagai Thanakaa |1|

Sagal Dhharam Punn Fal Paavahu Dhhoor Baanshhahu Sabh Jan Kaa |

Kehai Kabeer Sunahu Rae Santhahu Eihu Man Ouddan Pankhaeroo Ban Kaa |2|1|9|

Page -1253

## Chapter-6  Conscious Awareness (Simran)

True is the Master, True is His Name and Love is the language of the Infinite Lord. We beg to Him and the Great Giver gives us whatever we want. When He is the Giver of everything, what can we place before Him to come into His Presence? And what words should we utter to evoke His Love? In the Ambrosial hours before dawn, meditate on the True Name, and contemplate His Glorious Greatness. By the Lord's Mercy, you are blessed with the human body and by His Grace, the Gate of Liberation is found. O' Nanak, know this well that the True One Himself is All Pervading.

---

॥ ਜਪੁ ॥ ਗੁਰੂ ਨਾਨਕ ॥

ਸਾਚਾ ਸਾਹਿਬੁ ਸਾਚੁ ਨਾਇ ਭਾਖਿਆ ਭਾਉ ਅਪਾਰੁ ॥ਆਖਹਿ ਮੰਗਹਿ ਦੇਹਿ ਦੇਹਿ ਦਾਤਿ ਕਰੇ ਦਾਤਾਰੁ ॥

ਫੇਰਿ ਕਿ ਅਗੈ ਰਖੀਐ ਜਿਤੁ ਦਿਸੈ ਦਰਬਾਰੁ ॥ਮੁਹੌ ਕਿ ਬੋਲਣੁ ਬੋਲੀਐ ਜਿਤੁ ਸੁਣਿ ਧਰੇ ਪਿਆਰੁ ॥

ਅੰਮ੍ਰਿਤ ਵੇਲਾ ਸਚੁ ਨਾਓ ਵਡਿਆਈ ਵੀਚਾਰੁ ॥ਕਰਮੀ ਆਵੈ ਕਪੜਾ ਨਦਰੀ ਮੋਖੁ ਦੁਆਰੁ ॥

ਨਾਨਕ ਏਵੈ ਜਾਣੀਐ ਸਭੁ ਆਪੇ ਸਚਿਆਰੁ ॥੪॥

"JAP" First Guru:

Saachaa Saahib Saach Naae Bhaakhiaa Bhaao Apaar |
Aakhehi Mangehi Dhaehi Dhaehi Dhaath Karae Dhaathaar |
Faer K Agai Rakheeai Jith Dhisai Dharabaar |
Muha K Bolan Boleeai Jith Sun Dhharae Piaar |
Anmrith Vaelaa Sach Naao Vaddiaaee Veechaar |
Karamee Aavai Kaparraa Nadharee Mokh Dhuaar |
Naanak Eaevai Jaaneeai Sabh Aapae Sachiaar |4|   Page-2

Rise early in the morning before dawn and meditate on the Lord's Name; then remember Him every moment day and night. Says Nanak, anxieties shall not afflict you and negativities that disturb internal peace shall disappear.

ਗਉੜੀ ਬਾਵਨ ਅਖਰੀ ਮਹਲਾ ੫ ॥
ਸਲੋਕੁ ॥
ਝਾਲਾਘੇ ਉਠਿ ਨਾਮੁ ਜਪਿ ਨਿਸਿ ਬਾਸੁਰ ਆਰਾਧਿ ॥ ਕਾਰ੍ਹਾ ਤੁਝੈ ਨ ਬਿਆਪਈ ਨਾਨਕ ਮਿਟੈ ਉਪਾਧਿ ॥੧॥
Gourree Baavan Akharee Fifth Guru |
Salok |
Jhaalaaghae Outh Naam Jap Nis Baasur Aaraadhh |
Kaarhaa Thujhai N Biaapee Naanak Mittai Oupaadhh |1| Page-255

That one, in whose heart the Lord populates His Name, even minutely, the praises of such a blessed one cannot be sung. The Lord's Name is the greatest happiness and Ambrosial Nectar, and it resides in the minds of His devotees.

---

ਗਾਉੜੀ ਸੁਖਮਨੀ ਮਹਲਾ ੫ ॥
ਕਿਨਕਾ ਏਕ ਜਿਸੁ ਜੀਅ ਬਸਾਵੈ ॥ ਤਾ ਕੀ ਮਹਿਮਾ ਗਨੀ ਨ ਆਵੈ ॥
ਸੁਖਮਨੀ ਸੁਖ ਅੰਮ੍ਰਿਤ ਪ੍ਰਭ ਨਾਮੁ ॥ ਭਗਤ ਜਨਾ ਕੈ ਮਨਿ ਬਿਸ੍ਰਾਮ ॥ ਰਹਾਉ ॥
Gourree Sukhamanee Fifth Guru |
Kinakaa Eaek Jis Jeea Basaavai | Thaa Kee Mehimaa Ganee N Aavai |
Sukhamanee Sukh Anmrith Prabh Naam | Bhagath Janaa Kai Man Bisraam |Pause |
Page-262

To the truly God Oriented, being awake or asleep is immaterial as in their every breath, they are immersed in His Bliss; they are the embodiment of the Omnipresent Lord. It is through God's Grace that the True Guru is found and one meditates on His Name day and night; I also wish to be ever in their Holy Company so that I may be ushered into His Presence.

---

ਸਲੋਕੁ ਮਹਲਾ ੪ ॥
ਕਿਆ ਸਵਣਾ ਕਿਆ ਜਾਗਣਾ ਗੁਰਮੁਖਿ ਤੇ ਪਰਵਾਣੁ ॥
ਜਿਨਾ ਸਾਸ ਗਿਰਾਸ ਨ ਵਿਸਰੈ ਸੇ ਪੂਰੇ ਪੁਰਖ ਪਰਧਾਨ ॥
ਕਰਮੀ ਸਤਿਗੁਰੁ ਪਾਈਐ ਅਨਦਿਨੁ ਲਗੈ ਧਿਆਨੁ ॥ ਤਿਨ ਕੀ ਸੰਗਾਤ ਮਿਲਿ ਰਹਾ ਦਰਗਹ ਪਾਈ ਮਾਨੁ ॥

Salok Fourth Guru |
Kiaa Savanaa Kiaa Jaaganaa Guramukh Thae Paravaan |
Jinaa Saas Giraas N Visarai Sae Poorae Purakh Paradhhaan |
Karamee Sathigur Paaeeai Anadhin Lagai Dhhiaan |
Thin Kee Sangath Mil Rehaa Dharageh Paaee Maan |    Page-312

# Conscious Awareness (Simran)

Says Kabeer, remember a small thing and repeat the two
letters of God's Name "RaaMaa" (Raa – Maa); if the
Husband Lord so wishes, He will save you!

---

ਗਉੜੀ ਕਬੀਰ ਜੀ ॥
ਕਹੁ ਕਬੀਰ ਅਖਰ ਦੁਇ ਭਾਖ ॥ ਹੋਇਗਾ ਖਸਮੁ ਤੳ ਲੇਇਗਾ ਰਾਖ ॥੩॥੩੩॥
Gourree Kabeer Jee |
Kahu Kabeer Akhar Dhue Bhaakh |Hoeigaa Khasam Th Laeeigaa Raakh |3|33|
Page-329

---

Those who have forgotten the Name of the Lord, are deluded
by doubt and duality. Abandoning the tree and clinging to
the branches, how can one find shade?

---

ਆਸਾ ਮਹਲਾ ੧ ॥
ਜਿਨੑੀ ਨਾਮੁ ਵਿਸਾਰਿਆ ਦੂਜੈ ਭਰਮਿ ਭੁਲਾਈ ॥ ਮੂਲੁ ਛੋਡਿ ਡਾਲੀ ਲਗੇ ਕਿਆ ਪਾਵਹਿ ਛਾਈ ॥੧॥
Aasaa First Guru |
Jinhee Naam Visaariaa Dhoojai Bharam Bhulaaee |
Mool Shhodd Ddaalee Lagae Kiaa Paavehi Shhaaee |1|    Page-420

O' my brother, repeat the Lord's Name over, and over again, but do so slowly and calmly, and with love and attention; so, that the Lord Himself behind the words is not lost. Make your body like the clay pot (in which curd is churned to extract butter), churn in it the Wordless Word; do not let your mind wander away, then extract the Ambrosial Nectar of God's Name within you.

---

ਆਸਾ ਸ੍ਰੀ ਕਬੀਰ ਜੀਉ ਕੇ ਚਉਪਦੇ ਇਕਤੁਕੇ ॥
ਹਰਿ ਕਾ ਬਿਲੋਵਨਾ ਬਿਲੋਵਹੁ ਮੇਰੇ ਭਾਈ ॥ਸਹਜਿ ਬਿਲੋਵਹੁ ਜੈਸੇ ਤਤੁ ਨ ਜਾਈ ॥੧॥ ਰਹਾਉ ॥
ਤਨੁ ਕਰਿ ਮਟੁਕੀ ਮਨ ਮਾਹਿ ਬਿਲੋਈ ॥ਇਸੁ ਮਟੁਕੀ ਮਹਿ ਸਬਦੁ ਸੰਜੋਈ ॥੨॥

Aasaa Sree Kabeer Jeeo Kae Choupadhae Eikathukae |
Churn the churn of the Lord, O my Siblings of Destiny.
Sehaj Bilovahu Jaisae Thath N Jaaee |1| Pause |
Than Kar Mattukee Man Maahi Biloee |
Eis Mattukee Mehi Sabadh Sanjoee |2|     Page-478

The body is the fortress of the Infinite Lord; it is obtained with great fortune. The Lord Himself lives in this body, Himself is the Enjoyer of pleasures, Himself remains detached, and is unaffected by the worldly illusion (Maya). He does whatever pleases Him, and whatever He does, happens. The God Oriented meditate on the Lord's Name, and their perceived separation from the Lord is ended.

---

ਮਹਲਾ ੩ ॥ ਪਉੜੀ ॥
ਕਾਇਆ ਕੋਟੁ ਅਪਾਰੁ ਹੈ ਮਿਲਣਾ ਸੰਜੋਗੀ ॥ ਕਾਇਆ ਅੰਦਰਿ ਆਪਿ ਵਸਿ ਰਹਿਆ ਆਪੇ ਰਸ ਭੋਗੀ ॥
ਆਪਿ ਅਤੀਤੁ ਅਲਿਪਤੁ ਹੈ ਨਿਰਜੋਗੁ ਹਰਿ ਜੋਗੀ ॥ ਜੋ ਤਿਸੁ ਭਾਵੈ ਸੋ ਕਰੇ ਹਰਿ ਕਰੇ ਸੁ ਹੋਗੀ ॥
ਹਰਿ ਗੁਰਮੁਖਿ ਨਾਮੁ ਧਿਆਈਐ ਲਹਿ ਜਾਹਿ ਵਿਜੋਗੀ ॥੧੩॥

Third Guru | Pourree |
Kaaeiaa Kott Apaar Hai Milanaa Sanjogee |
Kaaeiaa Andhar Aap Vas Rehiaa Aapae Ras Bhogee |
Aap Atheeth Alipath Hai Nirajog Har Jogee |
Jo This Bhaavai So Karae Har Karae S Hogee |
Har Guramukh Naam Dhhiaaeeai Lehi Jaahi Vijogee |13|    Page-514

Deep within yourself, pray to the Lord Guru in adoration, and with your tongue, repeat the Guru's Name. Let your eyes behold the True Guru, and let your ears hear the Guru's Name. Attuned to the True Guru, you shall receive a place of honor in the Lord's Presence. Says Nanak, this treasure is bestowed on those who are blessed with His Mercy. In this world, they are known as the most pious, but they are indeed rare.

---

ਸਲੋਕੁ ਮਹਲਾ ੫ ॥
ਅੰਤਰਿ ਗੁਰੁ ਆਰਾਧਣਾ ਜਿਹਵਾ ਜਾਪ ਗੁਰ ਨਾਉ ॥ ਨੇਤ੍ਰੀ ਸਤਿਗੁਰੁ ਪੇਖਣਾ ਸ੍ਰਵਣੀ ਸੁਨਣਾ ਗੁਰ ਨਾਉ ॥
ਸਤਿਗੁਰ ਸੇਤੀ ਰਤਿਆ ਦਰਗਹ ਪਾਈਐ ਠਾਉ ॥ ਕਹੁ ਨਾਨਕ ਕਿਰਪਾ ਕਰੇ ਜਿਸ ਨੋ ਏਹ ਵਥੁ ਦੇਇ ॥
ਜਗ ਮਹਿ ਉਤਮ ਕਾਢੀਅਹਿ ਵਿਰਲੇ ਕੇਈ ਕੇਇ ॥੧॥
Salok Fifth Guru |
Anthar Gur Aaraadhhanaa Jihavaa Jap Gur Naao |
Naethree Sathigur Paekhanaa Sravanee Sunanaa Gur Naao |
Sathigur Saethee Rathiaa Dharageh Paaeeai Thaao |
Kahu Naanak Kirapaa Karae Jis No Eaeh Vathh Dhaee |
Jag Mehi Outham Kaadteeahi Viralae Kaeee Kaee |1|    Page-517

Kabeer's mother sobs, cries and bewails – O' Lord, how will
my grandchildren live? Kabeer has given up all his spinning
and weaving, and is all the time absorbed in repeating God's
Name. Says Kabeer, listen my mother, the Lord is the
provider of both the children and us. I do not want to separate
from my Beloved Lord even for a moment, but when I pass
the thread through the weaving reel, I forget Him. So, what
if people perceive me a lowly weaver of little intellect, but I
have earned the profit of Lord's Name in this world.

---

ਰਾਗੁ ਗੂਜਰੀ ਭਗਤਾ ਕੀ ਬਾਣੀ ॥ ਸ੍ਰੀ ਕਬੀਰ ਜੀਉ ॥
ਮੁਸ ਮੁਸ ਰੋਵੈ ਕਬੀਰ ਕੀ ਮਾਈ ॥ਏ ਬਾਰਿਕ ਕੈਸੇ ਜੀਵਹਿ ਰਘੁਰਾਈ ॥੧॥
ਤਨਨਾ ਬੁਨਨਾ ਸਭੁ ਤਜਿਓ ਹੈ ਕਬੀਰ ॥ਹਰਿ ਕਾ ਨਾਮੁ ਲਿਖਿ ਲੀਓ ਸਰੀਰ ॥੧॥ ਰਹਾਉ ॥
ਜਬ ਲਗੁ ਤਾਗਾ ਬਾਹਉ ਬੇਹੀ ॥ਤਬ ਲਗੁ ਬਿਸਰੈ ਰਾਮੁ ਸਨੇਹੀ ॥੨॥
ਓਛੀ ਮਤਿ ਮੇਰੀ ਜਾਤਿ ਜੁਲਾਹਾ ॥ਹਰਿ ਕਾ ਨਾਮੁ ਲਹਿਓ ਮੈ ਲਾਹਾ ॥੩॥
ਕਹਤ ਕਬੀਰ ਸੁਨਹੁ ਮੇਰੀ ਮਾਈ ॥ਹਮਰਾ ਇਨ ਕਾ ਦਾਤਾ ਏਕੁ ਰਘੁਰਾਈ ॥੪॥੨॥

Raag Goojaree Bhagathaa Kee Baanee
Sree Kabeer Jeeo
Mus Mus Rovai Kabeer Kee Maaee | Eae Baarik Kaisae Jeevehi Raghuraaee |1|
Thananaa Bunanaa Sabh Thajiou Hai Kabeer |
Har Kaa Naam Likh Leeou Sareer |1| Pause |
Jab Lag Thaagaa Baaho Baehee | Thab Lag Bisarai Raam Sanaehee |2|
Oushhee Math Maeree Jaath Julaahaa | Har Kaa Naam Lehiou Mai Laahaa |3|
Kehath Kabeer Sunahu Maeree Maaee |
Hamaraa Ein Kaa Dhaathaa Eaek Raghuraaee |4|2|    Page-524

O' my beautiful soul, do not delay even for a moment to repeat the God's Name as you may or may not have the next breath. O' my beautiful soul, fortunate is that day, time, moment, and instant when the Lord comes into my mind.

---

ਬਿਹਾਗੜਾ ਮਹਲਾ ੪ ॥

ਹਰਿ ਜਪਦਿਆ ਖਿਨੁ ਢਿਲ ਨ ਕੀਜਈ ਮੇਰੀ ਜਿੰਦੁੜੀਏ ਮਤੁ ਕਿ ਜਾਪੈ ਸਾਹੁ ਆਵੈ ਕਿ ਨ ਆਵੈ ਰਾਮ ॥
ਸਾ ਵੇਲਾ ਸੋ ਮੂਰਤੁ ਸਾ ਘੜੀ ਸੋ ਮੁਹਤੁ ਸਫਲੁ ਹੈ ਮੇਰੀ ਜਿੰਦੁੜੀਏ ਜਿਤੁ ਹਰਿ ਮੇਰਾ ਚਿਤਿ ਆਵੈ ਰਾਮ ॥

Bihaagarraa Fourth Guru |

Har Japadhiaa Khin Dtil N Keejee Maeree Jindhurreeeae Math K Jaapai Saahu Aavai K N Aavai Raam |

Saa Vaelaa So Moorath Saa Gharree So Muhath Safal Hai Maeree Jindhurreeeae Jith Har Maeraa Chith Aavai Raam |    Page-540

O' Saints, salvation comes only from meditating on the Lord's Name. That is why, sitting, standing, night and day, do the good deed of remembering on the Lord.

---

ਸੋਰਠਿ ਮਹਲਾ ੫ ॥
ਸੰਤਹੁ ਰਾਮ ਨਾਮ ਨਿਸਤਰੀਐ ॥
ਉਠਤ ਬੈਠਤ ਹਰਿ ਹਰਿ ਧਿਆਈਐ ਅਨਦਿਨੁ ਸੁਕ੍ਰਿਤੁ ਕਰੀਐ ॥੧॥ ਰਹਾਉ ॥
Sorath Fifth Guru |
Santhahu Raam Naam Nisathareeai |
Oothath Baithath Har Har Dhhiaaeeai Anadhin Sukirath Kareeai |1| Pause |
Page-621

---

O' brother, the one who by great fortune meditates on the Lord, all types of worries and anxieties vanish from within him. The Guru has blessed His servant Nanak with the understanding, that by meditating on the Lord, we can cross over the terrifying world-ocean.

---

ਧਨਾਸਰੀ ਮਹਲਾ ੪ ॥
ਜਹ ਹਰਿ ਸਿਮਰਨੁ ਭਇਆ ਤਹ ਉਪਾਧਿ ਗਤੁ ਕੀਨੀ ਵਡਭਾਗੀ ਹਰਿ ਜਪਨਾ ॥
ਜਨ ਨਾਨਕ ਕਉ ਗੁਰਿ ਇਹ ਮਤਿ ਦੀਨੀ ਜਾਪ ਹਰਿ ਭਵਜਲੁ ਤਰਨਾ ॥੨॥੬॥੧੨॥
Dhhanaasaree Fourth Guru |
Jeh Har Simaran Bhaeiaa Theh Oupaadhh Gath Keenee Vaddabhaagee Har Japanaa |
Jan Naanak Ko Gur Eih Math Dheenee Jap Har Bhavajal Tharanaa |2|6|12|    Page-670

O' brother, meditate on the Lord, meditate on the Lord, meditate on the Lord forever! Without meditating on the Lord's Name in meditation, a great many have drowned in the worldly ocean. You have wandered in many incarnations, as a pig, dog, etc., but still feel no shame! Forsaking the Ambrosial Name of the Lord, why do you eat poison?

---

ਰਾਗੁ ਧਨਾਸਰੀ ਬਾਣੀ ਭਗਤ ਕਬੀਰ ਜੀ ਕੀ
ਰਾਮ ਸਿਮਰਿ ਰਾਮ ਸਿਮਰਿ ਰਾਮ ਸਿਮਰਿ ਭਾਈ ॥ਰਾਮ ਨਾਮ ਸਿਮਰਨ ਬਿਨੁ ਬੂਡਤੇ ਅਧਿਕਾਈ ॥੧॥ ਰਹਾਉ
॥ਸੂਕਰ ਕੂਕਰ ਜੋਨਿ ਭ੍ਰਮੇ ਤਊ ਲਾਜ ਨ ਆਈ ॥
ਰਾਮ ਨਾਮ ਛਾਡਿ ਅੰਮ੍ਰਿਤ ਕਾਹੇ ਬਿਖੁ ਖਾਈ ॥੩॥
Raag Dhhanaasaree Baanee Bhagath Kabeer Jee Kee
Raam Simar Raam Simar Raam Simar Bhaaee ||Raam Naam Simaran Bin
Booddathae Adhhikaaee ||1|| Rehaao ||Sookar Kookar Jon Bhramae Thoo Laaj N
Aaee ||Raam Naam Shhaadd Anmrith Kaahae Bikh Khaaee ||3||      Page-692

---

O' God, meditating on Your Name and remembrance is giving to us the spiritual life. You dwell near those upon whom You show mercy.

---

ਸੂਹੀ ਮਹਲਾ ੫ ॥
ਜੀਵਨ ਰੂਪੁ ਸਿਮਰਣੁ ਪ੍ਰਭ ਤੇਰਾ ॥ ਜਿਸੁ ਕ੍ਰਿਪਾ ਕਰਹਿ ਬਸਹਿ ਤਿਸੁ ਨੇਰਾ ॥੨॥
Soohee Fifth Guru |
Jeevan Roop Simaran Prabh Thaeraa | Jis Kirapaa Karehi Basehi This Naeraa |2|
Page-743

One who accepts the wisdom of the True Guru's Teachings, is absorbed into the True Guru. The Lord's Name abides deep within the nucleus of one who realizes the *Bani* of the Guru's Word within his soul.

O' brother, in totally submitting to the Guru, understanding of the \*"four ages" is gained as one obtains the treasure of the Lord's Name. Celibacy, self-discipline, and pilgrimages were the essence of religion in the past ages; but in this Dark Age of Kala-Yuga, Praising of the Lord's Name is the essence of religion.

\* According to Hindu Mythology the existence has four Yugas (millions of years' period), first "Sata Yuga", the age of Truth; second "Treta Yuga", the age where Truth was partly forsaken for falsehood; third "Duapar Yuga", when two legs of Truth or religion were intact; and fourth Kala Yuga, the dark age.

---

ਬਿਲਾਵਲੁ ਮਹਲਾ ੩ ॥

ਸਤਿਗੁਰ ਕੀ ਜਿਸ ਨੋ ਮਤਿ ਆਵੈ ਸੋ ਸਤਿਗੁਰ ਮਾਹਿ ਸਮਾਨਾ ॥

ਇਹ ਬਾਣੀ ਜੋ ਜੀਅਹੁ ਜਾਣੈ ਤਿਸੁ ਅੰਤਰਿ ਰਵੈ ਹਰਿ ਨਾਮਾ ॥੧॥ ਰਹਾਉ ॥

ਚਹੁ ਜੁਗਾ ਕਾ ਹੁਣਿ ਨਿਬੇੜਾ ਨਰ ਮਨੁਖਾ ਨੋ ਏਕੁ ਨਿਧਾਨਾ ॥

ਜਤੁ ਸੰਜਮ ਤੀਰਥ ਓਨਾ ਜੁਗਾ ਕਾ ਧਰਮੁ ਹੈ ਕਲਿ ਮਹਿ ਕੀਰਤਿ ਹਰਿ ਨਾਮਾ ॥੨॥

Bilaaval Mehalaa 3 ||

Sathigur Kee Jis No Math Aavai So Sathigur Maahi Samaanaa ||

Eih Baanee Jo Jeeahu Jaanai This Anthar Ravai Har Naamaa ||1|| Rehaao ||

Chahu Jugaa Kaa Hun Nibaerraa Nar Manukhaa No Eaek Nidhhaanaa ||

Jath Sanjam Theerathh Ounaa Jugaa Kaa Dhharam Hai Kal Mehi Keerath Har Naamaa ||2|| Page-797

O' brother, meditate on the Lord of the Universe, and never ever forget Him. Inculcating Conscious Awareness (Simran) is the blessed opportunity of this human incarnation. This is your chance, and this is your time. Look deep into your own heart, and reflect on this seriously. Says Kabeer, I am repeatedly trying to tell you this in different ways; it is up to you to be a winner or loser in the game of life.

---

ਭੈਰਉ ਬਾਣੀ ਭਗਤਾ ਕੀ ॥ ਕਬੀਰ ਜੀਉ
ਭਜਹੁ ਗੋਬਿੰਦ ਭੂਲਿ ਮਤ ਜਾਹੁ ॥ਮਾਨਸ ਜਨਮ ਕਾ ਏਹੀ ਲਾਹੁ ॥੧॥ ਰਹਾਉ ॥
ਇਹੀ ਤੇਰਾ ਅਉਸਰੁ ਇਹ ਤੇਰੀ ਬਾਰ ॥ਘਟ ਭੀਤਰਿ ਤੂ ਦੇਖੁ ਬਿਚਾਰਿ ॥
ਕਹਤ ਕਬੀਰੁ ਜੀਤਿ ਕੈ ਹਾਰਿ ॥ਬਹੁ ਬਿਧ ਕਹਿਓ ਪੁਕਾਰਿ ਪੁਕਾਰਿ ॥੫॥੧॥੯॥
Bhairo Baanee Bhagathaa Kee ‖ Kabeer Jeeo
Bhajahu Guobindh Bhool Math Jaahu |
Maanas Janam Kaa Eaehee Laahu |1| Pause|
Eihee Thaeraa Aousar Eih Thaeree Baar | Ghatt Bheethar Thoo Dhaekh Bichaar |
Kehath Kabeer Jeeth Kai Haar | Bahu Bidhh Kehiou Pukaar Pukaar |5|1|9|    Page-1159

Kabeer, if you must rob, and plunder; then plunder the Lord's Name. Otherwise, in the world hereafter, you will regret and repent, when the breath of life leaves the body.

ਸਲੋਕ ਭਗਤ ਕਬੀਰ ਜੀਉ ਕੇ
ਕਬੀਰ ਲੁਟਨਾ ਹੈ ਤ ਲੂਟ ਲੈ ਰਾਮ ਨਾਮ ਹੈ ਲੂਟ ॥
ਿਫਿਰ ਪਾਛੈ ਪਛੁਤਾਹੁਗੇ ਪ੍ਰਾਨ ਜਾਹਿਗੇ ਛੂਟ ॥੪੧॥

Salok Bhagath Kabeer Jeeo Kae
Kabeer Loottanaa Hai Th Loott Lai Raam Naam Hai Loott |
Fir Paashhai Pashhuthaahugae Praan Jaahingae Shhoott |41|    Page-1366

Kabeer, why are you sleeping so deluded by the worldly illusion? Why don't you wake up and meditate on the Lord? One day you shall sleep with your legs outstretched as never to get up again.

ਸਲੋਕ ਭਗਤ ਕਬੀਰ ਜੀਉ ਕੇ
ਕਬੀਰ ਸੂਤਾ ਕਿਆ ਕਰਹਿ ਉਠਿ ਕਿ ਨ ਜਪਾਹਿ ਮੁਰਾਰ ॥
ਇਕ ਦਿਨ ਸੋਵਨੁ ਹੋਇਗੋ ਲਾਂਬੇ ਗੋਡ ਪਸਾਰ ॥੧੨੮॥

Salok Bhagath Kabeer Jeeo Kae
Kabeer Soothaa Kiaa Karehi Outh K N Japehi Muraar |
Eik Dhin Sovan Hoeigo Laanbae Godd Pasaar |128|    Page-1371

Says Trilochan, O' dear friend Naam Dayv, the worldly illusion has enticed you. Why are you stamping these clothes for selling and not meditating on the Lord's Name? Naam Dayv answers, O Trilochan, with your hands and feet, do all the work to earn a living, but utter God's Name with your mouth and stay consciously aware of the Immaculate Lord.

Note: Principal tenets of Guru Nanak's teachings are to stay consciously aware of the Lord, work to make an honest living leading a family life, and sharing your bread with others.

---

ਸਲੋਕ ਭਗਤ ਕਬੀਰ ਜੀਉ ਕੇ
ਨਾਮਾ ਮਾਇਆ ਮੋਹਿਆ ਕਹੈ ਤਿਲੋਚਨੁ ਮੀਤ ॥
ਕਾਹੇ ਛੀਪਹੁ ਛਾਇਲੈ ਰਾਮ ਨ ਲਾਵਹੁ ਚੀਤੁ ॥੨੧੨॥
ਨਾਮਾ ਕਹੈ ਤਿਲੋਚਨਾ ਮੁਖ ਤੇ ਰਾਮੁ ਸੰਮੑਾਲਿ ॥
ਹਾਥ ਪਾਉ ਕਰਿ ਕਾਮੁ ਸਭੁ ਚੀਤੁ ਨਿਰੰਜਨ ਨਾਲਿ ॥੨੧੩॥

Naamaa Maaeiaa Mohiaa Kehai Thilochan Meeth |
Kaahae Shheepahu Shhaaeilai Raam N Laavahu Cheeth ||212||
Naamaa Kehai Thilochanaa Mukh Thae Raam Sanmhaal ||
Haathh Paao Kar Kaam Sabh Cheeth Niranjan Naal ||213||     Page-1375

## Chapter-7  Surrender, Virtues & Faults

Due to my countless faults, I have been suffering the birth
and death cycles; how can I tell who is my mother, who the
father, or from where have I come?  We are formed from the
fire of the womb and a bubble of the sperm; for what purpose
are we created?  O' my Lord Master, who can know your
Glorious Virtues, but I am so full of countless faults. The
fortunate ones due to Your Mercy realize that You dwell
within us ever weighing our deeds.  Like the seas and the
oceans are overflowing with water, so vast are my own sins.
Please, shower me with Your Mercy, and take pity upon me;
You can carry across even sinking stones!

---

ਗਉੜੀ ਚੇਤੀ ਮਹਲਾ ੧ ॥
ਕਤ ਕੀ ਮਾਈ ਬਾਪੁ ਕਤ ਕੇਰਾ ਕਿਦੂ ਥਾਵਹੁ ਹਮ ਆਏ ॥
ਅਗਨਿ ਬਿੰਬ ਜਲ ਭੀਤਰਿ ਨਿਪਜੇ ਕਾਹੇ ਕੰਮਿ ਉਪਾਏ ॥੧॥
ਮੇਰੇ ਸਾਹਿਬਾ ਕਉਣੁ ਜਾਨੈ ਗੁਣ ਤੇਰੇ ॥ਕਹੇ ਨ ਜਾਨੀ ਅਉਗਣ ਮੇਰੇ ॥੧॥ ਰਹਾਉ ॥
ਲੈ ਕੈ ਤਕੜੀ ਤੋਲਣਿ ਲਾਗਾ ਘਟ ਹੀ ਮਹਿ ਵਟਜਾਰਾ ॥੪॥
ਜੇਤਾ ਸਮੁੰਦੁ ਸਾਗਰੁ ਨੀਰਿ ਭਰਿਆ ਤੇਤੇ ਅਉਗਣ ਹਮਾਰੇ ॥
ਦਇਆ ਕਰਹੁ ਕਿਛੁ ਮਿਹਰ ਉਪਾਵਹੁ ਡੂਬਦੇ ਪਥਰ ਤਾਰੇ ॥੫॥
Gourree Chaethee 1ˢᵗ Guru |
Kath Kee Maaee Baap Kath Kaeraa Kidhoo Thhaavahu Ham Aaeae |Agan Binb Jal
Bheethar Nipajae Kaahae Kanm Oupaaeae |1|Maerae Saahibaa Koun Jaanai Gun Thaerae
|Kehae N Jaanee Aougan Maerae |1| Pause |Lai Kai Thakarree Tholan Laagaa Ghatt Hee
Mehi Vanajaaraa |4|Jaethaa Samundh Saagar Neer Bhariaa Thaethae Aougan Hamaarae
|Dhaeiaa Karahu Kishh Mihar Oupaavahu Ddubadhae Paththar Thaarae |5|  Page-156

O' my Lord, the one who thirsts for Your Vision, he stays detached from Maya and enjoys peaceful bliss. Please listen to Your servant Nanak's prayer; infuse only Your Name in his heart.

---

ਆਸਾ ਮਹਲਾ ੫ ॥

ਦਰਸ ਤੇਰੇ ਕੀ ਪਿਆਸ ਮਨਿ ਲਾਗੀ ॥ ਸਹਜ ਅਨੰਦ ਬਸੈ ਬੈਰਾਗੀ ॥੩॥

ਨਾਨਕ ਕੀ ਅਰਦਾਸਿ ਸੁਣੀਜੈ ॥ ਕੇਵਲ ਨਾਮੁ ਰਿਦੇ ਮਹਿ ਦੀਜੈ ॥੪॥੨੬॥੭੭॥

Aasaa 5th Guru |

Dharas Thaerae Kee Piaas Man Laagee | Sehaj Anandh Basai Bairaagee |3|

Naanak Kee Aradhaas Suneejai | Kaeval Naam Ridhae Mehi Dheejai |4|26|77|

Page-389

---

O Nanak, meeting the True Guru, one comes to know the Perfect Way of living life. While laughing, playing, dressing, eating, and doing all the worldly tasks, one can be Liberated.

---

ਮਹਲਾ ੫ ॥

ਨਾਨਕ ਸਤਿਗੁਰਿ ਭੇਟਿਐ ਪੂਰੀ ਹੋਵੈ ਜੁਗਤਿ ॥

ਹਸੰਦਿਆ ਖੇਲੰਦਿਆ ਪੈਨੰਦਿਆ ਖਾਵੰਦਿਆ ਵਿਚੇ ਹੋਵੈ ਮੁਕਤਿ ॥੨॥

Naanak Sathigur Bhaettiai Pooree Hovai Jugath |Hasandhiaa Khaelandhiaa Painandhiaa Khaavandhiaa Vichae Hovai Mukath |2|   Page-522

O' my mother, my body is overflowing with faults; how can I meet my Beloved Lord who is the embodiment of all the Virtues?

---

ਵਡਹੰਸੁ ਮਹਲਾ ੪ ॥

ਮੈ ਅਵਗਣ ਭਰਪੂਰਿ ਸਰੀਰੇ ॥ ਹਉ ਕਿਉ ਕਰਿ ਮਿਲਾ ਅਪਣੇ ਪ੍ਰੀਤਮ ਪੂਰੇ ॥੨॥

Vaddehans 4th Guru |Mai Avagan Bharapoor Sareerae | Ho Kio Kar Milaa Apanae Preetham Poorae |2| Page-561

---

Wealth and supernatural powers are all emotional attachments; through them, the Name of the Lord, does not come to dwell in one's mind. Serving the Lord- Guru, the mind becomes immaculately pure, and the darkness of spiritual ignorance is dispelled. The jewel of the Lord's Name is revealed in the home of one's own being; O' Nanak, one merges in celestial bliss.

---

ਸਲੋਕੁ ਮਹਲਾ ੩ ॥

ਰਿਧਿ ਸਿਧਿ ਸਭੁ ਮੋਹੁ ਹੈ ਨਾਮੁ ਨ ਵਸੈ ਮਨਿ ਆਇ ॥

ਗੁਰ ਸੇਵਾ ਤੇ ਮਨੁ ਨਿਰਮਲੁ ਹੋਵੈ ਅਗਿਆਨੁ ਅੰਧੇਰਾ ਜਾਇ ॥

ਨਾਮੁ ਰਤਨੁ ਘਰਿ ਪਰਗਟੁ ਹੋਆ ਨਾਨਕ ਸਹਜਿ ਸਮਾਇ ॥੧॥

Ridhh Sidhh Sabh Mohu Hai Naam N Vasai Man Aae |Gur Saevaa Thae Man Niramal Hovai Agiaan Andhhaeraa Jaae |Naam Rathan Ghar Paragatt Hoaa Naanak Sehaj Samaae |1| Page-593

I have come to perceive, that when the Lord-Magician beats His tambourine, the entire Creation comes to see the show; and when the Magician winds up the show, He Himself Enjoys Alone!
What is the use of reading and listening to the religious scriptures, such as the Vedas and Purina's, if you have not become tranquil and come into the Lord's Presence?

---

ਰਾਗੁ ਸੋਰਠਿ ਬਾਣੀ ਭਗਤ ਕਬੀਰ ਜੀ ॥
ਬਾਜੀਗਰ ਡੰਕ ਬਜਾਈ ॥ ਸਭ ਖਲਕ ਤਮਾਸੇ ਆਈ ॥
ਬਾਜੀਗਰ ਸ੍ਵਾਂਗੁ ਸਕੇਲਾ ॥ ਅਪਨੇ ਰੰਗ ਰਵੈ ਅਕੇਲਾ ॥੨॥
ਕਿਆ ਪੜੀਐ ਕਿਆ ਗੁਨੀਐ ॥ ਕਿਆ ਬੇਦ ਪੁਰਾਨਾਂ ਸੁਨੀਐ ॥
ਪੜੇ ਸੁਨੇ ਕਿਆ ਹੋਈ ॥ ਜਉ ਸਹਜ ਨ ਮਿਲਿਓ ਸੋਈ ॥੧॥
Raag Sorath Baanee Bhagath Kabeer Jee |
Baajeegar Ddank Bajaaee | Sabh Khalak Thamaasae Aaee |Baajeegar Svaang Sakaelaa
|Apanae Rang Ravai Akaelaa |2|Kiaa Parreeai Kiaa Guneeai |Kiaa Baedh Puraanaan Suneeai
|Parrae Sunae Kiaa Hoee |Parrae Sunae Kiaa Hoee |    Page-655

O' brother, we cannot meet the Lord by our own efforts, nor through any particular service; He comes and meets us most unexpectedly! The one who is blessed by my Lord Master's Grace, practices the Teachings of the Guru's Word.

ਧਨਾਸਰੀ ਮਹਲਾ ੫ ॥
ਘਾਲ ਨ ਮਿਲਿਓ ਸੇਵ ਨ ਮਿਲਿਓ ਮਿਲਿਓ ਆਇ ਅਚਿੰਤਾ ॥
ਜਾ ਕਉ ਦਇਆ ਕਰੀ ਮੇਰੈ ਠਾਕੁਰਿ ਤਿਨਿ ਗੁਰਹਿ ਕਮਾਨੋ ਮੰਤਾ ॥੩॥

Dhhanaasaree 5<sup>th</sup> Guru |
Ghaal N Miliou Saev N Miliou Miliou Aae Achinthaa |Jaa Ko Dhaeiaa Karee Maerai Thaakur Thin Gurehi Kamaano Manthaa |3|  Page-672

O' Merciful Lord, unite me with You; I have come and fallen at Your door, surrendered completely. O' Merciful to the meek, save me; wandering and wandering, I am now very tired and exhausted!

ਮਹਲਾ ੫ ॥ ਪਉੜੀ ॥
ਮੇਲਿ ਲੈਹੁ ਦਇਆਲ ਢਹਿ ਪਏ ਦੁਆਰਿਆ ॥ਰਖਿ ਲੇਵਹੁ ਦੀਨ ਦਇਆਲ ਭ੍ਰਮਤ ਬਹੁ ਹਾਰਿਆ ॥

5<sup>th</sup> Guru|Pourree |
Mael Laihu Dhaeiaal Dtehi Peae Dhuaariaa |
Rakh Laevahu Dheen Dhaeiaal Bhramath Bahu Haariaa |  Page-709

The Lord Himself is absolute; He is The One and Only; but He Himself is also manifested in many forms. Whatever pleases Him, O Nanak, that alone is good.

---

ਤਿਲੰਗ ਮਹਲਾ ੪ ॥
ਆਪੇ ਹਰਿ ਇਕ ਰੰਗੁ ਹੈ ਆਪੇ ਬਹੁ ਰੰਗੀ ॥ਜੋ ਤਿਸੁ ਭਾਵੈ ਨਾਨਕਾ ਸਾਈ ਗਲ ਚੰਗੀ ॥੨੨॥੨॥
Thilang 4th Guru |
Aapae Har Eik Rang Hai Aapae Bahu Rangee |
Jo This Bhaavai Naanakaa Saaee Gal Changee |22|2|  Page-726

---

O' foolish man, you have knowingly and fully understanding ruined your own affairs. You did not restrain yourself from committing sins and did not eradicate the ego of wealth and worldly objects. So, Says Nanak, listen to the Teachings imparted by the Guru, and surrender Fully to the Lord.

---

ਤਿਲੰਗ ਮਹਲਾ ੯ ॥
ਜਾਨਿ ਬੂਝ ਕੈ ਬਾਵਰੇ ਤੈ ਕਾਜੁ ਬਿਗਾਰਿਓ ॥ਪਾਪ ਕਰਤ ਸੁਕਚਿਓ ਨਹੀ ਨਹ ਗਰਬੁ ਨਿਵਾਰਿਓ ॥੨॥
ਜਿਹ ਬਿਧਿ ਗੁਰ ਉਪਦੇਸਿਆ ਸੋ ਸੁਨੁ ਰੇ ਭਾਈ ॥ਨਾਨਕ ਕਹਤ ਪੁਕਾਰਿ ਕੈ ਗਹੁ ਪ੍ਰਭ ਸਰਨਾਈ ॥੩॥੩॥
Thilang 9th Guru |
Jaan Boojh Kai Baavarae Thai Kaaj Bigaariou |Paap Karath Sukachiou Nehee Neh Garab Nivaariou |2|Jih Bidhh Gur Oupadhaesiaa So Sun Rae Bhaaee |Naanak Kehath Pukaar Kai Gahu Prabh Saranaaee |3|3|  Page-727

O' brother, only if someone would come, and lead me to my Beloved Darling; I would sell myself to him. I am yearning for the Blessed Vision of the Lord. O' Merciful Lord, if You bless me with happiness, I will worship and adore You, but even in pain, I will meditate on You. If You give me hunger, I will stay satiated and will celebrate happiness even during sufferings. Poor Nanak has fallen at Your Door; O' Lord by Your Glorious Greatness, please unite me with You.

---

ਰਾਗੁ ਸੂਹੀ ਅਸਟਪਦੀਆ ਮਹਲਾ ੪ ॥
ਕੋਈ ਆਣਿ ਮਿਲਾਵੈ ਮੇਰਾ ਪ੍ਰੀਤਮੁ ਪਿਆਰਾ ਹਉ ਤਿਸੁ ਪਹਿ ਆਪੁ ਵੇਚਾਈ ॥੧॥ਦਰਸਨੁ ਹਰਿ ਦੇਖਣ ਕੈ ਤਾਈ ॥ਕ੍ਰਿਪਾ ਕਰਹਿ ਤਾ ਸਤਿਗੁਰੁ ਮੇਲਹਿ ਹਰਿ ਹਰਿ ਨਾਮੁ ਧਿਆਈ ॥੧॥ ਰਹਾਉ ॥ਜੇ ਸੁਖੁ ਦੇਹਿ ਤ ਤੁਝਹਿ ਅਰਾਧੀ ਦੁਖਿ ਭੀ ਤੁਝੈ ਧਿਆਈ ॥੨॥ਜੇ ਭੁਖ ਦੇਹਿ ਤ ਇਤ ਹੀ ਰਾਜਾ ਦੁਖ ਵਿਚਿ ਸੂਖ ਮਨਾਈ ॥ ਨਾਨਕੁ ਗਰੀਬੁ ਢਹਿ ਪਇਆ ਦੁਆਰੈ ਹਰਿ ਮੇਲਿ ਲੈਹੁ ਵਡਿਆਈ ॥੬॥
Raag Soohee Asattapadheeaa 4th Guru |
Koee Aan Milaavai Maeraa Preetham Piaaraa Ho This Pehi Aap Vaechaaee |1|
Dharasan Har Dhaekhan Kai Thaaee |Kirapaa Karehi Thaa Sathigur Maelehi Har Har Naam Dhhiaaee |1|Pause |Jae Sukh Dhaehi Th Thujhehi Araadhhee Dhukh Bhee Thujhai Dhhiaaee |2|Jae Bhukh Dhaehi Th Eith Hee Raajaa Dhukh Vich Sookh Manaaee |3|Than Man Kaatt Kaatt Sabh Arapee Vich Aganee Aap Jalaaee |4|Pakhaa Faeree Paanee Dtovaa Jo Dhaevehi So Khaaee |5|
Naanak Gareeb Dtehi Paeiaa Dhuaarai Har Mael Laihu Vaddiaaee |6|   Page-757

O' my Husband Lord, even if I am prone to mistakes and do not tread the righteous path, I am still called "Yours". Those who love anyone other than You, certainly die regretting and repeating their lives. I shall never leave my Husband Lord's side. My Beloved Lover is forever beautiful; He is my support and inspiration. Says Nanak, when in His Love, I became fully calm within, and overcoming my pride surrendered to Him, then my Beloved met me. I have received what was pre-ordained with the eternal blessing of the Guru.

---

ਰਾਗੁ ਸੂਹੀ ਮਹਲਾ ੫ ਅਸਟਪਦੀਆ ਘਰੁ ੧੦ ॥
ਜੇ ਭੁਲੀ ਜੇ ਚੁਕੀ ਸਾਈ. ਭੀ ਤਹਿੰਜੀ ਕਾਢੀਆ ॥ਜਿਨੑੂਹਾ ਨੇਹੁ ਦੂਜਾਣੇ ਲਗਾ ਝੂਰਿ ਮਰਹੁ ਸੇ ਵਾਢੀਆ ॥੧॥
ਹਉ ਨਾ ਛੋਡਉ ਕੰਤ ਪਾਸਰਾ ॥ਸਦਾ ਰੰਗੀਲਾ ਲਾਲੁ ਪਿਆਰਾ ਏਹੁ ਮਹਿੰਜਾ ਆਸਰਾ ॥੧॥ ਰਹਾਉ ॥
ਹੋਇ ਨਿਮਾਣੀ ਢਹਿ ਪਈ ਮਿਲਿਆ ਸਹਜਿ ਸੁਭਾਇ ॥
ਪੂਰਬਿ ਲਿਖਿਆ ਪਾਇਆ ਨਾਨਕ ਸੰਤ ਸਹਾਇ ॥੮॥੧॥੪॥

Raag Soohee 5th Guru Asattapadheeaa |
Jae Bhulee Jae Chukee Saaeanaee Bhee Thehinjee Kaadteeaa |
Jinhaa Naehu Dhoojaanae Lagaa Jhoor Marahu Sae Vaadteeaa |1|
Ho Naa Shhoddo Kanth Paasaraa |
Sadhaa Rangeelaa Laal Piaaraa Eaehu Mehinjaa Aasaraa |1| Pause|
Hoe Nimaanee Dtehi Pee Miliaa Sehaj Subhaae |
Poorab Likhiaa Paaeiaa Naanak Santh Sehaae |8|1|4|  Page-761

I have come from far away traversing many incarnations, seeking the Protection of Your Sanctuary. I have kept this hope in my mind, that You will completely take away all my pain and sufferings!

ਸੂਹੀ ਮਹਲਾ ੫ ਗੁਣਵੰਤੀ ॥
ਹਉ ਆਇਆ ਦੂਰਹੁ ਚਲਿ ਕੈ ਮੈ ਤਕੀ ਤਉ ਸਰਣਾਇ ਜੀਉ ॥
ਮੈ ਆਸਾ ਰਖੀ ਚਿਤਿ ਮਹਿ ਮੇਰਾ ਸਭੋ ਦੁਖੁ ਗਵਾਇ ਜੀਉ ॥
Soohee Mehalaa 5 Gunavanthee |
Ho Aaeiaa Dhoorahu Chal Kai Mai Thakee Tho Saranaae Jeeo |Mai Aasaa Rakhee
Chith Mehi Maeraa Sabho Dhukh Gavaae Jeeo |   Page-763

How Great, How Great is my Husband Lord! O' Lord and Master, You, created the creation and brought us into being. You created the oceans, mountains, vegetation and the rain making clouds. You Yourself created everything; Yourself dwell in everything and are still not affected by anything.

ਸਲੋਕ ਮਃ ੧ ॥
ਵਾਹੁ ਖਸਮ ਤੂ ਵਾਹੁ ਜਿਨਿ ਰਚਿ ਰਚਨਾ ਹਮ ਕੀਏ ॥
ਸਾਗਰ ਲਹਰਿ ਸਮੁੰਦ ਸਰ ਵੇਲਿ ਵਰਸ ਵਰਾਹੁ ॥ਆਪਿ ਖੜੋਵਹਿ ਆਪਿ ਕਰਿ ਆਪੀਨੈ ਆਪਾਹੁ ॥
Salok Ma 1 ||
Vaahu Khasam Thoo Vaahu Jin Rach Rachanaa Ham Keeeae ||
Saagar Lehar Samundh Sar Vael Varas Varaahu ||
Aap Kharrovehi Aap Kar Aapeenai Aapaahu ||   Page-788

Says Kabeer, I have the intense longing to die within, and fall dead at the Lord's door through complete surrender to the Lord. Then the Merciful Lord may come to ask," who is it that has fallen at my door?"

---

ਸਲੋਕ ਭਗਤ ਕਬੀਰ ਜੀਉ ਕੇ ॥
ਕਬੀਰ ਮੁਹਿ ਮਰਨੇ ਕਾ ਚਾਉ ਹੈ ਮਰਉ ਤ ਹਰਿ ਕੈ ਦੁਆਰ ॥
ਮਤ ਹਰਿ ਪੁਛੈ ਕਉਨੁ ਹੈ ਪਰਾ ਹਮਾਰੈ ਬਾਰ ॥੬੧॥
Salok Bhagath Kabeer Jeeo Kae|
Kabeer Muhi Maranae Kaa Chaao Hai Maro Th Har Kai Dhuaar |
Math Har Pooshhai Koun Hai Paraa Hamaarai Baar |61|   Page-1367

I am full of sins and demerits and have no virtues at all.
Abandoning the Ambrosial Nectar, I drink poison instead. I
am attached to the worldly illusion and deluded by doubt; I
am engrossed in love of my children and spouse. I have
heard about the most exalted path of "Company of the Holy"
(*Saad Sangat*), in which the fear of death is overcome.
Keerat the poet offers this one prayer: O" Guru Raam Daas,
save me; Please take me into Your Sanctuary!

---

ਸਵਈਏ ਮਹਲੇ ਚਉਥੇ ਕੇ ੪ ॥
ਹਮ ਅਵਗੁਨਿ ਭਰੇ ਏਕੁ ਗੁਨੁ ਨਾਹੀ ਅੰਮ੍ਰਿਤੁ ਛਾਡਿ ਬਿਖੈ ਬਿਖੁ ਖਾਈ ॥
ਮਾਯਾ ਮੋਹ ਭਰਮ ਪੈ ਭੂਲੇ ਸੁਤ ਦਾਰਾ ਸਿਉ ਪ੍ਰੀਤਿ ਲਗਾਈ ॥
ਇਕੁ ਉਤਮ ਪੰਥੁ ਸੁਨਿਓ ਗੁਰ ਸੰਗਤਿ ਤਿਹ ਮਿਲੰਤ ਜਮ ਤ੍ਰਾਸ ਮਿਟਾਈ ॥
ਇਕ ਅਰਦਾਸਿ ਭਾਟ ਕੀਰਤਿ ਕੀ ਗੁਰ ਰਾਮਦਾਸ ਰਾਖਹੁ ਸਰਣਾਈ ॥੪॥੫੮॥
Saveeeae Mehalae Chouthhae Kae 4|
Ham Avagun Bharae Eaek Gun Naahee Anmrith Shhaadd Bikhai Bikh Khaaee |
Maayaa Moh Bharam Pai Bhoolae Suth Dhaaraa Sio Preeth Lagaaee |
Eik Outham Panthh Suniou Gur Sangath Thih Milanth Jam Thraas Mittaaee |
Eik Aradhaas Bhaatt Keerath Kee Gur Raamadhaas Raakhahu Saranaaee |4|58|
Page-1406

---

## Chapter-8   Death, Heaven & Hell

Do not long for a place in Heaven after death, nor live in fear of possibly going to Hell. Whatever is going to happen, will happen by His Will; hence do not keep any desires in your mind. O my mind, in the end no one will give you any support; hence do not commit misdeeds to carry others' burden. This world is like the perch of a bird on the tree.

ਗਉੜੀ ਪੂਰਬੀ ਕਬੀਰ ਜੀ ॥
ਸੁਰਗ ਬਾਸੁ ਨ ਬਾਛੀਐ ਡਰੀਐ ਨ ਨਰਕਿ ਨਿਵਾਸੁ ॥
ਹੋਨਾ ਹੈ ਸੋ ਹੋਈ ਹੈ ਮਨਹਿ ਨ ਕੀਜੈ ਆਸ ॥੧॥
ਗਉੜੀ ॥ਰੇ ਮਨ ਤੇਰੋ ਕੋਇ ਨਹੀ ਖਿੰਚਿ ਲੇਇ ਜਿਨਿ ਭਾਰੁ ॥ਬਿਰਖ ਬਸੇਰੋ ਪੰਖਿ ਕੋ ਤੈਸੋ ਇਹੁ ਸੰਸਾਰੁ ॥੧॥

Gourree Poorabee | Kabeer Jee |
Surag Baas N Baashheeai Ddareeai N Narak Nivaas |
Honaa Hai So Hoee Hai Manehi N Keejai Aas |1|
Gourree |Rae Man Thaero Koe Nehee Khinch Laee Jin Bhaar |
Birakh Basaero Pankh Ko Thaiso Eihu Sansaar |1|   Page-337

O' Father, tell me: where has, the soul gone? It used to dwell within the body, consciously dancing, speaking, and teaching!

---

ਆਸਾ ਸ੍ਰੀ ਕਬੀਰ ਜੀਉ |
ਬਾਬਾ ਬੋਲਤੇ ਤੇ ਕਹਾ ਗਏ ਦੇਹੀ ਕੇ ਸੰਗਿ ਰਹਤੇ ॥
ਸੁਰਤਿ ਮਾਹਿ ਜੋ ਨਿਰਤੇ ਕਰਤੇ ਕਥਾ ਬਾਰਤਾ ਕਹਤੇ ॥੧॥ ਰਹਾਉ ॥
Aasaa Sree Kabeer Jeeo |
Baabaa Bolathae Thae Kehaa Geae Dhaehee Kae Sang Rehathae |
Surath Maahi Jo Nirathae Karathae Kathhaa Baarathaa Kehathae |1| Pause |
Page-480

---

I realized God, when I understood that there is only one clay from which God has created many forms. Says Kabeer, I have abandoned the paradise of your conception and reconciled my mind to hell!

---

ਆਸਾ ਸ੍ਰੀ ਕਬੀਰ ਜੀਉ
ਮਾਟੀ ਏਕ ਭੇਖ ਧਰਿ ਨਾਨਾ ਤਾ ਮਹਿ ਬ੍ਰਹਮੁ ਪਛਾਨਾ ॥
ਕਹੈ ਕਬੀਰਾ ਭਿਸਤ ਛੋਡਿ ਕਰਿ ਦੋਜਕ ਸਿਉ ਮਨੁ ਮਾਨਾ ॥੫॥੪॥੧੭॥
Aasaa Sree Kabeer Jeeo |
Maattee Eaek Bhaekh Dhhar Naanaa Thaa Mehi Breham Pashhaanaa |
Kehai Kabeeraa Bhisath Shhodd Kar Dhojak Sio Man Maanaa ||5||4||17||
Page-480

While living in this world, if one dies from it; then by so dying, he attains Liberation. Says Nanak, one only finds the True Guru, when he loses his own "self"!

ਮਹਲਾ ੩ ॥
ਜੀਵਤੁ ਮਰੈ ਮਰੈ ਫੁਨਿ ਜੀਵੈ ਤਾਂ ਮੋਖੰਤਰੁ ਪਾਏ ॥
ਨਾਨਕ ਸਤਿਗੁਰੁ ਤਦ ਹੀ ਪਾਏ ਜਾਂ ਵਿਚਹੁ ਆਪੁ ਗਵਾਏ ॥੨॥
Third Guru |
Jeevath Marai Marai Fun Jeevai Thaan Mokhanthar Paaeae |
Naanak Sathigur Thadh Hee Paaeae Jaan Vichahu Aap Gavaaeae |2|    Page-550

O' my Lord, liberation, truthful living, and happiness all come from serving You, to those whom You shower Your Grace. You alone instill the faith in us to sing Your Praises. Heaven is where Your Praises are sung!

ਸੂਹੀ ਮਹਲਾ ੫ ॥
ਮੁਕਤਿ ਭੁਗਤਿ ਜੁਗਤਿ ਤੇਰੀ ਸੇਵਾ ਜਿਸੁ ਤੂੰ ਆਪਿ ਕਰਾਇਹਿ ॥
ਤਹਾ ਬੈਕੁੰਠੁ ਜਹ ਕੀਰਤਨੁ ਤੇਰਾ ਤੂੰ ਆਪੇ ਸਰਧਾ ਲਾਇਹਿ ॥੨॥
Soohee Fifth Guru |
Mukath Bhugath Jugath Thaeree Saevaa Jis Thoon Aap Karaaeihi |
Thehaa Baikunth Jeh Keerathan Thaeraa Thoon Aapae Saradhhaa Laaeihi |2|   Page-749

O' Kabeer, you see everybody in this world is dying, but no one knows how to Truly die? Whosoever dies within, does not have to die ever again!
Third Guru: What do I know? How will I die? What sort of death will it be? If the Lord Master is not forgotten from the mind, then dying will be easy!
The world is terrified of death; everyone longs to live. By Guru's Grace, if one dies from ego while living, he realizes the Lord's Will. Says Nanak, one who dies such a death, lives forever.

---

ਬਿਹਾਗੜੇ ਕੀ ਵਾਰ ਮਹਲਾ ੪ ॥ ਸਲੋਕ ॥
ਕਬੀਰਾ ਮਰਤਾ ਮਰਤਾ ਜਗੁ ਮੁਆ ਮਰਿ ਭਿ ਨ ਜਾਨੈ ਕੋਇ ॥ ਐਸੀ ਮਰਨੀ ਜੋ ਮਰੈ ਬਹੁਰਿ ਨ ਮਰਨਾ ਹੋਇ ॥੧॥
ਮਹਲਾ ੩ ॥
ਕਿਆ ਜਾਣਾ ਕਿਵ ਮਰਹਗੇ ਕੈਸਾ ਮਰਣਾ ਹੋਇ ॥ ਜੇ ਕਰਿ ਸਾਹਿਬੁ ਮਨਹੁ ਨ ਵੀਸਰੈ ਤਾ ਸਹਿਲਾ ਮਰਣਾ ਹੋਇ ॥
ਮਰਣੈ ਤੇ ਜਗਤੁ ਡਰੈ ਜੀਵਿਆ ਲੋੜੈ ਸਭੁ ਕੋਇ ॥ ਗੁਰ ਪਰਸਾਦੀ ਜੀਵਤੁ ਮਰੈ ਹੁਕਮੈ ਬੂਝੈ ਸੋਇ ॥
ਨਾਨਕ ਐਸੀ ਮਰਨੀ ਜੋ ਮਰੈ ਤਾ ਸਦ ਜੀਵਣੁ ਹੋਇ ॥੨॥
Bihaagarrae Kee Vaar Fourth Guru
Salok |
Kabeeraa Marathaa Marathaa Jag Muaa Mar Bh N Jaanai Koe |
Aisee Maranee Jo Marai Bahur N Maranaa Hoe |1|
Third Guru |
Kiaa Jaanaa Kiv Marehagae Kaisaa Maranaa Hoe |
Jae Kar Saahib Manahu N Veesarai Thaa Sehilaa Maranaa Hoe |
Maranai Thae Jagath Ddarai Jeeviaa Lorrai Sabh Koe |
Gur Parasaadhee Jeevath Marai Hukamai Boojhai Soe |
Naanak Aisee Maranee Jo Marai Thaa Sadh Jeevan Hoe |2|    Page-555

Dying in the Wordless Word, you shall be free of all sins, become eternally alive and never die again. The Ambrosial Nectar of the Lord's Name is ever-sweet to the mind; but only few obtain trough the Wordless Word. The Great Giver keeps this Gift of the Name in His own hands and gives it to only those that He pleases. O' Nanak, imbued with the Lord's Name, they find peace, and in the Court of the Lord, they are exalted.

---

ਸੋਰਠਿ ਮਹਲਾ ੩ ॥
ਸਬਦਿ ਮਰਹੁ ਫਿਰਿ ਜੀਵਹੁ ਸਦ ਹੀ ਤਾ ਫਿਰਿ ਮਰਣੁ ਨ ਹੋਈ ॥
ਅੰਮ੍ਰਿਤੁ ਨਾਮੁ ਸਦਾ ਮਨਿ ਮੀਠਾ ਸਬਦੇ ਪਾਵੈ ਕੋਈ ॥੩॥
ਦਾਤੈ ਦਾਤਿ ਰਖੀ ਹਥਿ ਅਪਨੈ ਜਿਸੁ ਭਾਵੈ ਤਿਸੁ ਦੇਈ ॥
ਨਾਨਕ ਨਾਮਿ ਰਤੇ ਸੁਖੁ ਪਾਇਆ ਦਰਗਹ ਜਾਪਹਿ ਸੇਈ ॥੪॥੧੧॥
Sorath Third Guru |
Sabadh Marahu Fir Jeevahu Sadh Hee Thaa Fir Maran N Hoee |
Anmrith Naam Sadhaa Man Meethaa Sabadhae Paavai Koee |3|
Dhaathai Dhaath Rakhee Hathh Apanai Jis Bhaavai This Dhaeee |
Naanak Naam Rathae Sukh Paaeiaa Dharageh Jaapehi Saeee |4|11|    Page-604

We human beings live by each breath, do not know the extent of our life and the time of death. Prays Nanak, contemplate on the Lord, to whom our sole and breath of life belong. O' man, blinded by the worldly illusion, open your eyes and understand that your life in this world is for a limited time. Says Nanak, so long as we live, we should listen to and sing the Lord's Praises. I have searched and searched but found no place to have a permanent abode, hence I decided to die while living.

---

ਧਨਾਸਰੀ ਮਹਲਾ ੧ ॥
ਹਮ ਆਦਮੀ ਹਾਂ ਇਕ ਦਮੀ ਮੁਹਲਤਿ ਮੁਹਤੁ ਨ ਜਾਣਾ ॥ ਨਾਨਕੁ ਬਿਨਵੈ ਤਿਸੈ ਸਰੇਵਹੁ ਜਾ ਕੇ ਜੀਅ ਪਰਾਣਾ ॥੧॥
ਅੰਧੇ ਜੀਵਨਾ ਵੀਚਾਰਿ ਦੇਖਿ ਕੇਤੇ ਕੇ ਦਿਨਾ ॥੧॥ ਰਹਾਉ ॥
ਜਬ ਲਗੁ ਦੁਨੀਆ ਰਹੀਐ ਨਾਨਕ ਕਿਛੁ ਸੁਣੀਐ ਕਿਛੁ ਕਹੀਐ ॥
ਭਾਲਿ ਰਹੇ ਹਮ ਰਹਣੁ ਨ ਪਾਇਆ ਜੀਵਤਿਆ ਮਰਿ ਰਹੀਐ ॥੫॥੨॥
Dhhanaasaree First Guru |
Ham Aadhamee Haan Eik Dhamee Muhalath Muhath N Jaanaa |
Naanak Binavai Thisai Saraevahu Jaa Kae Jeea Paraanaa |1|
Andhhae Jeevanaa Veechaar Dhaekh Kaethae Kae Dhinaa |1| Pause |
Jab Lag Dhuneeaa Reheeai Naanak Kishh Suneeai Kishh Keheeai |
Bhaal Rehae Ham Rehan N Paaeiaa Jeevathiaa Mar Reheeai |5||2| Page-660

Like the iced-water loses its hardness with the Sun's rays and becomes one with the ocean, singing the Lord's Praises, one's dry self is wetted, merges with the Lord, and becomes Perfect. He then sees the One God everywhere and hears God speaking in everyone. He sees God in the entire Creation and does not recognize anything other than God. Prays Nanak, they alone know this, who have tasted the subtle essence of the Lord' Name.

---

ਬਿਲਾਵਲੁ ਮਹਲਾ ੫ ॥

ਸੂਰਜ ਕਿਰਣਿ ਮਿਲੇ ਜਲ ਕਾ ਜਲੁ ਹੂਆ ਰਾਮ ॥ ਜੋਤੀ ਜੋਤਿ ਰਲੀ ਸੰਪੂਰਨੁ ਥੀਆ ਰਾਮ ॥

ਬ੍ਰਹਮੁ ਦੀਸੈ ਬ੍ਰਹਮੁ ਸੁਣੀਐ ਏਕੁ ਏਕੁ ਵਖਾਣੀਐ ॥ ਆਤਮ ਪਸਾਰਾ ਕਰਣਹਾਰਾ ਪ੍ਰਭ ਬਿਨਾ ਨਹੀ ਜਾਣੀਐ ॥

ਆਪਿ ਕਰਤਾ ਆਪਿ ਭੁਗਤਾ ਆਪਿ ਕਾਰਣੁ ਕੀਆ ॥

ਬਿਨਵੰਤਿ ਨਾਨਕ ਸੇਈ ਜਾਣਹਿ ਜਿਨੑੀ ਹਰਿ ਰਸੁ ਪੀਆ ॥੪॥੨॥

Bilaaval Fifth Guru |
Sooraj Kiran Milae Jal Kaa Jal Hooaa Raam |
Jothee Joth Ralee Sanpooran Thheeaa Raam |
Breham Dheesai Breham Suneeai Eaek Eaek Vakhaaneeai |
Aatham Pasaaraa Karanehaaraa Prabh Binaa Nehee Jaaneeai |
Aap Karathaa Aap Bhugathaa Aap Kaaran Keeaa |
Binavanth Naanak Saeee Jaanehi Jinhee Har Ras Peeaa |4|2|    Page-846

Why am I so full of pride when the truth is that even my body is of little common use after death, while an animal's body serves many causes? I never think of the bad deeds I do every day, why am I not aware of the results, Father? The bones burn like a bundle of logs and hair burn like a bale of hay. Says Kabeer, the man only wakes up from his slumber and repents, when the club of death hits him over the head.

---

ਰਾਗੁ ਗੋਂਡ ਬਾਣੀ ਭਗਤਾ ਕੀ ਕਬੀਰ ਜੀ ॥
ਨਰੁ ਮਰੈ ਨਰੁ ਕਾਮਿ ਨ ਆਵੈ ॥ ਪਸੁ ਮਰੈ ਦਸ ਕਾਜ ਸਵਾਰੈ ॥੧॥
ਅਪਨੇ ਕਰਮ ਕੀ ਗਤਿ ਮੈ ਕਿਆ ਜਾਨਉ ॥ ਮੈ ਕਿਆ ਜਾਨਉ ਬਾਬਾ ਰੇ ॥੧॥ ਰਹਾਉ ॥
ਹਾਡ ਜਲੇ ਜੈਸੇ ਲਕਰੀ ਕਾ ਤੂਲਾ ॥ ਕੇਸ ਜਲੇ ਜੈਸੇ ਘਾਸ ਕਾ ਪੂਲਾ ॥੨॥
ਕਹੁ ਕਬੀਰ ਤਬ ਹੀ ਨਰੁ ਜਾਗੈ ॥ ਜਮ ਕਾ ਡੰਡੁ ਮੂੰਡ ਮਹਿ ਲਾਗੈ ॥੩॥੨॥
Raag Gonadd Baanee Bhagathaa Kee Kabeer Jee |
Naroo Marai Nar Kaam N Aavai | Pasoo Marai Dhas Kaaj Savaarai |1|
Apanae Karam Kee Gath Mai Kiaa Jaano | Mai Kiaa Jaano Baabaa Rae |1| Pause |Haadd
Jalae Jaisae Lakaree Kaa Thoolaa | Kaes Jalae Jaisae Ghaas Kaa Poolaa |2|Kahu Kabeer
Thab Hee Nar Jaagai | Jam Kaa Ddandd Moondd Mehi Laagai |3|2|   Page-870

When we say, somebody has died; in reality, the five elements of which the body is made, namely, air, water, space, fire, and earth, merge with those elements and the soul merges with the eternal Light. The one who weeps is due to his not understanding the Truth. Check, with the God Oriented Saints, life and death is just a wondrous play. The Creator Lord created this Creation. It comes and goes, subject to the Will of the Infinite Lord. No one dies; or can die. The soul does not perish; it is imperishable. Says Nanak, the Guru has dispelled my doubt; no one dies or comes and goes.

---

ਰਾਮਕਲੀ ਮਹਲਾ ੫ ॥
ਪਵਨੈ ਮਹਿ ਪਵਨੁ ਸਮਾਇਆ ॥ ਜੋਤੀ ਮਹਿ ਜੋਤਿ ਰਲਿ ਜਾਇਆ ॥
ਮਾਟੀ ਮਾਟੀ ਹੋਈ ਏਕ ॥ ਰੋਵਨਹਾਰੇ ਕੀ ਕਵਨ ਟੇਕ ॥੧॥
ਕਉਨੁ ਮੂਆ ਰੇ ਕਉਨੁ ਮੂਆ ॥
ਬ੍ਰਹਮ ਗਿਆਨੀ ਮਿਲਿ ਕਰਹੁ ਬੀਚਾਰਾ ਇਹੁ ਤਉ ਚਲਤੁ ਭਇਆ ॥੧॥ ਰਹਾਉ ॥
ਇਹੁ ਤਉ ਰਚਨੁ ਰਚਿਆ ਕਰਤਾਰਿ ॥ ਆਵਤ ਜਾਵਤ ਹੁਕਮਿ ਅਪਾਰਿ ॥
ਨਹ ਕੋ ਮੂਆ ਨ ਮਰਣੈ ਜੋਗੁ ॥ ਨਹ ਬਿਨਸੈ ਅਬਿਨਾਸੀ ਹੋਗੁ ॥੩॥
ਕਹੁ ਨਾਨਕ ਗੁਰਿ ਭਰਮੁ ਚੁਕਾਇਆ ॥ ਨਾ ਕੋਈ ਮਰੈ ਨ ਆਵੈ ਜਾਇਆ ॥੪॥੧੦॥
Raamakalee Fifth Guru |
Pavanai Mehi Pavan Samaaeiaa | Jothee Mehi Joth Ral Jaaeiaa |
Maattee Maattee Hoee Eaek | Rovanehaarae Kee Kavan Ttaek |1|
Koun Mooaa Rae Koun Mooaa |
Breham Giaanee Mil Karahu Beechaaraa Eihu Tho Chalath Bhaeiaa |1| Pause |
Eihu Tho Rachan Rachiaa Karathaar | Aavath Jaavath Hukam Apaar |
Neh Ko Mooaa N Maranai Jog | Neh Binasai Abinaasee Hog |3|
Kahu Naanak Gur Bharam Chukaaeiaa | Naa Koee Marai N Aavai Jaaeiaa |4|10|
Page-885

What is hell, and what is poor heaven? The Saints reject them both. I have no obligation to either of them, by the Grace of my Guru. Now, I have reached the highest state of internal bliss; I have met the Lord, the Sustainer of the World! The Lord and Kabeer have become one; no one can tell the difference.

---

ਰਾਮਕਲੀ ਬਾਣੀ ਭਗਤਾ ਕੀ ਕਬੀਰ ਜੀਉ ॥
ਕਵਨ ਨਰਕੁ ਕਿਆ ਸੁਰਗੁ ਬਿਚਾਰਾ ਸੰਤਨ ਦੋਉ ਰਾਦੇ ॥
ਹਮ ਕਾਹੂ ਕੀ ਕਾਣਿ ਨ ਕਢਤੇ ਅਪਨੇ ਗੁਰ ਪਰਸਾਦੇ ॥੫॥
ਅਬ ਤਉ ਜਾਇ ਚਢੇ ਸਿੰਘਾਸਨਿ ਮਿਲੇ ਹੈ ਸਾਰਿੰਗਪਾਨੀ ॥
ਰਾਮ ਕਬੀਰਾ ਏਕ ਭਏ ਹੈ ਕੋਇ ਨ ਸਕੈ ਪਛਾਨੀ ॥੬॥੩॥

Raamakalee Baanee Bhagathaa Kee Kabeer Jeeou|
Kavan Narak Kiaa Surag Bichaaraa Santhan Dhooo Raadhae |
Ham Kaahoo Kee Kaan N Kadtathae Apanae Gur Parasaadhae |5|
Ab Tho Jaae Chadtae Singhaasan Milae Hai Saaringapaanee |
Raam Kabeeraa Eaek Bheae Hai Koe N Sakai Pashhaanee ||6||3||    Page-969

The body-bride keeps saying to the soul, "O' my beloved youthful husband, please stay with me forever. Without you, I am of no use; promise to me that you will never leave". The soul-husband replies, "I am a slave to the Lord's Will. He is the Great Master who is Perfect and Fearless. I will remain with you so long as He Wills, but when He calls, I will get up and depart".

---

ਮਾਰੂ ਸੋਲਹੇ ਮਹਲਾ ੫
ਧਨ ਕਹੈ ਤੂ ਵਸੁ ਮੈ ਨਾਲੇ ॥ਪ੍ਰਿਅ ਸੁਖਵਾਸੀ ਬਾਲ ਗੁਪਾਲੇ ॥
ਤੁਝੈ ਬਿਨਾ ਹਉ ਕਿਤ ਹੀ ਨ ਲੇਖੈ ਵਚਨੁ ਦੇਹਿ ਛੋਡਿ ਨ ਜਾਸਾ ਹੇ ॥੭॥
ਪਿਰਿ ਕਹਿਆ ਹਉ ਹੁਕਮੀ ਬੰਦਾ ॥ਓਹੁ ਭਾਰੋ ਠਾਕੁਰੁ ਜਿਸੁ ਕਾਣਿ ਨ ਛੰਦਾ ॥
ਜਿਚਰੁ ਰਾਖੈ ਤਿਚਰੁ ਤੁਮ ਸੰਗਿ ਰਹਣਾ ਜਾ ਸਦੇ ਤ ਊਠਿ ਸਿਧਾਸਾ ਹੇ ॥੮॥
Maaroo Solehae 5th Guru|
Dhhan Kehai Thoo Vas Mai Naalae |Pria Sukhavaasee Baal Gupaalae |
Thujhai Binaa Ho Kith Hee N Laekhai Vachan Dhaehi Shhodd N Jaasaa Hae |7|
Pir Kehiaa Ho Hukamee Bandhaa |Ouhu Bhaaro Thaakur Jis Kaan N Shhandhaa |
Jichar Raakhai Thichar Thum Sang Rehanaa Jaa Sadhae Th Ooth Sidhhaasaa Hae |8|
Page-1072

O" father, now I shall not live in this village. The accountant "Chitar Gupat", recording scribes of the conscious and the unconscious, asks for an account of each, and every moment. Says Kabeer, listen, O' Saints: settle your accounts of the senses in this life. Then pray, O' Lord, please forgive Your servant now, in this life; so, that he may not have to return again to this terrifying world-ocean.

ਰਾਗੁ ਮਾਰੂ ਬਾਣੀ ਕਬੀਰ ਜੀਉ ਕੀ॥
ਬਾਬਾ ਅਬ ਨ ਬਸਉ ਇਹ ਗਾਉ ॥ਘਰੀ ਘਰੀ ਕਾ ਲੇਖਾ ਮਾਗੈ ਕਾਇਥੁ ਚੇਤੁ ਨਾਉ ॥੧॥ ਰਹਾਉ ॥
ਕਹੈ ਕਬੀਰੁ ਸੁਨਹੁ ਰੇ ਸੰਤਹੁ ਖੇਤ ਹੀ ਕਰਹੁ ਨਿਬੇਰਾ ॥ਅਬ ਕੀ ਬਾਰ ਬਖਸਿ ਬੰਦੇ ਕਉ ਬਹੁਰਿ ਨ ਭਉਜਲਿ ਫੇਰਾ
॥੩॥੭॥
Raag Maaroo Baanee Kabeer Jeeo Kee ||
Baabaa Ab N Baso Eih Gaao || Gharee Gharee Kaa Laekhaa Maagai Kaaeithh
Chaethoo Naao ||1|| Rehaao || Kehai Kabeer Sunahu Rae Santhahu Khaeth Hee
Karahu Nibaeraa || Ab Kee Baar Bakhas Bandhae Ko Bahur N Bhoujal Faeraa
||3||7||  Page-1104

The Lord says, O' man, first accept dying from your ego and give up the desire of living a selfish life. If you become so humble as the dust of everybody's feet, then you can come near Me.

ਸਲੋਕ ਮਹਲਾ ੫ ॥
ਪਹਿਲਾ ਮਰਣੁ ਕਬੂਲਿ ਜੀਵਣ ਕੀ ਛਡਿ ਆਸ ॥ ਹੋਹੁ ਸਭਨਾ ਕੀ ਰੇਣੁਕਾ ਤਉ ਆਉ ਹਮਾਰੈ ਪਾਸਿ ॥੧॥
Salok 5ᵗʰ Guru|
Pehilaa Maran Kabool Jeevan Kee Shhadd Aas |
Hohu Sabhanaa Kee Raenukaa Tho Aao Hamaarai Paas |1|  Page-1102

Kabeer, the world is afraid of dying from attachments; but such a death fills my mind with bliss. It is only by such death that the Lord is obtained; who is the Perfect Bliss.

ਸਲੋਕ ਭਗਤ ਕਬੀਰ ਜੀਉ ਕੇ ॥
ਕਬੀਰ ਜਿਸੁ ਮਰਨੇ ਤੇ ਜਗੁ ਡਰੈ ਮੇਰੇ ਮਨਿ ਆਨੰਦੁ ॥
ਮਰਨੇ ਹੀ ਤੇ ਪਾਈਐ ਪੂਰਨੁ ਪਰਮਾਨੰਦੁ ॥੨੨॥
Salok Bhagath Kabeer Jeeo Kae |
Kabeer Jis Maranae Thae Jag Ddarai Maerae Man Aanandh |
Maranae Hee Thae Paaeeai Pooran Paramaanandh |22|  Page-1365

Everybody says that "I want to go to Heaven", but I do not know where that Heaven is that they want to reach? They have not realized the mystery of their own self, but just speak of Heaven. O' my mind, so long as you have a desire for Heaven, you cannot find a place at the Lord's feet!

---

ਭੈਰਉ ਬਾਣੀ ਭਗਤਾ ਕੀ ਕਬੀਰ ਜੀਉ ॥
ਸਭੁ ਕੋਈ ਚਲਨ ਕਹਤ ਹੈ ਊਹਾਂ ॥ ਨਾ ਜਾਨਉ ਬੈਕੁੰਠੁ ਹੈ ਕਹਾਂ ॥੧॥ ਰਹਾਉ ॥
ਆਪ ਆਪ ਕਾ ਮਰਮੁ ਨ ਜਾਨਾਂ ॥ਬਾਤਨ ਹੀ ਬੈਕੁੰਠੁ ਬਖਾਨਾਂ ॥੧॥
ਜਬ ਲਗੁ ਮਨ ਬੈਕੁੰਠ ਕੀ ਆਸ ॥ਤਬ ਲਗੁ ਨਾਹੀ ਚਰਨ ਨਿਵਾਸ ॥੨॥
Bhairao, The Word of the Saints, Kabeer Jeeo |
Sabh Koee Chalan Kehath Hai Oohaan |
Naa Jaano Baikunth Hai Kehaan |1| Pause |
Aap Aap Kaa Maram N Jaanaan | Baathan Hee Baikunth Bakhaanaan |1|
Jab Lag Man Baikunth Kee Aas | Thab Lag Naahee Charan Nivaas |2|
Page-1161

Says Kabeer, the death's club is terrible; it cannot be endured.
I have met the Guru and with the Grace of God; He has
attached me to the hem of His robe.

---

ਸਲੋਕ ਭਗਤ ਕਬੀਰ ਜੀਉ ਕੇ ॥
ਕਬੀਰ ਜਮ ਕਾ ਠੇਂਗਾ ਬੁਰਾ ਹੈ ਓਹੁ ਨਹੀ ਸਹਿਆ ਜਾਇ ॥
ਏਕੁ ਜੁ ਸਾਧੂ ਮੁਹਿ ਮਿਲਿਓ ਤਿਨ੍ਹ ਲੀਆ ਅੰਚਲਿ ਲਾਇ ॥੭੮॥

Salok Bhagath Kabeer Jeeo Kae |
Kabeer Jam Kaa Thaenagaa Buraa Hai Ouhu Nehee Sehiaa Jaae |
Eaek J Saadhhoo Muohi Miliou Thinih Leeaa Anchal Laae |78| Page-1368

---

O' Fareed, the beautiful crane perches on the river bank,
playing joyfully and a hawk suddenly pounces on it; he then
forgets all the joyful playing! Similarly, the Hawk of Death
attacks a man when he is enjoying and is totally unaware!
God does whatever man never even thinks of!

---

ਸਲੋਕ ਸੇਖ ਫਰੀਦ ਕੇ ॥
ਫਰੀਦਾ ਦਰੀਆਵੈ ਕੰਨ੍ਹੈ ਬਗੁਲਾ ਬੈਠਾ ਕੇਲ ਕਰੇ ॥ਕੇਲ ਕਰੇਦੇ ਹੰਝ ਨੋ ਅਚਿੰਤੇ ਬਾਜ ਪਏ ॥
ਬਾਜ ਪਏ ਤਿਸੁ ਰਬ ਦੇ ਕੇਲਾਂ ਵਿਸਰੀਆਂ ॥ਜੋ ਮਨਿ ਚਿਤਿ ਨ ਚੇਤੇ ਸਨਿ ਸੋ ਗਾਲੀ ਰਬ ਕੀਆਂ ॥੯੯॥

Salok Saekh Fareedh Kae |
Fareedhaa Dhareeaavai Kannhai Bagulaa Baithaa Kael Karae |
Kael Karaedhae Hanjh No Achinthae Baaj Peae |
Baaj Peae This Rab Dhae Kaelaan Visareeaaan |
Jo Man Chith N Chaethae San So Gaalee Rab Keeaaan |99| Page-1383

The heavy body of man is nourished by water and grain. The mortal comes into the world with high hopes which are rarely met. But when the Messenger of Death comes, breaking down all the doors, it binds and gags the mortal, before the eyes of his beloved relatives. Behold, the mortal being is going away, carried on the shoulders of four men. O' Fareed, in the Court of the Lord, only those good deeds will be of any use that are done while living in this world.

---

ਸਲੋਕ ਸੇਖ ਫਰੀਦ ਕੇ
ਸਾਢੇ ਤ੍ਰੈ ਮਣ ਦੇਹੁਰੀ ਚਲੈ ਪਾਣੀ ਅੰਨਿ ॥ਆਇਓ ਬੰਦਾ ਦੁਨੀ ਵਿਚਿ ਵਤਿ ਆਸੂਣੀ ਬੰਨ੍ਹਿ ॥
ਮਲਕਲ ਮਉਤ ਜਾਂ ਆਵਸੀ ਸਭ ਦਰਵਾਜੇ ਭੰਨਿ ॥ਤਿਨ੍ਹਾ ਪਿਆਰਿਆ ਭਾਈਆਂ ਅਗੈ ਦਿਤਾ ਬੰਨ੍ਹਿ ॥
ਵੇਖਹੁ ਬੰਦਾ ਚਲਿਆ ਚਹੁ ਜਣਿਆ ਦੈ ਕੰਨ੍ਹਿ ॥
ਫਰੀਦਾ ਅਮਲ ਜਿ ਕੀਤੇ ਦੁਨੀ ਵਿਚਿ ਦਰਗਹ ਆਏ ਕੰਮਿ ॥੧੦੦॥
Salok Saekh Fareedh Kae |
Saadtae Thrai Man Dhaehuree Chalai Paanee Ann |
Aaeiou Bandhaa Dhunee Vich Vath Aasoonee Bannih |
Malakal Mouth Jaan Aavasee Sabh Dharavaajae Bhann |
Thinhaa Piaariaa Bhaaeeaaan Agai Dhithaa Bannih |
Vaekhahu Bandhaa Chaliaa Chahu Janiaa Dhai Kannih |
Fareedhaa Amal J Keethae Dhunee Vich Dharageh Aaeae Kanm |100|   Page-1383

## Chapter-9  Prayer

O' Lord, I have not meditated on Your Name, nor done any good deeds, practice self-restraint, or pursue righteous living. I have neither served the Holy Saints nor acknowledged the Lord, my King. Says Nanak, "we humans are full of contemptible actions, but seek Your Sanctuary and benevolent forgiveness".

ਆਸਾ ਮਹਲਾ ੫ ॥

ਜਪੁ ਤਪੁ ਸੰਜਮੁ ਧਰਮੁ ਨ ਕਮਾਇਆ ॥ਸੇਵਾ ਸਾਧ ਨ ਜਾਨਿਆ ਹਰਿ ਰਾਇਆ ॥

ਕਹੁ ਨਾਨਕ ਹਮ ਨੀਚ ਕਰੰਮਾ ॥ਸਰਣਿ ਪਰੇ ਕੀ ਰਾਖਹੁ ਸਰਮਾ ॥੨॥੪॥

Aasaa 5th Guru |Jap Thap Sanjam Dhharam N Kamaaeiaa |Saevaa Saadhh N Jaaniaa Har Raaeiaa |Kahu Naanak Ham Neech Karanmaa |Saran Parae Kee Raakhahu Saramaa |2|4| Page-12

Prayer

O' my father! Please give me the Name of the Lord as my dowry. Give me the Lord's Name as my wedding gown, and the Lord' Name as my jewelry, with which I will shine and look beautiful. The blessed bride who receives such dowry is glorified throughout the world and this dowry of His Name can never be matched.

---

ਸਿਰੀਰਾਗੁ ਮਹਲਾ ੪ ਘਰੁ ੨ ਛੰਤ
ਹਰਿ ਪ੍ਰਭੁ ਮੇਰੇ ਬਾਬੁਲਾ ਹਰਿ ਦੇਵਹੁ ਦਾਨੁ ਮੈ ਦਾਜੋ ॥
ਹਰਿ ਕਪੜੋ ਹਰਿ ਸੋਭਾ ਦੇਵਹੁ ਜਿਤੁ ਸਵਰੈ ਮੇਰਾ ਕਾਜੋ ॥
ਖੰਡਿ ਵਰਭੰਡਿ ਹਰਿ ਸੋਭਾ ਹੋਈ ਇਹੁ ਦਾਨੁ ਨ ਰਲੈ ਰਲਾਇਆ ॥

Sireeraag Mehalaa 4 Ghar 2 Shhantha ॥
Har Prabh Maerae Baabulaa Har Dhaevahu Dhaan Mai Dhaajo ||
Har Kaparro Har Sobhaa Dhaevahu Jith Savarai Maeraa Kaajo ||
Khandd Varabhandd Har Sobhaa Hoee Eihu Dhaan N Ralai Ralaaeiaa || Page-78

---

Says Nanak, "O' the All-powerful Lord, I bow down to You, and fall to the ground in humble adoration, countless times. Please reach out and give me Your Hand to save me from wavering in Your Faith.

---

ਗਉੜੀ ਬਾਵਨ ਅਖਰੀ ਮਹਲਾ ੫ ॥ਸਲੋਕੁ ॥
ਡੰਡਉਤਿ ਬੰਦਨ ਅਨਿਕ ਬਾਰ ਸਰਬ ਕਲਾ ਸਮਰਥ ॥ ਡੋਲਨ ਤੇ ਰਾਖਹੁ ਪ੍ਰਭੂ ਨਾਨਕ ਦੇ ਕਰਿ ਹਥ ॥੧॥
Gourree Baavan Akharee 5th Guru | Salok |
Ddanddouth Bandhan Anik Baar Sarab Kalaa Samarathh |Ddolan Thae Raakhahu Prabhoo Naanak Dhae Kar Hathh |1|   Page-256

---

# Prayer

O' my Lord Master, I pray unto You that this body and soul that You have given, are Your blessing. You are our Father and Mother and we are your children; we enjoy so many pleasures and comforts due to Your Grace. No one knows Your limits, O' Highest of the High, Most Gracious God. The entire creation is functioning under Your Will; nothing is outside Your Command. You alone know Yourself and Your Greatness. Nanak, your slave, is forever a sacrifice.

---

ਗਉੜੀ ਸੁਖਮਨੀ ਮਃ ੫ ॥
ਅਸਟਪਦੀ ॥
ਤੂ ਠਾਕੁਰੁ ਤੁਮ ਪਹਿ ਅਰਦਾਸਿ ॥ ਜੀਉ ਪਿੰਡੁ ਸਭੁ ਤੇਰੀ ਰਾਸਿ ॥
ਤੁਮ ਮਾਤ ਪਿਤਾ ਹਮ ਬਾਰਿਕ ਤੇਰੇ ॥ ਤੁਮਰੀ ਕ੍ਰਿਪਾ ਮਹਿ ਸੂਖ ਘਨੇਰੇ ॥
ਕੋਇ ਨ ਜਾਨੈ ਤੁਮਰਾ ਅੰਤੁ ॥ ਊਚੇ ਤੇ ਊਚਾ ਭਗਵੰਤ ॥
ਸਗਲ ਸਮਗ੍ਰੀ ਤੁਮਰੈ ਸੂਤ੍ਰਿ ਧਾਰੀ ॥ ਤੁਮ ਤੇ ਹੋਇ ਸੁ ਆਗਿਆਕਾਰੀ ॥
ਤੁਮਰੀ ਗਤਿ ਮਿਤਿ ਤੁਮ ਹੀ ਜਾਨੀ ॥ ਨਾਨਕ ਦਾਸ ਸਦਾ ਕੁਰਬਾਨੀ ॥੮॥੪॥
Gourree Sukhamanee 5<sup>th</sup> Guru |
Asattapadhee |
Thoo Thaakur Thum Pehi Aradhaas | Jeeo Pindd Sabh Thaeree Raas |
Jeeo Pindd Sabh Thaeree Raas | Thumaree Kirapaa Mehi Sookh Ghanaerae |
Koe N Jaanai Thumaraa Anth | Oochae Thae Oochaa Bhagavanth |
Sagal Samagree Thumarai Soothr Dhhaaree | Thum Thae Hoe S Aagiaakaaree |
Thumaree Gath Mith Thum Hee Jaanee |
Naanak Dhaas Sadhaa Kurabaanee ||8||4||    Page-268

Prayer

O' my Lord, bestow Your Mercy: come and dwell within my heart. If You become my helper, then I can repeat Your Name deep in my mind. O' my Dear Beloved, you are my Husband Lord. Please bless Your humble servant so that by continuously listening to Your Name, I may yearn to behold You. Please help me to fulfil my goal of being in Your Presence.

---

ਆਸਾ ਮਹਲਾ ੫ ॥
ਮਨ ਮਹਿ ਰਾਮ ਨਾਮਾ ਜਾਪਿ ॥
ਕਰਿ ਕਿਰਪਾ ਵਸਹੁ ਮੇਰੈ ਹਿਰਦੈ ਹੋਇ ਸਹਾਈ ਆਪਿ ॥੧॥ ਰਹਾਉ ॥
ਸੁਣਿ ਸੁਣਿ ਨਾਮੁ ਤੁਮਾਰਾ ਪ੍ਰੀਤਮ ਪ੍ਰਭ ਪੇਖਨ ਕਾ ਚਾਉ ॥
ਦਇਆ ਕਰਹੁ ਕਿਰਮ ਅਪੁਨੇ ਕਉ ਇਹੈ ਮਨੋਰਥੁ ਸੁਆਉ ॥੨॥
Aasaa Mehalaa 5 |
Mana Mehi Raam Naamaa Jaap |
Kar Kirapaa Vasahu Maerai Hiradhai Hoe Sehaaee Aap |1|Rehaao |
Sun Sun Naam Thumaaraa Preetham Prabh Paekhan Kaa Chaao |
Dhaeiaa Karahu Kiram Apunae Ko Eihai Manorathh Suaao |2|   Page-405/6

O' Lord God, shower Your Mercy upon us. We, the stone hearted, please carry us across the world-ocean. By binding us to the Wordless Word and Your Love, please pull us out of the molasses of worldly attachments. We are struck in the swamp of emotional entanglements and sliding downhill. O' Lord, please give me Your arm and pull me up!

ਆਸਾ ਮਹਲਾ ੪ ॥
ਹਰਿ ਦਇਆ ਪ੍ਰਭ ਧਾਰਹੁ ਪਾਖਣ ਹਮ ਤਾਰਹੁ ਕਢਿ ਲੇਵਹੁ ਸਬਦਿ ਸੁਭਾਇ ਜੀਉ ॥
ਮੋਹ ਚੀਕੜਿ ਫਾਥੇ ਨਿਘਰਤ ਹਮ ਜਾਤੇ ਹਰਿ ਬਾਂਹ ਪ੍ਰਭੂ ਪਕਰਾਇ ਜੀਉ ॥
Aasaa Mehalaa 4 |
Har Dhaeiaa Prabh Dhhaarahu Paakhan Ham Thaarahu Kadt Laevahu Sabadh
Subhaae Jeeo |Moh Cheekarr Faathhae Nigharath Ham Jaathae Har Baanh
Prabhoo Pakaraae Jeeo |   Page-446

Prayer

O' my Beautiful Lord! I am your little child, I just don't
know! Why are you not forgiving my sins? The son may
commit many mistakes, but his mother does not remember
and forgets them all. If the stupid son becomes angry and
tries to harm his mother, even then she does not hold it
against him in her mind!

ਆਸਾ ਸ੍ਰੀ ਕਬੀਰ ਜੀਉ ਕੇ ॥
ਸੁਤੁ ਅਪਰਾਧ ਕਰਤ ਹੈ ਜੇਤੇ ॥ਜਨਨੀ ਚੀਤਿ ਨ ਰਾਖਸਿ ਤੇਤੇ ॥੧॥
ਰਾਮਈਆ ਹਉ ਬਾਰਿਕੁ ਤੇਰਾ ॥੧॥ਕਾਹੇ ਨ ਖੰਡਸਿ ਅਵਗਨੁ ਮੇਰਾ ॥੧॥ ਰਹਾਉ ॥
ਜੇ ਅਤਿ ਕ੍ਰੋਪ ਕਰੇ ਕਰਿ ਧਾਇਆ ॥ਤਾ ਭੀ ਚੀਤਿ ਨ ਰਾਖਸਿ ਮਾਇਆ ॥੨॥
Aasaa Sree Kabeer Jeeo Kae |
Suth Aparaadhh Karath Hai Jaethae | Jananee Cheeth N Raakhas Thaethae |1|
Raameeaa Ho Baarik Thaeraa | Kaahae N Khanddas Avagan Maeraa |1|Rehaao |
Jae Ath Krop Karae Kar Dhhaaeiaa | Thaa Bhee Cheeth N Raakhas Maaeiaa |2|
Page-478

Spiritual Gems                                                    120

Prayer

O' my Lord, You, are so Great and Powerful, but my intellect is minute and incapable of understanding. Your Glance and Grace are forever Perfect and You cherish equally even the ungrateful ones. O' the Creator, the Infinite Lord, you are beyond our intellectual reach; I am so lowly and know nothing. Abandoning Your Precious Name, I keep collecting sea shells. I am of animal like nature and ignorant!

---

ਬਿਹਾਗੜਾ ਮਹਲਾ ੫ ॥
ਤੂ ਸਮਰਥੁ ਵਡਾ ਮੇਰੀ ਮਤਿ ਥੋਰੀ ਰਾਮ ॥ ਪਾਲਹਿ ਅਕਿਰਤਘਨਾ ਪੂਰਨ ਦ੍ਰਿਸਟਿ ਤੇਰੀ ਰਾਮ ॥
ਅਗਾਧਿ ਬੋਧਿ ਅਪਾਰ ਕਰਤੇ ਮੋਹਿ ਨੀਚੁ ਕਛੂ ਨ ਜਾਨਾ ॥
ਰਤਨੁ ਤਿਆਗਿ ਸੰਗ੍ਰਹਨ ਕਉਡੀ ਪਸੂ ਨੀਚੁ ਇਆਨਾ ॥
Bihaagarraa 5th Guru |
Thoo Samarathh Vaddaa Maeree Math Thhoree Raam |
Paalehi Akirathaghanaa Pooran Dhrisatt Thaeree Raam |
Agaadhh Bodhh Apaar Karathae Mohi Neech Kashhoo N Jaanaa |
Agaadhh Bodhh Apaar Karathae Mohi Neech Kashhoo N Jaanaa |
Thiaag Chalathee Mehaa Chanchal Dhokh Kar Kar Joree |      Page-547

Prayer

O' the All-Powerful Great Giver, you can destroy and create
life; with clasped hands, the entire Creation stands begging
before You. O Great Giver, I see no one equal to you; You
give by Your Grace to the beings of all the continents,
worlds, regions, and universes.

ਮਹਲਾ ੩ ॥ਪਉੜੀ ॥
ਤੂ ਭੰਨਣ ਘੜਣ ਸਮਰਥੁ ਦਾਤਾਰੁ ਹਹਿ ਤੁਧੁ ਅਗੈ ਮੰਗਣ ਨੋ ਹਥ ਜੋੜਿ ਖਲੀ ਸਭ ਹੋਈ ॥
ਤੁਧੁ ਜੇਵਡੁ ਦਾਤਾਰੁ ਮੈ ਕੋਈ ਨਦਰਿ ਨ ਆਵਈ ਤੁਧੁ ਸਭਮੈ ਨੋ ਦਾਨੁ ਦਿਤਾ ਖੰਡੀ ਵਰਭੰਡੀ ਪਾਤਾਲੀ ਪੁਰਈ ਸਭ
ਲੋਈ ॥੩॥
3rd Guru |Pourree |
Thoo Bhannan Gharran Samarathh Dhaathaar Hehi Thudhh Agai Mangan No
Hathh Jorr Khalee Sabh Hoee |
Thudhh Jaevadd Dhaathaar Mai Koee Nadhar N Aavee Thudhh Sabhasai No
Dhaan Dhithaa Khanddee Varabhanddee Paathaalee Puree Sabh Loee |3|
Page-549

Prayer

O' Dear Beloved Lord, you are my Husband; please live by
Your Husband's role and unite me with You. Whether good
or bad, I am still Yours!

---

ਸੋਰਠਿ ਮਹਲਾ ੫ ॥
ਪ੍ਰਭ ਜੀਉ ਖਸਮਾਨਾ ਕਰਿ ਪਿਆਰੇ ॥ ਬੁਰੇ ਭਲੇ ਹਮ ਥਾਰੇ ॥ ਰਹਾਉ ॥
Sorath Mehalaa 5 |
Prabh Jeeo Khasamaanaa Kar Piaarae |
Burae Bhalae Ham Thhaarae | Pause |    Page-631

---

O' brother, we cannot meet the Lord by our own efforts, nor
by doing any particular service. He comes and meets us
entirely on His own, when we are least thinking about it!
One who is blessed by my Lord Master's Grace, practices the
Teachings of the Guru's Word.

---

ਧਨਾਸਰੀ ਮਹਲਾ ੫ ॥
ਘਾਲ ਨ ਮਿਲਿਓ ਸੇਵ ਨ ਮਿਲਿਓ ਮਿਲਿਓ ਆਇ ਅਚਿੰਤਾ ॥
ਜਾ ਕਉ ਦਇਆ ਕਰੀ ਮੇਰੈ ਠਾਕੁਰਿ ਤਿਨਿ ਗੁਰਹਿ ਕਮਾਨੋ ਮੰਤਾ ॥੩॥
Dhhanaasaree Mehalaa 5 |
Ghaal N Miliou Saev N Miliou Miliou Aae Achinthaa |
Jaa Ko Dhaeiaa Karee Maerai Thaakur Thin Gurehi Kamaano Manthaa |3|
Page-672

---

Prayer

O' my Lord, you are the Merciful Protector of all. My eyes have become purified (stopped seeing evil) upon Your Blessed Vision and touching my forehead with the dust of Your Feet. With joy and happiness, I sing the Glorious Praises of my Lord and pray; "O' Lord of the Universe, please come and abide in my heart".

ਧਨਾਸਰੀ ਮਹਲਾ ੫ ॥
ਨੇਤ੍ਰ ਪੁਨੀਤ ਭਏ ਦਰਸ ਪੇਖੇ ਮਾਥੈ ਪਰਉ ਰਵਾਲ ॥
ਰਸਿ ਰਸਿ ਗੁਣ ਗਾਵਉ ਠਾਕੁਰ ਕੇ ਮੋਰੈ ਹਿਰਦੈ ਬਸਹੁ ਗੋਪਾਲ ॥੧॥
ਤੁਮ ਤਉ ਰਾਖਨਹਾਰ ਦਇਆਲ ॥
Dhhanaasaree Mehalaa 5 |
Naethr Puneeth Bheae Dharas Paekhae Maathhai Paro Ravaal |
Ras Ras Gun Gaavo Thaakur Kae Morai Hiradhai Basahu Gopaal |1|
Thum Tho Raakhanehaar Dhaeiaal |    Page-680

Prayer

The Lord can remove the three ailments of body, mind, and spirit. He is the Destroyer of pain and Fountain of pleasure; no obstacles come in the path of those who pray before God.

---

ਟੋਡੀ ਮਹਲਾ ੫ ॥
ਤੀਨੇ ਤਾਪ ਨਿਵਾਰਣਹਾਰਾ ਦੁਖ ਹੰਤਾ ਸੁਖ ਰਾਸਿ ॥
ਤਾ ਕਉ ਬਿਘਨੁ ਨ ਕੋਊ ਲਾਗੈ ਜਾ ਕੀ ਪ੍ਰਭ ਆਗੈ ਅਰਦਾਸਿ ॥੧॥
Ttoddee Mehalaa 5 |
Theenae Thaap Nivaaranehaaraa Dhukh Hanthaa Sukh Raas |
Thaa Ko Bighan N Kooo Laagai Jaa Kee Prabh Aagai Aradhaas ||1||   Page-714

---

Says Nanak, O' Lord I pray to You with clasped hands, "Please Bless and fulfil me, if You so wish".
When the Lord through His Mercy gives one the boon of His devotion, he contemplates on His Name forever.

---

ਸੂਹੀ ਮਹਲਾ ੫ ॥
ਦੁਇ ਕਰ ਜੋੜਿ ਕਰਉ ਅਰਦਾਸਿ ॥ ਤੁਧੁ ਭਾਵੈ ਤਾ ਆਣਹਿ ਰਾਸਿ ॥
ਕਰਿ ਕਿਰਪਾ ਅਪਨੀ ਭਗਤੀ ਲਾਇ ॥ ਜਨ ਨਾਨਕ ਪ੍ਰਭ ਸਦਾ ਧਿਆਇ ॥੪॥੨॥
Soohee Mehalaa 5 |
Dhue Kar Jorr Karo Aradhaas | Thudhh Bhaavai Thaa Aanehi Raas |
Kar Kirapaa Apanee Bhagathee Laae | Jan Naanak Prabh Sadhaa Dhhiaae |4|2|   Page-736

Prayer

Which, of Your many Glorious Virtues should I sing and recount, Lord? You are my Lord and Master, the treasure of excellence. I cannot express Your Glorious Praises. You are my Lord/Master, lofty and benevolent. You alone are my strength, and my Court; unto You alone I pray. There is no other place where I can offer my prayers; my pains and pleasures I can only say to You.

---

ਸੂਹੀ ਮਹਲਾ ੪ ॥
ਤੇਰੇ ਕਵਨ ਕਵਨ ਗੁਣ ਕਹਿ ਕਹਿ ਗਾਵਾ ਤੂ ਸਾਹਿਬ ਗੁਣੀ ਨਿਧਾਨਾ ॥
ਤੁਮਰੀ ਮਹਿਮਾ ਬਰਨਿ ਨ ਸਾਕਉ ਤੂੰ ਠਾਕੁਰ ਊਚ ਭਗਵਾਨਾ ॥੧॥
ਮੈ ਤਾਣੁ ਦੀਬਾਣੁ ਤੂਹੈ ਮੇਰੇ ਸੁਆਮੀ ਮੈ ਤੁਧੁ ਆਗੈ ਅਰਦਾਸਿ ॥
ਮੈ ਹੋਰੁ ਥਾਉ ਨਾਹੀ ਜਿਸੁ ਪਹਿ ਕਰਉ ਬੇਨੰਤੀ ਮੇਰਾ ਦੁਖੁ ਸੁਖੁ ਤੁਝ ਹੀ ਪਾਸਿ ॥੨॥
Soohee Mehalaa 4 |
Thaerae Kavan Kavan Gun Kehi Kehi Gaavaa Thoo Saahib Gunee Nidhhaanaa |
Thumaree Mehimaa Baran N Saako Thoon Thaakur Ooch Bhagavaanaa |1|
Mai Thaan Dheebaan Thoohai Maerae Suaamee Mai Thudhh Aagai Aradhaas |
Mai Hor Thhaao Naahee Jis Pehi Karo Baenanthee Maeraa Dhukh Sukh Thujh
Hee Paas |2|    Page-735

Prayer

O' brother, listen to the story of a foolish man who does insignificant service, but demands too much of a reward. He cannot attain the Lord's Presence, but says, he has already achieved it! He shows off his stubbornness and competes with those who have been accepted by the Beloved Lord. O' Nanak, pray to the Lord and say; "the poor human is incapable, lacks compassion, and is lustful; but he is still Yours, please forgive him for his sins".

---

ਸੂਹੀ ਮਹਲਾ ੫ ॥
ਸੇਵਾ ਥੋਰੀ ਮਾਗਨੁ ਬਹੁਤਾ ॥ ਮਹਲੁ ਨ ਪਾਵੈ ਕਹਤੋ ਪਹੁਤਾ ॥੧॥
ਜੋ ਪ੍ਰਿਅ ਮਾਨੇ ਤਿਨ ਕੀ ਰੀਸਾ ॥ ਕੂੜੇ ਮੂਰਖ ਕੀ ਹਾਠੀਸਾ ॥੧॥ ਰਹਾਉ ॥
ਕਹੁ ਨਾਨਕ ਪ੍ਰਭ ਬਿਨਉ ਸੁਨੀਜੈ ॥ ਕੁਚਲ ਕਠੋਰੁ ਕਾਮੀ ਮੁਕਤੁ ਕੀਜੈ ॥੪॥

Soohee Mehalaa 5 |Saevaa Thhoree Maagan Bahuthaa | Mehal N Paavai Kehatho Pahuthaa |1|Jo Pria Maanae Thin Kee Reesaa | Koorrae Moorakh Kee Haatheesaa |1| Rehaao | Kahu Naanak Prabh Bino Suneejai | Kuchal Kathor Kaamee Mukath Keejai |4|  Page-738

Prayer

O' my sister, I never learnt how to live a righteous life; I am
so full of demerits that they cannot be contained within me.
In this state, how can I go to please my Husband Lord? At
His Door, there are so many brides who surpass one another;
nobody even knows my name there! Virtue is in You, O
Lord; I am totally without virtue. This is Nanak's only prayer:
You give all Your nights to the virtuous brides. I know I am
unworthy, but isn't there a night for me as well?

---

ਰਾਗੁ ਸੂਹੀ ਮਹਲਾ ੧ ॥
ਮੰਝੁ ਕੁਚਜੀ ਅੰਮਾਵਣਿ ਡੋਸੜੇ ਹਉ ਕਿਉ ਸਹੁ ਰਾਵਣਿ ਜਾਉ ਜੀਉ ॥ ਇਕ ਦੂ ਇਕਿ ਚੜੰਦੀਆ ਕਉਣੁ ਜਾਣੈ ਮੇਰਾ
ਨਾਉ ਜੀਉ ॥ਸੁਇਨਾ ਰੁਪਾ ਰੰਗੁਲਾ ਮੋਤੀ ਤੈ ਮਾਣਿਕੁ ਜੀਉ ॥ਸੇ ਵਸਤੂ ਸਹਿ ਦਿਤੀਆ ਮੈ ਤਿਨ੍ਹ ਸਿਉ ਲਾਇਆ
ਚਿਤੁ ਜੀਉ ॥ਅੰਬਰਿ ਕੂੰਜਾ ਕੁਰਲੀਆ ਬਗ ਬਹਿਠੇ ਆਇ ਜੀਉ ॥ ਸਾ ਧਨ ਚਲੀ ਸਾਹੁਰੈ ਕਿਆ ਮੁਹੁ ਦੇਸੀ ਅਗੈ
ਜਾਇ ਜੀਉ ॥ਤੁਧੁ ਗੁਣ ਮੈ ਸਭਿ ਅਵਗਣਾ ਇਕ ਨਾਨਕ ਕੀ ਅਰਦਾਸਿ ਜੀਉ ॥ ਸਭਿ ਰਾਤੀ ਸੋਹਾਗਣੀ ਮੈ
ਡੋਹਾਗਣਿ ਕਾਈ ਰਾਤਿ ਜੀਉ ॥੧॥
Raag Soohee 1st Guru |
Mannj Kuchajee Anmaavan Ddosarrae Ho Kio Sahu Raavan Jaao Jeeo |Eik Dhoo Eik
Charrandheeaa Koun Jaanai Maeraa Naao Jeeo |Sueinaa Rupaa Rangulaa Mothee Thai
Maanik Jeeo |Sae Vasathoo Sehi Dhitheeaa Mai Thinh Sio Laaeiaa Chith Jeeo |Anbar
Koonjaa Kuraleeaa Bag Behithae Aae Jeeo |Saa Dhhan Chalee Saahurai Kiaa Muhu
Dhaesee Agai Jaae Jeeo |Thudhh Gun Mai Sabh Avaganaa Eik Naanak Kee Aradhaas Jeeo
|Sabh Raathee Sohaaganee Mai Ddohaagan Kaaee Raath Jeeo |1|    Page-762

Prayer

O' the Great Giver, never forget me; please bless me with Your Name. Nanak's happiness is in the singing of Your Praises, day and night.

ਸੂਹੀ ਮਹਲਾ ੫ ॥
ਵਿਸਰੁ ਨਾਹੀ ਦਾਤਾਰ ਆਪਣਾ ਨਾਮੁ ਦੇਹੁ ॥
ਗੁਣ ਗਾਵਾ ਦਿਨੁ ਰਾਤਿ ਨਾਨਕ ਚਾਉ ਏਹੁ ॥੮॥੨॥੫॥੧੬॥
Soohee Mehalaa 5 ||
Visar Naahee Dhaathaar Aapanaa Naam Dhaehu ||
Gun Gaavaa Dhin Raath Naanak Chaao Eaehu ||8||2||5||16||     Page-762

O' Creator of the Universe, the Lord Master; You are the All-Powerful Cause of causes. We are by nature akin to making mistakes forever and ever, but it is Your Ingrained Nature to forgive and save the sinners.

ਬਿਲਾਵਲੁ ਮਹਲਾ ੫ ॥
ਤੁਮ੍ਹ ਸਮਰਥਾ ਕਾਰਨ ਕਰਨ ॥ਹਮਰੋ ਸਹਾਉ ਸਦਾ ਸਦ ਭੂਲਨ ਤੁਮ੍ਹਰੋ ਬਿਰਦੁ ਪਤਿਤ ਉਧਰਨ ॥
Bilaaval 5th Guru |
Thumh Samarathhaa Kaaran Karan |Hamaro Sehaao Sadhaa Sadh Bhoolan Thumharo Biradh Pathith Oudhharan |     Page-828

# Prayer

O' Lord, my life's boat is loaded with sins, is wobbly and unsteady. The wind of worldly illusions is blowing hard and I am fearful that it may tip over and sink! I have overcome my hesitation and come to seek Your Protection. O' Lord, please Bless me so that I may surely sing Your Praises.

---

ਰਾਮਕਲੀ ਮਹਲਾ ੧ ॥
ਹਮ ਡੋਲਤ ਬੇੜੀ ਪਾਪ ਭਰੀ ਹੈ ਪਵਣੁ ਲਗੈ ਮਤੁ ਜਾਈ ॥
ਸਨਮੁਖ ਸਿਧ ਭੇਟਣ ਕਉ ਆਏ ਨਿਹਚਉ ਦੇਹਿ ਵਡਿਆਈ ॥੧॥
Raamakalee 1<sup>st</sup> Guru |
Ham Ddolath Baerree Paap Bharee Hai Pavan Lagai Math Jaaee |
Sanamukh Sidhh Bhaettan Ko Aaeae Nihacho Dhaehi Vaddiaaee |1| Page-878

# Prayer

O' Generous Giver, Lord of the meek; have Mercy on me, please do not consider my merits and demerits. O my Lord and Master, how can raw clay be washed? Such is the reality of us humans! You have created and adorned the earthen vessels and infused Your Light within them. As is the destiny pre-ordained by You, such are the deeds we perform.

ਰਾਗੁ ਰਾਮਕਲੀ ਮਹਲਾ ੫ ॥
ਕਿਰਪਾ ਕਰਹੁ ਦੀਨ ਕੇ ਦਾਤੇ ਮੇਰਾ ਗੁਣੁ ਅਵਗਣੁ ਨ ਬੀਚਾਰਹੁ ਕੋਈ ॥ਮਾਟੀ ਕਾ ਕਿਆ ਧੋਪੈ ਸੁਆਮੀ ਮਾਣਸ ਕੀ ਗਤਿ ਏਹੀ ॥੧॥
ਕਾਚੇ ਭਾਡੇ ਸਾਜਿ ਨਿਵਾਜੇ ਅੰਤਰਿ ਜੋਤਿ ਸਮਾਈ ॥
ਜੈਸਾ ਲਿਖਤੁ ਲਿਖਿਆ ਧੁਰਿ ਕਰਤੈ ਹਮ ਤੈਸੀ ਕਿਰਤਿ ਕਮਾਈ ॥੨॥
Raag Raamakalee 5th Guru |
Kirapaa Karahu Dheen Kae Dhaathae Maeraa Gun Avagan N Beechaarahu Koee |
Maattee Kaa Kiaa Dhhopai Suaamee Maanas Kee Gath Eaehee |1|
Kaachae Bhaaddae Saaj Nivaajae Anthar Joth Samaaee |
Jaisaa Likhath Likhiaa Dhhur Karathai Ham Thaisee Kirath Kamaaee |2|    Page-882

Spiritual Gems                                                    131

Prayer

O' my Lord, to beg anything from You other than Your
Name is asking for misery after misery. Please bless me with
Your Name for contentment and to satisfy the hunger of my
mind. Says Nanak, the True Guru who has made the woods
and meadows green again; is it any wonder that He can Bless
the humans as well?

---

ਮਹਲਾ ੫ ॥
ਵਿਣੁ ਤੁਧੁ ਹੋਰੁ ਜਿ ਮੰਗਣਾ ਸਿਰਿ ਦੁਖਾ ਕੈ ਦੁਖ ॥
ਦੇਹਿ ਨਾਮੁ ਸੰਤੋਖੀਆ ਉਤਰੈ ਮਨ ਕੀ ਭੁਖ ॥
ਗੁਰਿ ਵਣੁ ਤਿਣੁ ਹਰਿਆ ਕੀਤਿਆ ਨਾਨਕ ਕਿਆ ਮਨੁਖ ॥੨॥

5th Guru |
Vin Thudhh Hor J Manganaa Sir Dhukhaa Kai Dhukh |
Dhaehi Naam Santhokheeaa Outharai Man Kee Bhukh |
Gur Van Thin Hariaa Keethiaa Naanak Kiaa Manukh |2|    Page-958

The tidal waves of greed constantly assault me. O' the Lord with Beautiful Hair, my body is drowning. Please carry me across the world-ocean, O' Lord of the Universe. Carry me across, my Beloved Father. I cannot steer my ship in this storm and cannot find the other shore, Beloved Lord. Please be merciful, and unite me with the True Guru; carry me across, O' the Beautiful Haired Lord. Says Naam Dayv, I do not know how to swim; please give me Your Arm, give me Your Arm, O' Beloved Father.

---

ਬਸੰਤੁ ਬਾਣੀ ਨਾਮਦੇਉ ਜੀ ਕੀ ॥
ਲੋਭ ਲਹਰਿ ਅਤਿ ਨੀਝਰ ਬਾਜੈ ॥ਕਾਇਆ ਡੂਬੈ ਕੇਸਵਾ ॥੧॥
ਸੰਸਾਰੁ ਸਮੁੰਦੇ ਤਾਰਿ ਗਬਿੰਦੇ ॥ਤਾਰਿ ਲੈ ਬਾਪ ਬੀਠੁਲਾ ॥੧॥ ਰਹਾਉ ॥
ਅਨਿਲ ਬੇੜਾ ਹਉ ਖੇਵਿ ਨ ਸਾਕਉ ॥ਤੇਰਾ ਪਾਰੁ ਨ ਪਾਇਆ ਬੀਠੁਲਾ ॥੨॥
ਹੋਹੁ ਦਇਆਲੁ ਸਤਿਗੁਰੁ ਮੇਲਿ ਤੂ ਮੋ ਕਉ ॥ਪਾਰਿ ਉਤਾਰੇ ਕੇਸਵਾ ॥੩॥
ਨਾਮਾ ਕਹੈ ਹਉ ਤਰਿ ਭੀ ਨ ਜਾਨਉ ॥ਮੋ ਕਉ ਬਾਹ ਦੇਹਿ ਬਾਹ ਦੇਹਿ ਬੀਠੁਲਾ ॥੪॥੨॥
Basanth Baanee Naamadhaeo Jee Kee |
Lobh Lehar Ath Neejhar Baajai | Kaaeiaa Ddoobai Kaesavaa |1|
Sansaar Samundhae Thaar Guobindhae | Thaar Lai Baap Beethulaa |1|Pause |
Anil Baerraa Ho Khaev N Saako | Thaeraa Paar N Paaeiaa Beethulaa |2|
Hohu Dhaeiaal Sathigur Mael Thoo Mo Ko | Paar Outhaarae Kaesavaa |3|
Naamaa Kehai Ho Thar Bhee N Jaano | Mo Ko Baah Dhaehi Baah Dhaehi Beethulaa |4|2|
Page-1196

Prayer

The thirsty rain bird chirps in the ambrosial hours of the
morning before dawn, begging for a drop of water; its prayer
is instantly heard in the Court of the Lord! The clouds are
ordered to mercifully shower down immediately!

ਸਲੋਕ ਮਹਲਾ ੩ ॥
ਬਾਬੀਹਾ ਅੰਮ੍ਰਿਤ ਵੇਲੈ ਬੋਲਿਆ ਤਾਂ ਦਰਿ ਸੁਣੀ ਪੁਕਾਰ ॥ਮੇਘੈ ਨੋ ਫੁਰਮਾਨੁ ਹੋਆ ਵਰਸਹੁ ਕਿਰਪਾ ਧਾਰਿ ॥
Salok 3rd Guru |
Baabeehaa Anmrith Vaelai Boliaa Thaan Dhar Sunee Pukaar |
Maeghai No Furamaan Hoaa Varasahu Kirapaa Dhhaar | Page-1285

O' Lord, we humans are akin to committing`` sins, to which
there is no limit. Please be Merciful and forgive me, I am a
great sinner and offender. If You count my sins, I can never
get a turn to be pardoned; it is only through Your Mercy that
I can be saved.

ਸਲੋਕ ਮਹਲਾ ੩
ਅਸੀ ਖਤੇ ਬਹੁਤੁ ਕਮਾਵਦੇ ਅੰਤੁ ਨ ਪਾਰਾਵਾਰੁ ॥
ਹਰਿ ਕਿਰਪਾ ਕਰਿ ਕੈ ਬਖਸਿ ਲੈਹੁ ਹਉ ਪਾਪੀ ਵਡ ਗੁਨਹਗਾਰੁ ॥
ਹਰਿ ਜੀਉ ਲੇਖੈ ਵਾਰ ਨ ਆਵਈ ਤੂੰ ਬਖਸਿ ਮਿਲਾਵਣਹਾਰੁ ॥
Salok 3rd Guru |
Asee Khathae Bahuth Kamaavadhae Anth N Paaraavaar ||
Har Kirapaa Kar Kai Bakhas Laihu Ho Paapee Vadd Gunehagaar | Har Jeeo Laekhai Vaar N
Aavee Thoon Bakhas Milaavanehaar || Page-1416

My looks are not attractive; how can I remember and conceive the beautiful Lord? My eyes are not good looking; how can I see the glimpse of that beloved Lord? My tongue is not ambrosial; how can I make an effective request to my beloved? I do not have such power of hearing that I can enjoy the honey-like words of my beloved Lord?

---

ਭਾਈ ਗੁਰਦਾਸ ।
ਨਾਹਿਨ ਅਨੂਪ ਰੂਪ ਚਿਤਵੈ ਕਿਉ ਚਿੰਤਾਮਨਿ ਲੋਨੇ ਹੈ ਨ ਲੋਇਨ ਜੋ ਲਾਲਨ ਬਿਲੋਕੀਐ ।
ਰਸਨਾ ਰਸੀਲੀ ਨਾਹਿ ਬੇਨਤੀ ਬਖਾਨਉ ਕੈਸੇ ਸੁਰਤਿ ਨ ਸ੍ਰਵਨਨ ਬਚਨ ਮਧੋਕੀਐ ।

Bhai Gurdas I

Naahin Anoop Roop Chitavai Kiu Chintaamani , Lonay Hai N Loin Jo Laalan Bilokeeai I
Rasanaa Raseelee Naahi Baynatee Bakhaanau Kaisay , Surati N Sravanan Bachan
Madhokeeai I Kabit 640

## Chapter-10 Love

O' my body, you will remain happy only so long as the soul stays with you; when the soul companion leaves, you will merge with the dust. Everyone shall go to their in-laws' house, the Husband Lord; everyone shall be given their ceremonial send-off. O' Nanak, blessed are the fortunate brides, who are wedded to the Lord and are in Love with the Lord.

ਸਿਰੀਰਾਗੁ ਮਹਲਾ ੫ ॥
ਤਿਚਰੁ ਵਸਹਿ ਸੁਹੇਲੜੀ ਜਿਚਰੁ ਸਾਥੀ ਨਾਲਿ ॥ਜਾ ਸਾਥੀ ਉਠੀ ਚਲਿਆ ਤਾ ਧਨ ਖਾਕੂ ਰਾਲਿ ॥੧॥
ਸਭਨਾ ਸਾਹੁਰੈ ਵੰਞਣਾ ਸਭਿ ਮੁਕਲਾਵਣਹਾਰ ॥
ਨਾਨਕ ਧੰਨੁ ਸੋਹਾਗਣੀ ਜਿਨ ਸਹ ਨਾਲਿ ਪਿਆਰੁ ॥੪॥੨੩॥੯੩॥
Sireeraag 5<sup>th</sup> Guru |
Thichar Vasehi Suhaelarree Jichar Saathhee Naal |
Jaa Saathhee Outhee Chaliaa Thaa Dhhan Khaakoo Raal |1|
Sabhanaa Saahurai Vannjanaa Sabh Mukalaavanehaar |
Naanak Dhhann Sohaaganee Jin Seh Naal Piaar |4|23|93|    Page-50

O' my mind, love the Lord like the lotus loves water; it is
tossed about by the waves, but still blooms in water. Love the
Lord like the fish loves water; the more water, the happier is
fish and cannot stay alive without it even for a moment. Love
the Lord like the rain-bird loves rain; the lakes may be
overflowing and the ground lush green, but the rain-bird thirsts
for a drop of rain to fall in his mouth!

---

ਸਿਰੀਰਾਗੁ ਮਹਲਾ ੧ ॥
ਰੇ ਮਨ ਐਸੀ ਹਰਿ ਸਿਉ ਪ੍ਰੀਤਿ ਕਰਿ ਜੈਸੀ ਜਲ ਕਮਲੇਹਿ ॥ਲਹਰੀ ਨਾਲਿ ਪਛਾੜੀਐ ਭੀ ਵਿਗਸੈ ਅਸਨੇਹਿ ॥
ਰੇ ਮਨ ਐਸੀ ਹਰਿ ਸਿਉ ਪ੍ਰੀਤਿ ਕਰਿ ਜੈਸੀ ਮਛੁਲੀ ਨੀਰ ॥
ਜਿਉ ਅਧਿਕਉ ਤਿਉ ਸੁਖੁ ਘਨੋ ਮਨਿ ਤਨਿ ਸਾਂਤਿ ਸਰੀਰ ॥
ਰੇ ਮਨ ਐਸੀ ਹਰਿ ਸਿਉ ਪ੍ਰੀਤਿ ਕਰਿ ਜੈਸੀ ਚਾਤ੍ਰਿਕ ਮੇਹ ॥ਸਰ ਭਰਿ ਥਲ ਹਰੀਆਵਲੇ ਇਕ ਬੂੰਦ ਨ ਪਵਈ ਕੇਹ ॥
Sireeraag 1st Guru |
Rae Man Aisee Har Sio Preeth Kar Jaisee Jal Kamalaehi |
Leharee Naal Pashhaarreeai Bhee Vigasai Asanaehi |
Rae Man Aisee Har Sio Preeth Kar Jaisee Mashhulee Neer |
Jio Adhhiko Thio Sukh Ghano Man Than Saanth Sareer |
Rae Man Aisee Har Sio Preeth Kar Jaisee Chaathrik Maeh |
Sar Bhar Thhal Hareeaavalae Eik Boondh N Pavee Kaeh |     Page-59

Love


O' Lord, let Your Name be my food, like the wild vegetation is
for the deer and live carefree like the deer. By the Guru's
Grace, if I can meet my Husband-Lord, I am a sacrifice to Him
again and again. Like the cuckoo bird loves the mango tree,
may I also fall in Love with the Lord and sing His praises in a
sweet voice? Then in a tranquil state I have the blessed Vision
of the Infinite Beautiful Lord! If my Love for the Lord
becomes like the fish with water, I may dwell forever in Him
who nourishes the entire creation. My Husband Lord dwells
on this shore, and the shore beyond; I will swim across like the
fish and hug Him with out-stretched arms!


---

ਗਉੜੀ ਬੈਰਾਗਣਿ ਮਹਲਾ ੧ ॥
ਹਰਣੀ ਹੋਵਾ ਬਨਿ ਬਸਾ ਕੰਦ ਮੂਲ ਚੁਣਿ ਖਾਉ ॥
ਗੁਰ ਪਰਸਾਦੀ ਮੇਰਾ ਸਹੁ ਮਿਲੈ ਵਾਰਿ ਵਾਰਿ ਹਉ ਜਾਉ ਜੀਉ ॥੧॥
ਕੋਕਿਲ ਹੋਵਾ ਅੰਬਿ ਬਸਾ ਸਹਜਿ ਸਬਦ ਬੀਚਾਰੁ ॥
ਸਹਜਿ ਸੁਭਾਇ ਮੇਰਾ ਸਹੁ ਮਿਲੈ ਦਰਸਨਿ ਰੂਪਿ ਅਪਾਰੁ ॥੨॥
ਮਛੁਲੀ ਹੋਵਾ ਜਲਿ ਬਸਾ ਜੀਅ ਜੰਤ ਸਭਿ ਸਾਰਿ ॥
ਉਰਵਾਰਿ ਪਾਰਿ ਮੇਰਾ ਸਹੁ ਵਸੈ ਹਉ ਮਿਲਉਗੀ ਬਾਹ ਪਸਾਰਿ ॥੩॥
Gourree Bairaagan Mehalaa 1 |
Haranee Hovaa Ban Basaa Kandh Mool Chun Khaao |
Gur Parasaadhee Maeraa Sahu Milai Vaar Vaar Ho Jaao Jeeo |1|
Kokil Hovaa Anb Basaa Sehaj Sabadh Beechaar |
Sehaj Subhaae Maeraa Sahu Milai Dharasan Roop Apaar |2|
Mashhulee Hovaa Jal Basaa Jeea Janth Sabh Saar |
Ouravaar Paar Maeraa Sahu Vasai Ho Milougee Baah Pasaar |3|   Page-157

I am not stained by just one sin, that could be washed clean by a single virtue. I have kept sleeping the entire night of my life in attachments, while my Husband-Lord stays awake. In this way, how can I become lovable to my Husband? I am in such deep sleep the entire night and my Husband is awake! Having the worldly desires within, I approach His Bed with hope, but do not know if He will like me or not? O' my mother! How do I know what will happen to me? Without the Blessed Vision of my Husband-Lord, I can never survive; have not tasted His Love, and my thirst is not quenched. My beautiful youth has gone, and now I can only repent and regret!

---

ਆਸਾ ਮਹਲਾ ੧ ॥

ਏਕ ਨ ਭਰੀਆ ਗੁਣ ਕਰਿ ਧੋਵਾ ॥ ਮੇਰਾ ਸਹੁ ਜਾਗੈ ਹਉ ਨਿਸਿ ਭਰਿ ਸੋਵਾ ॥੧॥

ਇਉ ਕਿਉ ਕੰਤ ਪਿਆਰੀ ਹੋਵਾ ॥ ਸਹੁ ਜਾਗੈ ਹਉ ਨਿਸ ਭਰਿ ਸੋਵਾ ॥੧॥ ਰਹਾਉ ॥

ਆਸ ਪਿਆਸੀ ਸੇਜੈ ਆਵਾ ॥ ਆਗੈ ਸਹ ਭਾਵਾ ਕਿ ਨ ਭਾਵਾ ॥੨॥

ਕਿਆ ਜਾਨਾ ਕਿਆ ਹੋਇਗਾ ਰੀ ਮਾਈ ॥ ਹਰਿ ਦਰਸਨ ਬਿਨੁ ਰਹਨੁ ਨ ਜਾਈ ॥੧॥ ਰਹਾਉ ॥

ਪ੍ਰੇਮ ਨ ਚਾਖਿਆ ਮੇਰੀ ਤਿਸ ਨ ਬੁਝਾਨੀ ॥ ਗਇਆ ਸੁ ਜੋਬਨੁ ਧਨ ਪਛੁਤਾਨੀ ॥੩॥

Aasaa 1<sup>st</sup> Guru |

Eaek N Bhareeaa Gun Kar Dhhovaa |

Maeraa Sahu Jaagai Ho Nis Bhar Sovaa |1|

Eio Kio Kanth Piaaree Hovaa | Sahu Jaagai Ho Nis Bhar Sovaa |1|Pause |

Aas Piaasee Saejai Aavaa | Aagai Seh Bhaavaa K N Bhaavaa |2|

Kiaa Jaanaa Kiaa Hoeigaa Ree Maaee |

Har Dharasan Bin Rehan N Jaaee |1|Pause|

Praem N Chaakhiaa Maeree This N Bujhaanee |

Gaeiaa S Joban Dhhan Pashhuthaanee |3|    Page-356

Love

The Angels yearning for the Blessed Vision of the Lord
suffered through pain and hunger at the sacred shrines. The
Yogis and the Celibates lived disciplined lives, and others
wore saffron robes and became hermits.
O' my Lord Master, countless people are imbued with Love to
have Your Blessed Vision. Your Names are so many, and
Your Forms are endless. No one can tell how many Glorious
Virtues You have.

ਆਸਾ ਮਹਲਾ ੧ ॥
ਦੇਵਤਿਆ ਦਰਸਨ ਕੈ ਤਾਈ ਦੂਖ ਭੂਖ ਤੀਰਥ ਕੀਏ ॥
ਜੋਗੀ ਜਤੀ ਜੁਗਤਿ ਮਹਿ ਰਹਤੇ ਕਰਿ ਕਰਿ ਭਗਵੇ ਭੇਖ ਭਏ ॥੧॥
ਤਉ ਕਾਰਣਿ ਸਾਹਿਬਾ ਰੰਗਿ ਰਤੇ ॥
ਤੇਰੇ ਨਾਮ ਅਨੇਕਾ ਰੂਪ ਅਨੰਤਾ ਕਹਣੁ ਨ ਜਾਹੀ ਤੇਰੇ ਗੁਣ ਕੇਤੇ ॥੧॥ਰਹਾਉ ॥
Aasaa 1st Guru |
Dhaevathiaa Dharasan Kai Thaaee Dhookh Bhookh Theerathh Keeeae |
Jogee Jathee Jugath Mehi Rehathae Kar Kar Bhagavae Bhaekh Bheae |1|
Tho Kaaran Saahibaa Rang Rathae |
Thaerae Naam Anaekaa Roop Ananthaa Kehan N Jaahee Thaerae Gun Kaethae
|1|Pause |
Page-358

Spiritual Gems                                                                                         140

They alone are Truthful, who love God deep within their hearts. Those who have one thing in their heart, and something else in their mouth, are known to be false. Those who are imbued with true Love for the Lord, are blessed by His Vision. Those who forget the Name of the Lord, are a burden on this earth. Those whom the Lord attaches to the hem of His robe, are the true Saints at His Door. Blessed are the mothers who gave birth to them, and fruitful is their coming into the world. O Lord, Sustainer and Cherisher, you are the Infinite, Unfathomable and Endless. Those who recognize the True Lord - I kiss their feet. I seek Your Protection - You are the Forgiving Lord. Please, bless Shaikh Fareed with the bounty of Your meditative worship.

---

ਆਸਾ ਸੇਖ ਫਰੀਦ ਜੀਉ ਕੀ ਬਾਣੀ ॥

ਦਿਲਹੁ ਮੁਹਬਤਿ ਜਿੰਨ੍ਹ ਸੇਈ ਸਚਿਆ ॥ ਜਿਨ੍ਹ ਮਨਿ ਹੋਰੁ ਮੁਖਿ ਹੋਰੁ ਸਿ ਕਾਂਢੇ ਕਚਿਆ ॥੧॥

ਰਤੇ ਇਸਕ ਖੁਦਾਇ ਰੰਗਿ ਦੀਦਾਰ ਕੇ ॥ ਵਿਸਰਿਆ ਜਿਨ੍ਹ ਨਾਮੁ ਤੇ ਭੁਇ ਭਾਰੁ ਥੀਏ ॥੧॥ ਰਹਾਉ ॥

ਆਪਿ ਲੀਏ ਲੜਿ ਲਾਇ ਦਰਿ ਦਰਵੇਸ ਸੇ ॥ਤਿਨ ਧੰਨੁ ਜਣੇਦੀ ਮਾਉ ਆਏ ਸਫਲੁ ਸੇ ॥੨॥

ਪਰਵਦਗਾਰ ਅਪਾਰ ਅਗਮ ਬੇਅੰਤ ਤੂ ॥ਜਿਨਾ ਪਛਾਤਾ ਸਚੁ ਚੁੰਮਾ ਪੈਰ ਮੂੰ ॥੩॥

ਤੇਰੀ ਪਨਹ ਖੁਦਾਇ ਤੂ ਬਖਸੰਦਗੀ ॥ ਸੇਖ ਫਰੀਦੈ ਖੈਰੁ ਦੀਜੈ ਬੰਦਗੀ ॥੪॥੧॥

Aasaa Saekh Fareedh Jeo Kee Baanee |Dhilahu Muhabath Jinnh Saeee Sachiaa | Jinh Man Hor Mukh Hor S Kaandtae Kachiaa |1|Rathae Eisak Khudhaae Rang Dheedhaar Kae |Visariaa Jinh Naam Thae Bhue Bhaar Thheeeae |1|Pause | Aap Leeeae Larr Laae Dhar Dharavaes Sae |Thin Dhhann Janaedhee Maao Aaeae Safal Sae |2|Paravadhagaar Apaar Agam Baeanth Thoo |Jinaa Pashhaathaa Sach Chunmaa Pair Moon |3|Thaeree Paneh Khudhaae Thoo Bakhasandhagee | Saekh Fareedhai Khair Dheejai Bandhagee |4|1|    Page-488

Love

O' peaceful night, grow longer - I am imbued in love for my Husband-Beloved. O painful sleep, grow shorter, so that I may forever clasp His Feet. The Lord lovingly embraces whoever comes to His Sanctuary - this is the way of the Lord Master. Prays Nanak, I have met my Husband Lord, who always plays with me!

---

ਬਿਹਾਗੜਾ ਮਹਲਾ ॥
ਵਡੁ ਸੁਖੁ ਰੈਨੜੀਐ ਪ੍ਰਿਅ ਪ੍ਰੇਮੁ ਲਗਾ ॥ ਘਟ ਦੁਖ ਨੀਦੜੀਐ ਪਰਸਉ ਸਦਾ ਪਗਾ ॥
ਜੋ ਸਰਣਿ ਆਵੈ ਤਿਸੁ ਕੰਠਿ ਲਾਵੈ ਇਹੁ ਬਿਰਦੁ ਸੁਆਮੀ ਸੰਦਾ ॥
ਬਿਨਵੰਤਿ ਨਾਨਕ ਹਰਿ ਕੰਤੁ ਮਿਲਿਆ ਸਦਾ ਕੇਲ ਕਰੰਦਾ ॥੪॥੧॥੪॥
Bihaagarraa 5th Guru |
Vadhh Sukh Rainarreeeae Pria Praem Lagaa |
Ghatt Dhukh Needharreeeae Paraso Sadhaa Pagaa |
Jo Saran Aavai This Kanth Laavai Eihu Biradh Suaamee Sandhaa |
Binavanth Naanak Har Kanth Miliaa Sadhaa Kael Karandhaa |4|1|4|   Page-544

Love


If You are the mountain, O' Lord, then I am the peacock.  If
You are the moon, then I am the partridge in love with it.  O'
Lord, if You will not break with me, then I will not break with
You.  For, if I were to break with You, with whom would I
then connect?  If You are the lamp, then I am the wick.  If You
are the sacred place of pilgrimage, then I am the pilgrim.  I am
joined in True Love with You and have broken with all others.

ਰਾਗੁ ਸੋਰਠਿ ਬਾਣੀ ਭਗਤ ਰਵਿਦਾਸ ਜੀ ਕੀ ॥
ਜਉ ਤੁਮ ਗਿਰਿਵਰ ਤਉ ਹਮ ਮੋਰਾ ॥ ਜਉ ਤੁਮ ਚੰਦ ਤਉ ਹਮ ਭਏ ਹੈ ਚਕੋਰਾ ॥੧॥
ਮਾਧਵੇ ਤੁਮ ਨ ਤੋਰਹੁ ਤਉ ਹਮ ਨਹੀ ਤੋਰਹਿ ॥ ਤੁਮ ਸਿਉ ਤੋਰਿ ਕਵਨ ਸਿਉ ਜੋਰਹਿ ॥੧॥ ਰਹਾਉ ॥
ਜਉ ਤੁਮ ਦੀਵਰਾ ਤਉ ਹਮ ਬਾਤੀ ॥ ਜਉ ਤੁਮ ਤੀਰਥ ਤਉ ਹਮ ਜਾਤੀ ॥੨॥
ਸਾਚੀ ਪ੍ਰੀਤਿ ਹਮ ਤੁਮ ਸਿਉ ਜੋਰੀ ॥ ਤੁਮ ਸਿਉ ਜੋਰਿ ਅਵਰ ਸੰਗਿ ਤੋਰੀ ॥੩॥
Raag Sorath Baanee Bhagath Ravidhaas Jee Kee  |
Jo Thum Girivar Tho Ham Moraa |
Jo Thum Chandh Tho Ham Bheae Hai Chakoraa |1|
Maadhhavae Thum N Thorahu Tho Ham Nehee Thorehi |
Thum Sio Thor Kavan Sio Jorehi |1| Pause |
Jo Thum Dheevaraa Tho Ham Baathee |
Jo Thum Theerathh Tho Ham Jaathee |2|
Saachee Preeth Ham Thum Sio Joree |Thum Sio Jor Avar Sang Thoree |3|
 Page-658

Says Ravi Daas, that the One Husband-Lord in several forms
dwells within everyone and Himself enjoys His Creation; He is
nearer to me than my hands, everything is happening in His
Will.
O' Lord, we have overcome the noose of attachments by
loving You. Now, even if You try to, how can You escape
from the bonds of our Love? O' Lord, You, know my Love
for You, what can You do? My love for You is like that of a
fish, who is caught, cut up, and cooked in many ways. Bit by
bit, it is eaten, but still, it does not forget the water!

---

ਰਾਗੁ ਸੋਰਠਿ ਬਾਣੀ ਭਗਤ ਰਵਿਦਾਸ ਜੀ ਕੀ _॥
ਸਰਬੇ ਏਕੁ ਅਨੇਕੈ ਸੁਆਮੀ ਸਭ ਘਟ ਭਗਵੈ ਸੋਈ ॥ ਕਹਿ ਰਵਿਦਾਸ ਹਾਥ ਪੈ ਨੇਰੈ ਸਹਜੇ ਹੋਇ ਸੁ ਹੋਈ ॥੪॥੧॥
ਜਉ ਹਮ ਬਾਂਧੇ ਮੋਹ ਫਾਸ ਹਮ ਪ੍ਰੇਮ ਬਧਨਿ ਤੁਮ ਬਾਧੇ ॥ ਅਪਨੇ ਛੂਟਨ ਕੋ ਜਤਨੁ ਕਰਹੁ ਹਮ ਛੂਟੇ ਤੁਮ ਆਰਾਧੇ
॥੧॥
ਮਾਧਵੇ ਜਾਨਤ ਹਹੁ ਜੈਸੀ ਤੈਸੀ ॥ ਅਬ ਕਹਾ ਕਰਹੁਗੋ ਐਸੀ ॥੧॥ ਰਹਾਉ ॥
ਮੀਨੁ ਪਕਰਿ ਫਾਂਕਿਓ ਅਰੁ ਕਾਟਿਓ ਰਾਂਧਿ ਕੀਓ ਬਹੁ ਬਾਨੀ ॥
ਖੰਡ ਖੰਡ ਕਰਿ ਭੋਜਨੁ ਕੀਨੋ ਤਊ ਨ ਬਿਸਰਿਓ ਪਾਨੀ ॥੨॥
Raag Sorath Baanee Bhagath Ravidhaas Jee Kee |
Sarabae Eaek Anaekai Suaamee Sabh Ghatt Bhuogavai Soee |
Kehi Ravidhaas Haathh Pai Naerai Sehajae Hoe S Hoee |4|1|
Jo Ham Baandhhae Moh Faas Ham Praem Badhhan Thum Baadhhae |
Apanae Shhoottan Ko Jathan Karahu Ham Shhoottae Thum Aaraadhhae |1|
Maadhhavae Jaanath Hahu Jaisee Thaisee |
Ab Kehaa Karahugae Aisee |1| Pause |
Meen Pakar Faankiou Ar Kaattiou Raandhh Keeou Bahu Baanee |
Khandd Khandd Kar Bhojan Keeno Thoo N Bisariou Paanee |2|    Page-658

Love

Says Ravi Daas, O' Lord, I have been separated from You for many incarnations, please have Mercy on me, so that I can dedicate this life in remembering You. It has been long since I came into Your Presence; I live to only fulfill this desire. I am fearful that my love for the Lord of the Universe may not diminish. I have paid dearly for this Love; got it in exchange for my soul!

---

ਧਨਾਸਰੀ ਭਗਤ ਰਵਿਦਾਸ ਜੀ ਕੀ ॥
ਬਹੁਤ ਜਨਮ ਬਿਛੁਰੇ ਥੇ ਮਾਧਉ ਇਹੁ ਜਨਮੁ ਤੁਮ੍ਹਾਰੇ ਲੇਖੇ ॥
ਕਹਿ ਰਵਿਦਾਸ ਆਸ ਲਗਿ ਜੀਵਉ ਚਿਰ ਭਇਓ ਦਰਸਨੁ ਦੇਖੇ ॥੨॥੧॥
ਮੇਰੀ ਪ੍ਰੀਤਿ ਗੋਬਿੰਦ ਸਿਉ ਜਿਨਿ ਘਟੈ ॥ ਮੈ ਤਉ ਮੋਲਿ ਮਹਗੀ ਲਈ ਜੀਅ ਸਟੈ ॥੧॥ ਰਹਾਉ ॥
Dhhanaasaree Bhagath Ravidhaas Jee Kee |
Bahuth Janam Bishhurae Thhae Maadhho Eihu Janam Thumhaarae Laekhae |
Kehi Ravidhaas Aas Lag Jeevo Chir Bhaeiou Dharasan Dhaekhae |2|1|
Maeree Preeth Gobindh Sio Jin Ghattai |
Mai Tho Mol Mehagee Lee Jeea Sattai |1| Pause |   Page-694

Spiritual Gems                                                                    145

O' the Lord of Wisdom! O' the Maker of our hearts sacred! O' the Ever Steady! O' the Liberator from bonds! Your Love abides in my mind and heart! The Divine Vision is indeed priceless; its value cannot be estimated. O' the Sacred Cherisher, you are my Husband, exalted of the exalted, of immeasurable Power, the Lord Master.

ਤਿਲੰਗ ਮਹਲਾ ੫ ॥
ਮੀਰਾਂ ਦਾਨਾਂ ਦਿਲ ਸੋਚ ॥ ਮੁਹਬਤੇ ਮਨਿ ਤਨਿ ਬਸੈ ਸਚੁ ਸਾਹ ਬੰਦੀ ਮੋਚ ॥੧॥ ਰਹਾਉ
ਦੀਦਨੇ ਦੀਦਾਰ ਸਾਹਿਬ ਕਛੁ ਨਹੀ ਇਸ ਕਾ ਮੋਲੁ ॥
ਪਾਕ ਪਰਵਦਗਾਰ ਤੂ ਖੁਦਿ ਖਸਮੁ ਵਡਾ ਅਤੋਲੁ ॥੧॥
Thilang 5ᵗʰ Guru |Meeraan Dhaanaan Dhil Soch |
Muhabathae Man Than Basai Sach Saah Bandhee Moch |1| Pause |
Dheedhanae Dheedhaar Saahib Kashh Nehee Eis Kaa Mol |
Paak Paravadhagaar Thoo Khudh Khasam Vaddaa Athol |1|    Page-724

I have fallen in Love with my Beloved Lord. The Lord has tied His Love String with me so strongly, that it can neither be broken nor loosened, even if I try to let go!

ਬਿਲਾਵਲੁ ਮਹਲਾ ੫ ॥
ਮੁ ਲਾਲਨ ਸਿਉ ਪ੍ਰੀਤਿ ਬਨੀ ॥ ਰਹਾਉ ॥
ਤੋਰੀ ਨ ਤੂਟੈ ਛੋਰੀ ਨ ਛੂਟੈ ਐਸੀ ਮਾਧੋ ਖਿੰਚ ਤਨੀ ॥੧॥
Bilaaval 5ᵗʰ Guru |Moo Laalan Sio Preeth Banee |Pause |Thoree N Thoottai Shhoree
N Shhoottai Aisee Maadhho Khinch Thanee |1|    Page-827

O' my Lord, carry me across the world ocean, save me! My Loving Father, please give me Your arm, me the ignorant do not know how to swim! Like the fish out of water wriggles, so is Naam Dayv in pain without the Lord's Name. As the man driven by sex loves another man's wife, so does Naam Dayv Love the Lord. As the earth scorches in the dazzling sunlight, so is poor Naam Dayv burning without the Lord's Name.

---

ਰਾਗੁ ਗੋਂਡ ਬਾਣੀ ਨਾਮਦੇਉ ਜੀ ਕੀ ॥

ਮੋ ਕਉ ਤਾਰਿ ਲੇ ਰਾਮਾ ਤਾਰਿ ਲੇ ॥ ਮੈ ਅਜਾਨੁ ਜਨੁ ਤਰਿਬੇ ਨ ਜਾਨਉ ਬਾਪ ਬੀਠੁਲਾ ਬਾਹ ਦੇ ॥੧॥ ਰਹਾਉ ॥

ਪਾਨੀਆ ਬਿਨੁ ਮੀਨੁ ਤਲਫੈ ॥ ਐਸੇ ਰਾਮ ਨਾਮਾ ਬਿਨੁ ਬਾਪੁਰੋ ਨਾਮਾ ॥੧॥ ਰਹਾਉ ॥

ਜੈਸੇ ਬਿਖੈ ਹੇਤ ਪਰ ਨਾਰੀ ॥ ਐਸੇ ਨਾਮੇ ਪ੍ਰੀਤਿ ਮੁਰਾਰੀ ॥੪॥

ਜੈਸੇ ਤਾਪਤੇ ਨਿਰਮਲ ਘਾਮਾ ॥ ਤੈਸੇ ਰਾਮ ਨਾਮਾ ਬਿਨੁ ਬਾਪੁਰੋ ਨਾਮਾ ॥੫॥੪॥

Raag Gonadd Baanee Naamadhaeo Jee Kee |
Mo Ko Thaar Lae Raamaa Thaar Lae |
Mai Ajaan Jan Tharibae N Jaano Baap Beethulaa Baah Dhae |1|Pause |
Paaneeaa Bin Meen Thalafai |Aisae Raam Naamaa Bin Baapuro Naamaa |1|Rehaao |
|3|Jaisae Bikhai Haeth Par Naaree |Aisae Naamae Preeth Muraaree |4|Jaisae
Thaapathae Niramal Ghaamaa |Thaisae Raam Naamaa Bin Baapuro Naamaa |5|4|
Page-873

The trader of the Ambrosial Name stays awake day and night; he never sleeps in the slumber of worldly attachments. He has been hit by the arrow of God's Love and he alone knows the pain of separation from the Lord! How can any physician know the cure for this pain?

---

ਰਾਗੁ ਮਾਰੂ ਮਹਲਾ ੧ ॥
ਅਹਿਨਿਸਿ ਜਾਗੈ ਨੀਦ ਨ ਸੋਵੈ ॥ਸੋ ਜਾਣੈ ਜਿਸੁ ਵੇਦਨ ਹੋਵੈ ॥
ਪ੍ਰੇਮ ਕੇ ਕਾਨ ਲਗੇ ਤਨ ਭੀਤਰਿ ਵੈਦੁ ਕਿ ਜਾਣੈ ਕਾਰੀ ਜੀਉ ॥੧॥
Raag Maaroo 1ˢᵗ Guru |
Ahinis Jaagai Needh N Sovai |So Jaanai Jis Vaedhan Hovai |
Praem Kae Kaan Lagae Than Bheethar Vaidh K Jaanai Kaaree Jeeo |1| Page-993

---

The love which the Lord's devotee feels for the Lord lasts forever. So long as he is alive, he remembers the Lord-Master and when departing, he keeps Him enshrined in his consciousness.

---

ਮਾਰੂ ਮਹਲਾ ੫ ॥
ਸੇਵਕ ਕੀ ਓੜਕਿ ਨਿਬਹੀ ਪ੍ਰੀਤਿ ॥
ਜੀਵਤ ਸਾਹਿਬੁ ਸੇਵਿਓ ਅਪਨਾ ਚਲਤੇ ਰਾਖਿਓ ਚੀਤਿ ॥੧॥ ਰਹਾਉ ॥
Maaroo 5ᵗʰ Guru |
Saevak Kee Ourrak Nibehee Preeth |
Jeevath Saahib Saeviou Apanaa Chalathae Raakhiou Cheeth |1|Pause |     Page-1000

# Love

O' Lord, Treasure of Mercy, please bless me, that I may sing Your Glorious Praises. I live in the hope O' Lord, when will You hug and hold me in Your Embrace? I am a foolish and ignorant child; Father, please teach me to learn! Your child makes mistakes again and again, but still, you are pleased with him, O' Father of the Universe. Those, upon whom God has Mercy Love Him and God Loves them. They merge with the God's Light and become one with Him.

---

ਕਲਿਆਨ ਮਹਲਾ ੪ ॥
ਪ੍ਰਭ ਕੀਜੈ ਕ੍ਰਿਪਾ ਨਿਧਾਨ ਹਮ ਹਰਿ ਗੁਨ ਗਾਵਹਗੇ ॥
ਹਉ ਤੁਮਰੀ ਕਰਉ ਨਿਤ ਆਸ ਪ੍ਰਭ ਮੋਹਿ ਕਬ ਗਲਿ ਲਾਵਹਿਗੇ ॥੧॥ ਰਹਾਉ ॥
ਹਮ ਬਾਰਿਕ ਮੁਗਧ ਇਆਨ ਪਿਤਾ ਸਮਝਾਵਹਿਗੇ ॥ਸੁਤ ਖਿਨ ਖਿਨ ਭੂਲਿ ਬਿਗਾਰਿ ਜਗਤ ਪਿਤ ਭਾਵਹਿਗੇ ॥੧॥
ਜੋ ਹਰਿ ਭਾਵਹਿ ਭਗਤ ਤਿਨਾ ਹਰਿ ਭਾਵਹਿਗੇ ॥ਜੋਤੀ ਜੋਤਿ ਮਿਲਾਇ ਜੋਤਿ ਰਲਿ ਜਾਵਹਗੇ ॥੩॥
Kaliaan 4th Guru |
Prabh Keejai Kirapaa Nidhhaan Ham Har Gun Gaavehagae |
Ho Thumaree Karo Nith Aas Prabh Mohi Kab Gal Laavehigae |1|Pause |
Ham Baarik Mugadhh Eiaan Pithaa Samajhaavehigae |
Suth Khin Khin Bhool Bigaar Jagath Pith Bhaavehigae |1|
Jo Har Bhaavehi Bhagath Thinaa Har Bhaavehigae |
Jothee Joth Milaae Joth Ral Jaavehagae |3|    Page-1321

Love

Kabeer, how can I describe the extent of joy of the Lord's Lotus Feet? Even trying to describe its sublime Glory is not appropriate; it must be seen to be comprehended.

ਸਲੋਕ ਭਗਤ ਕਬੀਰ ਜੀਉ ਕੇ ॥
ਕਬੀਰ ਚਰਨ ਕਮਲ ਕੀ ਮਉਜ ਕੋ ਕਹਿ ਕੈਸੇ ਉਨਮਾਨ ॥ਕਹਿਬੇ ਕਉ ਸੋਭਾ ਨਹੀ ਦੇਖਾ ਹੀ ਪਰਵਾਨੁ ॥੧੨੧॥
Salok Bhagath Kabeer Jeeo Kae |
Kabeer Charan Kamal Kee Mouj Ko Kehi Kaisae Ounamaan |
Kehibae Ko Sobhaa Nehee Dhaekhaa Hee Paravaan |121| Page-1370

I am not afraid of losing my youth, so long as I do not lose the Love of my Husband Lord. O' Fareed, so many youths, without His Love, have dried up and withered away.

ਸਲੋਕ ਸੇਖ ਫਰੀਦ ਕੇ
ਜੋਬਨ ਜਾਂਦੇ ਨਾ ਡਰਾਂ ਜੇ ਸਹ ਪ੍ਰੀਤਿ ਨ ਜਾਇ ॥ਫਰੀਦਾ ਕਿਤੀ ਜੋਬਨ ਪ੍ਰੀਤਿ ਬਿਨੁ ਸੁਕਿ ਗਏ ਕੁਮਲਾਇ ॥੩੪॥
Salok Saekh Fareedh Kae |
Joban Jaandhae Naa Ddaraan Jae Seh Preeth N Jaae |
Fareedhaa Kithanaee Joban Preeth Bin Suk Geae Kumalaae |34| Page-1379

Love

O' Fareed, the path is a muddy sludge, and the house of my Beloved is so far away but I have immense Love for Him. If I go out, my blanket will get soaked, but if I remain at home, my heart will be broken!
Come on blanket! Get soaked and drenched with the downpour of the Lord's Rain. I will go out and meet my God Loving Friends, so that my Love will not be broken!

---

ਸਲੋਕ ਸੇਖ ਫਰੀਦ ਕੇ ॥
ਫਰੀਦਾ ਗਲੀਏ ਚਿਕੜੁ ਦੂਰਿ ਘਰੁ ਨਾਲਿ ਪਿਆਰੇ ਨੇਹੁ ॥
ਚਲਾ ਤ ਭਿਜੈ ਕੰਬਲੀ ਰਹਾਂ ਤ ਤੁਟੈ ਨੇਹੁ ॥੨੪॥
ਭਿਜਉ ਸਿਜਉ ਕੰਬਲੀ ਅਲਹ ਵਰਸਉ ਮੇਹੁ ॥
ਜਾਇ ਮਿਲਾ ਤਿਨਾ ਸਜਣਾ ਤੁਟਉ ਨਾਹੀ ਨੇਹੁ ॥੨੫॥
Salok Saekh Fareedh Kae |
Fareedhaa Galeeeae Chikarr Dhoor Ghar Naal Piaarae Naehu |
Chalaa Th Bhijai Kanbalee Rehaan Th Thuttai Naehu |24|
Bhijo Sijo Kanbalee Aleh Varaso Maehu |
Jaae Milaa Thinaa Sajanaa Thutto Naahee Naehu |25|     Page-1379

Spiritual Gems                                                           151

Love

If you are fond of playing the game of love, then come to My street with your head on the palm of your hand. You can only place your feet on this Path, when you are ready to offer your head without any hesitation!

---

ਸਲੋਕ ਵਾਰਾਂ ਤੇ ਵਧੀਕ ॥ਮਹਲਾ ੧ ॥
ਜਉ ਤਉ ਪ੍ਰੇਮ ਖੇਲਣ ਕਾ ਚਾਉ ॥ਸਿਰੁ ਧਰਿ ਤਲੀ ਗਲੀ ਮੇਰੀ ਆਉ ॥
ਇਤੁ ਮਾਰਗਿ ਪੈਰੁ ਧਰੀਜੈ ॥ਸਿਰੁ ਦੀਜੈ ਕਾਣਿ ਨ ਕੀਜੈ ॥੨੦॥
Salok Vaaraan Thae Vadhheek ||Mehalaa 1 ||
Jo Tho Praem Khaelan Kaa Chaao ||Sir Dhhar Thalee Galee Maeree Aao ||
Eith Maarag Pair Dhhareejai ||ਸਿਰੁ ਦੀਜੈ ਕਾਣਿ ਨ ਕੀਜੈ ॥੨੦॥  Page-1412

Love

Hearing that Lord Krishana came and stayed over at poor
Bidar's home, Duryodhan remarked sarcastically; "You
abandoned my palace and went to stay in my servant's hut."
Then smilingly, Lord Krishana asked the King to come
forward and listen carefully; "I see no love and devotion in
you; I am not looking for my comfort". I see no one has even
a fraction of the love that Bidar bears in his heart. The Lord is
hungry of Love and Devotion only and nothing else!

Note: This is from the true story of the Indian Epic "Mahabharata" which
demonstrates the victory of good over evil, like the other Epic "Ramayana"
mentioned in Chapter 14. A great war (Mahabharata) is said to have
occurred between the Kauravas, led by King Duryodhan and the Pandavas
led by the warrior Arjun. Lord Krishana drove Arjun's chariot in the
battle! Bidar was a childhood friend of Lord Krishna.

---

ਵਾਰਾਂ ਭਾਈ ਗੁਰਦਾਸ ।
ਆਇਆ ਸੁਣਿਆ ਬਿਦਰ ਦੇ ਬੇਲੈ ਦੁਰਜੋਧਨ ਹੋਇ ਰੁਖਾ। ਘਰਿ ਅਸਾਡੇ ਛਡਿ ਕੈ ਗੋਲੇ ਦੇ ਘਰਿ ਜਾਹਿ ਕਿ ਸੁਖਾ ।
ਹਸਿ ਬੋਲੇ ਭਗਵਾਨ ਜੀ ਸੁਣਿਹੋ ਰਾਜਾ ਹੋਇ ਸਨਮੁਖਾ। ਤੇਰੇ ਭਾਉ ਨ ਦਿਸਈ ਮੇਰੇ ਨਾਹੀ ਅਪਦਾ ਦੁਖਾ ।
ਭਾਉ ਜਿਵੇਹਾ ਬਿਦਰ ਦੇ ਹੇਰੀ ਦੇ ਚਿਤਿ ਚਾਉ ਨ ਚੁਖਾ। ਗੋਬਿੰਦ ਭਾਉ ਭਗਤਿ ਦਾ ਭੁਖਾ ॥੭॥
Vaaran Bhai Gurdas.
Aaiaa Souniaa Bidar Day Bolai Durajodhanu Hoi Roukhaa.
Ghari Asaaday Chhadi Kai Golay Day Ghari Jaahi Ki Soukhaa.
Hasi Bolai Bhagavaan Jee Souniho Raajaa Hoi Sanamoukhaa.
Tayray Bhaau N Disaee Mayray Naahee Apadaa Doukhaa.
Bhaau Jivayhaa Bidar Day Horee Day Chiti Chaau N Choukhaa.
Gobind Bhaau Bhagati Daa Bhoukhaa ॥7॥  Vaar 10

## Chapter-11  Truth & Truthful Living

Many people stubbornly pursue ritualism based on their intellect and many contemplate on the ancient religious writings such as the Vedas (Hindu Scripture). There are also so many other ego entanglements that tie up the soul, but the God oriented eventually find the path to Liberation. Truth is High, but Higher still is Truthful living!

---

ਸਿਰੀਰਾਗੁ ਮਹਲਾ ੧ ॥
ਮਨਹਠ ਬੁਧੀ ਕੇਤੀਆ ਕੇਤੇ ਬੇਦ ਬੀਚਾਰ ॥ਕੇਤੇ ਬੰਧਨ ਜੀਅ ਕੇ ਗੁਰਮੁਖਿ ਮੋਖ ਦੁਆਰ ॥
ਸਚਹੁ ਓਰੈ ਸਭੁ ਕੋ ਉਪਰਿ ਸਚੁ ਆਚਾਰੁ ॥੫॥
Sireeraag 1ˢᵗ Guru |
Manehath Budhhee Kaetheeaa Kaethae Baedh Beechaar |
Kaethae Bandhhan Jeea Kae Guramukh Mokh Dhuaar |
Sachahu Ourai Sabh Ko Oupar Sach Aachaar |5|  Page-62

True are Your worlds and the Universe and its Systems. True are Your everlasting life systems and the entire creation. True are Your Kingdom and justice & True the Divine Will and Commands. True is Your praise and adoration and True is Your almighty power created Nature, O' the True King.

---

ਸਲੋਕੁ ॥ ਮਹਲਾ ੧ ॥

ਸਚੇ ਤੇਰੇ ਖੰਡ ਸਚੇ ਬ੍ਰਹਮੰਡ ॥ਸਚੇ ਤੇਰੇ ਲੋਅ ਸਚੇ ਆਕਾਰ ॥

ਸਚਾ ਤੇਰਾ ਅਮਰੁ ਸਚਾ ਦੀਬਾਣੁ ॥ਸਚਾ ਤੇਰਾ ਹੁਕਮੁ ਸਚਾ ਫੁਰਮਾਣੁ ॥

ਸਚੀ ਤੇਰੀ ਸਿਫਤਿ ਸਚੀ ਸਾਲਾਹ ॥ਸਚੀ ਤੇਰੀ ਕੁਦਰਤਿ ਸਚੇ ਪਾਤਿਸਾਹ ॥

Salok 1st Guru |

Sachae Thaerae Khandd Sachae Brehamandd |

Sachae Thaerae Loa Sachae Aakaar |

Sachaa Thaeraa Amar Sachaa Dheebaan |

Sachaa Thaeraa Hukam Sachaa Furamaan |

Sachee Thaeree Sifath Sachee Saalaah |

Sachee Thaeree Kudharath Sachae Paathisaah |   Page-463

Truth is known only when Truth lives in one's heart. The filth of falsehood departs, and the body is also rendered pure. One fully comprehends Truth only when one truly loves God. Being in Tune with God, the mind experiences bliss and is then liberated.

---

ਮਹਲਾ ੧ ॥
ਸਚੁ ਤਾ ਪਰੁ ਜਾਣੀਐ ਜਾ ਰਿਦੈ ਸਚਾ ਹੋਇ ॥ਕੂੜ ਕੀ ਮਲੁ ਉਤਰੈ ਤਨੁ ਕਰੇ ਹਛਾ ਧੋਇ ॥
ਸਚੁ ਤਾ ਪਰੁ ਜਾਣੀਐ ਜਾ ਸਚਿ ਧਰੇ ਪਿਆਰੁ ॥ ਨਾਉ ਸੁਣਿ ਮਨੁ ਰਹਸੀਐ ਤਾ ਪਾਏ ਮੋਖ ਦੁਆਰੁ ॥
1st Guru |
Sach Thaa Par Jaaneeai Jaa Ridhai Sachaa Hoe |
Koorr Kee Mal Outharai Than Karae Hashhaa Dhhoe |
Sach Thaa Par Jaaneeai Jaa Sach Dhharae Piaar |
Naao Sun Man Rehaseeai Thaa Paaeae Mokh Dhuaar |   Page-468

True friends are those, whom when we meet, our evil mindedness disappears. I have searched the entire world, O' Nanak, but such persons are indeed very rare.

---

ਮਹਲਾ ੫ ॥

ਜਿਨ੍ਹਾ ਦਿਸੰਦੜਿਆ ਦੁਰਮਤਿ ਵੰਞੈ ਮਿਤ੍ਰ ਅਸਾਡੜੇ ਸੇਈ ॥
ਹਉ ਢੁਢੇਦੀ ਜਗੁ ਸਬਾਇਆ ਜਨ ਨਾਨਕ ਵਿਰਲੇ ਕੇਈ ॥੨॥

5th Guru |

Jinhaa Dhisandharriaa Dhuramath Vannjai Mithr Asaaddarrae Saeee |
Ho Dtoodtaedhee Jag Sabaaeiaa Jan Naanak Viralae Kaeee |2|   Page- 520

---

True company is of those with whom we contemplate on the Lord's Name. O' Nanak, do not associate with the ones that look out only for their selfish interests.

---

ਮਹਲਾ ੫ ॥

ਸਚੀ ਬੈਸਕ ਤਿਨ੍ਹਾ ਸੰਗਿ ਜਿਨ ਸੰਗਿ ਜਪੀਐ ਨਾਉ ॥
ਤਿਨ੍ਹ ਸੰਗਿ ਸੰਗੁ ਨ ਕੀਚਈ ਨਾਨਕ ਜਿਨਾ ਆਪਣਾ ਸੁਆਉ ॥੨॥

5th Guru |

Sachee Baisak Thinhaa Sang Jin Sang Japeeai Naao |
Thinh Sang Sang N Keechee Naanak Jinaa Aapanaa Suaao |2|   Page- 520

---

True union is only of those who are united heart to heart, like the Lover and Beloved. No matter how much you wish, Communion cannot occur through mere talk or words.

---

ਤਿਲੰਗ ਮਹਲਾ ੧ ਘਰੁ ੨
ਜੋ ਦਿਲਿ ਮਿਲਿਆ ਸੁ ਮਿਲਿ ਰਹਿਆ ਮਿਲਿਆ ਕਹੀਐ ਰੇ ਸੋਈ ॥
ਜੇ ਬਹੁਤੇਰਾ ਲੋਚੀਐ ਬਾਤੀ ਮੇਲੁ ਨ ਹੋਈ ॥੭॥
Jo Dhil Miliaa S Mil Rehiaa Miliaa Keheeai Rae Soee |
Jae Bahuthaeraa Locheeai Baathee Mael N Hoee |7|  Page-725

My real friends and companions are those who are always with me wherever I am, here and hereafter. Where accounts are called for they are seen standing by my side to vouch for me.

---

ਸੂਹੀ ਮਹਲਾ ੧ ॥
ਸਜਣ ਸੇਈ ਨਾਲਿ ਮੈ ਚਲਦਿਆ ਨਾਲਿ ਚਲੰਨ੍ਹਿ ॥ਜਿਥੈ ਲੇਖਾ ਮੰਗੀਐ ਤਿਥੈ ਖੜੇ ਦਿਸੰਨਿ ॥੧॥ ਰਹਾਉ ॥
Soohee 1st Guru |
Sajan Saeee Naal Mai Chaladhiaa Naal Chalannih |
Jithhai Laekhaa Mangeeai Thithhai Kharrae Dhisann |1|Pause |  Page-729

The fool does not contemplate on the Lord's Name, but what is he thinking again and again? In the darkness, we need a lamp, to find what we are looking for. Although in his heart there is deception, yet the mouth is full of words of wisdom. What good is washing your body when the heart is full of filth. It is like washing a gourd (bitter squash) at the sixty-eight (per the Hindu legend) sacred shrines. But even then, its bitterness is never removed. Says Kabeer after deep contemplation, O' Lord please help me conquer the Maya (Illusion) and come into your holy Presence, thus crossing the terrifying world-ocean.

---

ਰਾਗੁ ਸੋਰਠਿ ਬਾਣੀ ਭਗਤ ਕਬੀਰ ਜੀ ॥
ਹਰਿ ਕਾ ਨਾਮੁ ਨ ਜਪਸਿ ਗਵਾਰਾ ॥ ਕਿਆ ਸੋਚਹਿ ਬਾਰੰ ਬਾਰਾ ॥੧॥ ਰਹਾਉ ॥
ਅੰਧਿਆਰੇ ਦੀਪਕੁ ਚਹੀਐ ॥ ਇਕ ਬਸਤੁ ਅਗੋਚਰ ਲਹੀਐ ॥
ਹਿਰਦੈ ਕਪਟੁ ਮੁਖ ਗਿਆਨੀ ॥ ਝੂਠੇ ਕਹਾ ਬਿਲੋਵਸਿ ਪਾਨੀ ॥੧॥
ਕਾਂਇਆ ਮਾਂਜਸਿ ਕਉਨ ਗੁਨਾਂ ॥ ਜਉ ਘਟ ਭੀਤਰਿ ਹੈ ਮਲਨਾਂ ॥੧॥ ਰਹਾਉ ॥
ਲਉਕੀ ਅਠਸਠਿ ਤੀਰਥ ਨ੍ਹਾਈ ॥ ਕਉਰਾਪਨੁ ਤਊ ਨ ਜਾਈ ॥੨॥
ਕਹਿ ਕਬੀਰ ਬੀਚਾਰੀ ॥ ਭਵ ਸਾਗਰੁ ਤਾਰਿ ਮੁਰਾਰੀ ॥੩॥੮॥
Raag Sorath Baanee Bhagath Kabeer Jee |
Har Kaa Naam N Japas Gavaaraa | Kiaa Sochehi Baaran Baaraa |1|Pause |
Andhhiaarae Dheepak Cheheeai | Eik Basath Agochar Leheeai |
Hridhai Kapatt Mukh Giaanee | Jhoothae Kehaa Bilovas Paanee |1|
Kaaneiaa Maanjas Koun Gunaan | Jo Ghatt Bheethar Hai Malanaan |1|Pause |
Loukee Athasath Theerathh Nhaaee | Kouraapan Thoo N Jaaee |2|
Kehi Kabeer Beechaaree | Bhav Saagar Thaar Muraaree |3|8|   Page-655

Build a beautiful raft of contemplation on the Lord's Name and have self-discipline, to carry you safely across the river of Maya (Illusion). No ocean, and/or rising tides can stop you; this is how comfortable your path shall become. O' Lord, the robe of my spiritual body is dyed permanently beautiful by contemplation on Your Name. O' my life journey's dear companions, do you know how will we meet the Lord? If we have the virtue of His Name in our packs, the Lord will unite us Himself!

ਸੂਹੀ ਮਹਲਾ ੧ ॥
ਜਪ ਤਪ ਕਾ ਬੰਧੁ ਬੇੜੁਲਾ ਜਿਤੁ ਲੰਘਹਿ ਵਹੇਲਾ ॥ ਨਾ ਸਰਵਰੁ ਨਾ ਉਛਲੈ ਐਸਾ ਪੰਥੁ ਸੁਹੇਲਾ ॥੧॥
ਤੇਰਾ ਏਕੋ ਨਾਮੁ ਮੰਜੀਠੜਾ ਰਤਾ ਮੇਰਾ ਚੋਲਾ ਸਦ ਰੰਗ ਢੋਲਾ ॥੧॥ ਰਹਾਉ ॥
ਸਾਜਨ ਚਲੇ ਪਿਆਰਿਆ ਕਿਉ ਮੇਲਾ ਹੋਈ ॥ ਜੇ ਗੁਣ ਹੋਵਹਿ ਗੰਠੜੀਐ ਮੇਲੇਗਾ ਸੋਈ ॥੨॥
Soohee 1<sup>St</sup> Guru |
Jap Thap Kaa Bandhh Baerrulaa Jith Langhehi Vehaelaa |
Naa Saravar Naa Ooshhalai Aisaa Panthh Suhaelaa |1|
Thaeraa Eaeko Naam Manjeetharraa Rathaa Maeraa Cholaa Sadh Rang Dtolaa
|1|Pause |Saajan Chalae Piaariaa Kio Maelaa Hoee | Jae Gun Hovehi Gantharreeai
Maelaegaa Soee |2|   Page-729

Do not call them husband and wife, who merely live under one roof. Husband and wife are only those who have two bodies but a single bond of the same eternal light.

---

ਮਹਲਾ ੩ ॥
ਧਨ ਪਿਰੁ ਏਹਿ ਨ ਆਖੀਅਨਿ ਬਹਨਿ ਇਕਠੇ ਹੋਇ ॥ ਏਕ ਜੋਤਿ ਦੁਇ ਮੂਰਤੀ ਧਨ ਪਿਰੁ ਕਹੀਐ ਸੋਇ ॥੩॥
3rd Guru |
Dhhan Pir Eaehi N Aakheean Behan Eikathae Hoe |
Eaek Joth Dhue Moorathee Dhhan Pir Keheeai Soe |3|    Page-788

---

Knowing each other by acquaintance, association, or worldly relationship is not a uniting of the two. However, if you are internally connected with Love of God as the common thread, then you are truly united.

---

ਮਹਲਾ ੨ ॥
ਮਿਲਿਐ ਮਿਲਿਆ ਨਾ ਮਿਲੈ ਮਿਲੈ ਮਿਲਿਆ ਜੇ ਹੋਇ ॥ਅੰਤਰ ਆਤਮੈ ਜੋ ਮਿਲੈ ਮਿਲਿਆ ਕਹੀਐ ਸੋਇ ॥੩॥
2nd Guru ||
Miliai Miliaa Naa Milai Milai Miliaa Jae Hoe |
Anthar Aathamai Jo Milai Miliaa Keheeai Soe |3|   Page-791

Do not call them blind, who have no eyes in their face. Only those are truly blind, O' Nanak, who wander away from the Husband Lord.

---

ਸਲੋਕ ਮਹਲਾ ੨ ॥
ਅੰਧੇ ਏਹਿ ਨ ਆਖੀਅਨਿ ਜਿਨ ਮੁਖਿ ਲੋਇਣ ਨਾਹਿ ॥ ਅੰਧੇ ਸੇਈ ਨਾਨਕਾ ਖਸਮਹੁ ਘੁਥੇ ਜਾਹਿ ॥੧॥
Salok Ma 2 |
Andhhae Eaehi N Aakheean Jin Mukh Loein Naahi |
Andhhae Saeee Naanakaa Khasamahu Ghuthhae Jaahi |1| Page-954

---

O Nanak, break away from the hypocrites, and seek out the Saints, and True friends. The false shall leave you, even while you are still alive; but the Saints and True friends shall not forsake you, even after death.

---

ਸਲੋਕ ਡਖਣੇ ਮਹਲਾ ੫ ॥
ਨਾਨਕ ਕਚੜਿਆ ਸਿਉ ਤੋੜਿ ਢੂਢਿ ਸਜਣ ਸੰਤ ਪਕਿਆ ॥
ਓਇ ਜੀਵੰਦੇ ਵਿਛੁੜਹਿ ਓਇ ਮੁਇਆ ਨ ਜਾਹੀ ਛੋੜਿ ॥੧॥
Salok Ddakhanae 5th Guru |
Naanak Kacharriaa Sio Thorr Dtoodt Sajan Santh Pakiaa |
Oue Jeevandhae Vishhurrehi Oue Mueiaa N Jaahee Shhorr |1| Page-1102

Says Nanak, O' my mind, listen carefully to the True Teachings. Opening His ledger, God will call you to account for your past deeds. Those egoistic rebels who have unpaid accounts shall be called out. Azrael, the Angel of Death, shall be standing ready to punish them. In those difficult moments, they will be struck and find no way to escape. Falsehood is of no avail, O' Nanak; only Truth will prevail in the end.

---

ਮਹਲਾ ੧ ॥
ਨਾਨਕੁ ਆਖੈ ਰੇ ਮਨਾ ਸੁਣੀਐ ਸਿਖ ਸਹੀ ॥ ਲੇਖਾ ਰਬੁ ਮੰਗੇਸੀਆ ਬੈਠਾ ਕਢਿ ਵਹੀ ॥
ਤਲਬਾ ਪਉਸਨਿ ਆਕੀਆ ਬਾਕੀ ਜਿਨਾ ਰਹੀ ॥ ਅਜਰਾਈਲੁ ਫਰੇਸਤਾ ਹੋਸੀ ਆਇ ਤਈ ॥
ਆਵਣੁ ਜਾਣੁ ਨ ਸੁਝਈ ਭੀੜੀ ਗਲੀ ਫਹੀ ॥ ਕੂੜ ਨਿਖੁਟੇ ਨਾਨਕਾ ਓੜਕਿ ਸਚਿ ਰਹੀ ॥੨॥
1st Guru |
Naanak Aakhai Rae Manaa Suneeai Sikh Sehee |
Laekhaa Rab Mangaeseeaa Baithaa Kadt Vehee |
Thalabaa Pousan Aakeeaa Baakee Jinaa Rehee |
Ajaraaeel Faraesathaa Hosee Aae Thee |
Aavan Jaan N Sujhee Bheerree Galee Fehee |
Koorr Nikhuttae Naanakaa Ourrak Sach Rehee |2|   Page-953

The man, who in this battlefield of life bravely fights evil and perversion, and believes this life to be the opportunity to do so, is truly a warrior. He hears battle drums in his sixth sense and feels wounded as though hit by the aim of an arrow! He alone is known as a true hero, who fights in defense of the meek and downtrodden. He may be cut apart, piece by piece, but he never leaves the battle field!

ਸਲੋਕ ਕਬੀਰ ॥

ਗਗਨ ਦਮਾਮਾ ਬਾਜਿਓ ਪਰਿਓ ਨੀਸਾਨੈ ਘਾਉ ॥ ਖੇਤੁ ਜੁ ਮਾਂਡਿਓ ਸੂਰਮਾ ਅਬ ਜੂਝਨ ਕੋ ਦਾਉ ॥੧॥

ਸੂਰਾ ਸੋ ਪਹਿਚਾਨੀਐ ਜੁ ਲਰੈ ਦੀਨ ਕੇ ਹੇਤ ॥ ਪੁਰਜਾ ਪੁਰਜਾ ਕਟਿ ਮਰੈ ਕਬਹੂ ਨ ਛਾਡੈ ਖੇਤੁ ॥੨॥੨॥

Salok Kabeer |

Gagan Dhamaamaa Baajiou Pariou Neesaanai Ghaao |

Khaeth J Maanddiou Sooramaa Ab Joojhan Ko Dhaao |1|

Sooraa So Pehichaaneeai J Larai Dheen Kae Haeth |

Purajaa Purajaa Katt Marai Kabehoo N Shhaaddai Khaeth |2|2|  Page-1105

The self-oriented egoistic are false; without the Lord's Name, and wander around like demons. They are black hearted within and are like an animal wrapped in human skin.

---

ਮਃ ੫ ॥ ਪਉੜੀ ॥

ਮਨਮੁਖ ਵਿਟੁ ਨਾਵੈ ਕੁੜਿਆਰ ਫਿਰਹਿ ਬੇਤਾਲਿਆ ॥

ਪਸੂ ਮਾਟਸ ਚੰਮਿ ਪਲੇਟੇ ਅੰਦਰਹੁ ਕਾਲਿਆ ॥

5th Guru Pourree ||

Manamukh Vin Naavai Koorriaar Firehi Baethaaliaa ||

Pasoo Maanas Chanm Palaettae Andharahu Kaaliaa ||    Page-1284

Says Kabeer, O' Mullah (the Muslim priest), why do you climb to the top of the mosque's minaret? The Lord is not hard of hearing! Look within your own heart for the One, for whose sake you shout out the call for prayers. O' Shaikh, when you do not have contentment within, what is the benefit of going on pilgrimage to Mecca? Kabeer, one whose heart is not at peace, for him God cannot be found anywhere.

---

ਸਲੋਕ ਭਗਤ ਕਬੀਰ ਜੀਉ ਕੇ ॥
ਕਬੀਰ ਮੁਲਾਂ ਮੁਨਾਰੇ ਕਿਆ ਚਢਹਿ ਸਾਂਈ ਨ ਬਹਰਾ ਹੋਇ ॥
ਜਾ ਕਾਰਨਿ ਤੂੰ ਬਾਂਗ ਦੇਹਿ ਦਿਲ ਹੀ ਭੀਤਰਿ ਜੋਇ ॥੧੮੪॥
ਸੇਖ ਸਬੂਰੀ ਬਾਹਰਾ ਕਿਆ ਹਜ ਕਾਬੇ ਜਾਇ ॥
ਕਬੀਰ ਜਾ ਕੀ ਦਿਲ ਸਾਬਤਿ ਨਹੀ ਤਾ ਕਉ ਕਹਾਂ ਖੁਦਾਇ ॥੧੮੫॥
Salok Bhagath Kabeer Jeeo Kae
Kabeer Mulaan Munaarae Kiaa Chadtehi Saanee N Beharaa Hoe |
Jaa Kaaran Thoon Baang Dhaehi Dhil Hee Bheethar Joe |184|
Saekh Sabooree Baaharaa Kiaa Haj Kaabae Jaae |
Kabeer Jaa Kee Dhil Saabath Nehee Thaa Ko Kehaan Khudhaae |185|
Page-1374

---

## Chapter-12 Universal Oneness

One Universal Infinite God, the Truth, Wordless Word, the Creator, Omnipresent, Fearless, Enemy-less (All Love), Timeless, All Pervading Image, Never Born, Never Dies, Has Come into Existence Himself, the Guru, by His Grace.

Note: The Guru Granth Sahib opens with this description of the Eternal Truth, known as the holy hymn "*mool mantra*", and it is repeated throughout the Holy Scripture before the start of many major *Gurbanis* of the Gurus and the Saints.

---

ੴ ਸਤਿ ਨਾਮੁ ਕਰਤਾ ਪੁਰਖੁ ਨਿਰਭਉ ਨਿਰਵੈਰੁ ਅਕਾਲ ਮੂਰਤਿ ਅਜੂਨੀ ਸੈਭੰ ਗੁਰ ਪ੍ਰਸਾਦਿ ॥
Ikoankaar Sathnaam Karathaa Purakh Nirabho Niravair Akaal Moorath Ajoonee Saibhan Gurprasaadh|    Page-1

Within and beyond all the earth and sky, there is only One Light of Universal Oneness. This neither Decreases nor, Increases at any time and its Intensity is Always Constant.

---

ਪਾਤਿਸ਼ਾਹੀ ੧੦ ॥
ਜਿਮੀ ਜਮਾਨ ਕੇ ਬਿਖੈ ਸਮਸਤਿ ਏਕ ਜੋਤਿ ਹੈ ॥ਨ ਘਾਟਿ ਹੈ ਨ ਬਾਧਿ ਹੈ ਨ ਘਾਟਿ ਬਾਧਿ ਹੋਤ ਹੈ ॥ਦਸਮ ਗਰੰਥ
10ᵗʰ Guru ॥
Jimee Jamaana Ke Bikhai Samasat(i) Eeka Jot(i) Hai ॥
Na Ghaatti Hai Na Baadhi Hai Na Ghaatti Baadhi Hota Hai ॥  Dasam Granth.

What was that time, and what was the moment? What was that day, and what was the date? What was that season, and what was the month, when the Universe was created? The Pundits (Hindu scholars) cannot tell, as otherwise it would be written in the Puranas (Hindu scripture). The Qazis (Muslim priests), do not know as otherwise it would be written in the Koran (Muslim scripture). The day and the date are also not known to the Yogis, nor anyone else can tell the month or the season. The Creator who created this Creation, only He, Himself knows it!

---

॥ ਜਪੁ ॥ ਕਵਣੁ ਸੁ ਵੇਲਾ ਵਖਤੁ ਕਵਣੁ ਕਵਣ ਥਿਤਿ ਕਵਣੁ ਵਾਰੁ ॥ਕਵਣਿ ਸਿ ਰੁਤੀ ਮਾਹੁ ਕਵਣੁ ਜਿਤੁ ਹੋਆ ਆਕਾਰੁ ॥ਵੇਲ ਨ ਪਾਈਆ ਪੰਡਤੀ ਜਿ ਹੋਵੈ ਲੇਖੁ ਪੁਰਾਣੁ ॥ ਵਖਤੁ ਨ ਪਾਇਓ ਕਾਦੀਆ ਜਿ ਲਿਖਨਿ ਲੇਖੁ ਕੁਰਾਣੁ ॥ਥਿਤਿ ਵਾਰੁ ਨਾ ਜੋਗੀ ਜਾਣੈ ਰੁਤਿ ਮਾਹੁ ਨਾ ਕੋਈ ॥ ਜਾ ਕਰਤਾ ਸਿਰਠੀ ਕਉ ਸਾਜੇ ਆਪੇ ਜਾਣੈ ਸੋਈ ॥
|Jap|
Kavan S Vaelaa Vakhath Kavan Kavan Thhith Kavan Vaar |Kavan S Ruthee Maahu Kavan Jith Hoaa Aakaar |Vael N Paaeeaa Panddathee J Hovai Laekh Puraan |
Vakhath N Paaeiou Kaadheeaa J Likhan Laekh Kuraan |Thhith Vaar Naa Jogee Jaanai Ruth Maahu Naa Koee |Jaa Karathaa Sirathee Ko Saajae Aapae Jaanai Soee |21| Page-4

Eyes seeing without lust, Ears hearing without malice, Feet avoiding to walk in bad directions, Hands not doing harmful tasks, Tongue not speaking ill of others: this is how one dies while living. O' Nanak understanding the Divine Will through the body's senses, makes one realize the Husband Lord.

ਸਲੋਕੁ ਮਹਲਾ ੨ ॥
ਅਖੀ ਬਾਝਹੁ ਵੇਖਣਾ ਵਿਣੁ ਕੰਨਾ ਸੁਨਣਾ ॥ ਪੈਰਾ ਬਾਝਹੁ ਚਲਣਾ ਵਿਣੁ ਹਥਾ ਕਰਣਾ ॥
ਜੀਭੈ ਬਾਝਹੁ ਬੋਲਣਾ ਇਉ ਜੀਵਤ ਮਰਣਾ ॥ ਨਾਨਕ ਹੁਕਮੁ ਪਛਾਣਿ ਕੈ ਤਉ ਖਸਮੈ ਮਿਲਣਾ ॥੧॥
Salok 2<sup>nd</sup> Guru |
Akhee Baajhahu Vaekhanaa Vin Kannaa Sunanaa | Pairaa Baajhahu Chalanaa Vin
Hathhaa Karanaa |Jeebhai Baajhahu Bolanaa Eio Jeevath Maranaa |
Naanak Hukam Pashhaan Kai Tho Khasamai Milanaa |1| Page-139

O' Brother, the poor human is like a wooden puppet, what can he do? Only the Master who is pulling the strings knows. As the Puppeteer Lord dresses the puppet, so is the role the puppet plays.

ਗਉੜੀ ਮਹਲਾ ੫ ॥
ਕਾਠ ਕੀ ਪੁਤਰੀ ਕਹਾ ਕਰੈ ਬਪੁਰੀ ਖਿਲਾਵਨਹਾਰੋ ਜਾਨੈ ॥
ਜੈਸਾ ਭੇਖੁ ਕਰਾਵੈ ਬਾਜੀਗਰੁ ਓਹੁ ਤੈਸੋ ਹੀ ਸਾਜੁ ਆਨੈ ॥੩॥
Gourree 5<sup>th</sup> Guru |
Kaath Kee Putharee Kehaa Karai Bapuree Khilaavanehaaro Jaanai |
Jaisaa Bhaekh Karaavai Baajeegar Ouhu Thaiso Hee Saaj Aanai |3| Page-206

Of all the religions, the best one is to contemplate on God's Name and maintain pure conduct. Of all religious rituals, the most sublime is to erase the filth of the dirty mind in the Company of the Holy. Of all places, the most sublime place, O Nanak, is that heart in which the Name of the Lord abides.

---

ਗਉੜੀ ਸੁਖਮਨੀ ਮਹਲਾ ੫ ॥ਸਲੋਕੁ ॥
ਸਰਬ ਧਰਮ ਮਹਿ ਸੇਸਟ ਧਰਮੁ ॥ਹਰਿ ਕੋ ਨਾਮੁ ਜਪਿ ਨਿਰਮਲ ਕਰਮੁ ॥
ਸਗਲ ਕ੍ਰਿਆ ਮਹਿ ਊਤਮ ਕਿਰਿਆ ॥ ਸਾਧਸੰਗਿ ਦੁਰਮਤਿ ਮਲੁ ਹਿਰਿਆ ॥
ਸਗਲ ਥਾਨ ਤੇ ਓਹੁ ਊਤਮ ਥਾਨੁ ॥ਨਾਨਕ ਜਿਹ ਘਟਿ ਵਸੈ ਹਰਿ ਨਾਮੁ ॥੮॥੩॥

Gourree Sukhamanee Ma 5 | Salok |
Sarab Dhharam Mehi Sraesatt Dhharam | Har Ko Naam Jap Niramal Karam |
Sagal Kiraaa Mehi Ootham Kiriaa | Saadhhasang Dhuramath Mal Hiriaa |
Sagal Thhaan Thae Ouhu Ootham Thhaan |
Naanak Jih Ghatt Vasai Har Naam |8|3|    Page-266

Many millions are the fields of creation and the galaxies.
Many millions are the etheric skies and the solar systems.
Many millions are the divine incarnations. In so many ways,
He has unfolded Himself. So many times, He has created,
engulfed and re-created the Creation. The One Infinite All
Pervading God is Forever and Forever.

---

ਗਉੜੀ ਸੁਖਮਨੀ ਮਹਲਾ ੫ ॥ਸਲੋਕੁ ॥
ਕਈ ਕੋਟਿ ਖਾਣੀ ਅਰੁ ਖੰਡ ॥ ਕਈ ਕੋਟਿ ਅਕਾਸ ਬ੍ਰਹਮੰਡ ॥
ਕਈ ਕੋਟਿ ਹੋਏ ਅਵਤਾਰ ॥ ਕਈ ਜੁਗਤਿ ਕੀਨੋ ਬਿਸਥਾਰ ॥
ਕਈ ਬਾਰ ਪਸਰਿਓ ਪਾਸਾਰ ॥ ਸਦਾ ਸਦਾ ਇਕੁ ਏਕੰਕਾਰ ॥
Gourree Sukhamanee Ma 5 | Salok |
Kee Kott Khaanee Ar Khandd | Kee Kott Akaas Brehamandd |
Kee Kott Hoeae Avathaar | Kee Jugath Keeno Bisathhaar |
Kee Baar Pasariou Paasaar | Sadhaa Sadhaa Eik Eaekankaar | Page-276

O' brother, My Guru always lives with me, and is part and parcel of me. Meditating on Him with His blessing, I cherish Him in my heart.

---

ਆਸਾ ਘਰੁ ੭ ਮਹਲਾ ੫ ॥

ਗੁਰੁ ਮੇਰੈ ਸੰਗਿ ਸਦਾ ਹੈ ਨਾਲੇ ॥ ਸਿਮਰਿ ਸਿਮਰਿ ਤਿਸੁ ਸਦਾ ਸਮੁਹਾਲੇ ॥੧॥ ਰਹਾਉ ॥

Aasaa Ghar 7 5th Guru |

Gur Maerai Sang Sadhaa Hai Naalae |Simar Simar This Sadhaa Samhaalae |1|

Pause | Page-394

---

The Lord God is pervading in everyone, so meditate on Him forever and ever. Why should you serve anyone else, who is born and then dies?

---

ਸਲੋਕੁ ਮਃ ੩ ॥

ਸਦਾ ਸਦਾ ਸੋ ਸੇਵੀਐ ਜੋ ਸਭ ਮਹਿ ਰਹੈ ਸਮਾਇ ॥

ਅਵਰੁ ਦੂਜਾ ਕਿਉ ਸੇਵੀਐ ਜੰਮੈ ਤੈ ਮਰਿ ਜਾਇ ॥

Salok Ma 3 ||

Sadhaa Sadhaa So Saeveeai Jo Sabh Mehi Rehai Samaae ||

Avar Dhoojaa Kio Saeveeai Janmai Thai Mar Jaae || Page-509

O' Great Giver, You, are all-powerful to create and destroy.
With clasped hands the entire creation stands begging from
you. I see no one can match you in magnanimity. You, O'
Great Giver give in charity to all beings, worlds, systems,
regions, and universes.

ਮਹਲਾ ੩ ॥ਪਉੜੀ ॥
ਤੂ ਭੰਨਣ ਘੜਣ ਸਮਰਥੁ ਦਾਤਾਰੁ ਹਹਿ ਤੁਧੁ ਅਗੈ ਮੰਗਣ ਨੋ ਹਥ ਜੋੜਿ ਖਲੀ ਸਭ ਹੋਈ ॥
ਤੁਧੁ ਜੇਵਡੁ ਦਾਤਾਰੁ ਮੈ ਕੋਈ ਨਦਰਿ ਨ ਆਵਈ ਤੁਧੁ ਸਭਸੈ ਨੋ ਦਾਨੁ ਦਿਤਾ ਖੰਡੀ ਵਰਭੰਡੀ ਪਾਤਾਲੀ ਪੁਰਈ ਸਭ
ਲੋਈ ॥੩॥
3rd Guru | Pourree |
Thoo Bhannan Gharran Samarathh Dhaathaar Hehi Thudhh Agai Mangan No
Hathh Jorr Khalee Sabh Hoee |Thudhh Jaevadd Dhaathaar Mai Koee Nadhar N
Aavee Thudhh Sabhasai No Dhaan Dhithaa Khanddee Varabhanddee Paathaalee
Puree Sabh Loee |3| Page-549

O' Lord, you are so wonderful and Your Creation is equally
amazing! You, Yourself, are the Cause and Yourself, the
Creator. By Your Will, people are born, and by Your Will,
they die.

ਵਡਹੰਸੁ ਮਹਲਾ ੫ ॥
ਤੂ ਅਚਰਜੁ ਕੁਦਰਤਿ ਤੇਰੀ ਬਿਸਮਾ ॥੧॥ ਰਹਾਉ ॥
ਤੁਧੁ ਆਪੇ ਕਾਰਣੁ ਆਪੇ ਕਰਣਾ ॥ਹੁਕਮੇ ਜੰਮਣੁ ਹੁਕਮੇ ਮਰਣਾ ॥੨॥
Vaddehans 5th Guru |
Thoo Acharaj Kudharath Thaeree Bisamaa |1| Pause |Thudhh Aapae Kaaran
Aapae Karanaa |Hukamae Janman Hukamae Maranaa |2| Page-563

The One God is our Father; we all are children of the One God. O' Father, You, are my Guru. Listen, friends, my soul is a sacrifice, to you Lord; please reveal to me the Blessed Vision of Your Presence.

---

ਸੋਰਠਿ ਮਹਲਾ ੫ ॥
ਏਕੁ ਪਿਤਾ ਏਕਸ ਕੇ ਹਮ ਬਾਰਿਕ ਤੂ ਮੇਰਾ ਗੁਰ ਹਾਈ ॥
ਸੁਣਿ ਮੀਤਾ ਜੀਉ ਹਮਾਰਾ ਬਲਿ ਬਲਿ ਜਾਸੀ ਹਰਿ ਦਰਸਨੁ ਦੇਹੁ ਦਿਖਾਈ ॥੧॥
Sorath 5th Guru |
Eaek Pithaa Eaekas Kae Ham Baarik Thoo Maeraa Gur Haaee |
Sun Meethaa Jeeo Hamaaraa Bal Bal Jaasee Har Dharasan Dhaehu Dhikhaaee |1|
Page-611

The All-Pervading Creator Himself came to my rescue, and not even a single hair of mine was bent out of shape (absolutely no harm was done to me). O Saints, the purifying pool of Ambrosial Nectar of Guru Ram Das is sublime. Whosoever bathes in it, his family and ancestry are saved, and his soul is saved as well.

ਸੋਰਠਿ ਮਹਲਾ ੫ ॥
ਵਿਚਿ ਕਰਤਾ ਪੁਰਖੁ ਖਲੋਆ ॥ ਵਾਲੁ ਨ ਵਿੰਗਾ ਹੋਆ ॥
ਸੰਤਹੁ ਰਾਮਦਾਸ ਸਰੋਵਰੁ ਨੀਕਾ ॥ਜੋ ਨਾਵੈ ਸੋ ਕੁਲੁ ਤਰਾਵੈ ਉਧਾਰੁ ਹੋਆ ਹੈ ਜੀ ਕਾ ॥੧॥ ਰਹਾਉ ॥
Sorath 5th Guru |
Vich Karathaa Purakh Khaloaa |Vaal N Vingaa Hoaa |
Santhahu Raamadhaas Sarovar Neekaa |
Jo Naavai So Kul Tharaavai Oudhhaar Hoaa Hai Jee Kaa |1|Pause |   Page-623

The Creator who pervades the Universe also dwells within the body; whosoever seeks Him, finds Him there. Peepaa prays, the Lord is the supreme essence; He reveals Himself through the True Guru.

ਧਨਾਸਰੀ ਬਾਣੀ ਭਗਤਾਂ ਕੀ ਪੀਪਾ ॥
ਜੋ ਬ੍ਰਹਮੰਡੇ ਸੋਈ ਪਿੰਡੇ ਜੋ ਖੋਜੈ ਸੋ ਪਾਵੈ ॥
ਪੀਪਾ ਪ੍ਰਣਵੈ ਪਰਮ ਤਤੁ ਹੈ ਸਤਿਗੁਰੁ ਹੋਇ ਲਖਾਵੈ ॥੨॥੩॥
Dhhanaasaree Baanee Bhagathaan Kee  Peepaa ||
Jo Brehamanddae Soee Pinddae Jo Khojai So Paavai ||
Peepaa Pranavai Param Thath Hai Sathigur Hoe Lakhaavai ||2||3||   Page-695

From the beginning of existence, in the middle, and in the end, it is only God Himself. O Nanak, there is no one else other than Him at all. (*meaning, creation is part and parcel of God*)

---

ਰਾਗੁ ਸੂਹੀ ਮਹਲਾ ੫ ॥

ਆਦਿ ਮਧਿ ਅੰਤਿ ਪ੍ਰਭੁ ਸੋਈ ॥ਨਾਨਕ ਤਿਸੁ ਬਿਨੁ ਅਵਰੁ ਨ ਕੋਈ ॥੮॥੧॥੨॥

Raag Soohee Mehalaa 5 |

Aadh Madhh Anth Prabh Soee |Naanak This Bin Avar N Koee |8|1|2|   Page-760

---

My Dear Lord and Master, my Friend, speaks so sweetly. I have grown weary of testing Him, but still, He never speaks harshly to me. He does not know any bitter words; the Perfect Lord God does not even consider my faults and demerits.

---

ਰਾਗੁ ਸੂਹੀ ਮਹਲਾ ੫ ਛੰਤ ॥

ਮਿਠ ਬੋਲੜਾ ਜੀ ਹਰਿ ਸਜਣੁ ਸੁਆਮੀ ਮੋਰਾ ॥ਹਉ ਸੰਮਲਿ ਥਕੀ ਜੀ ਓਹੁ ਕਦੇ ਨ ਬੋਲੈ ਕਉਰਾ ॥

ਕਉੜਾ ਬੋਲਿ ਨ ਜਾਨੈ ਪੂਰਨ ਭਗਵਾਨੈ ਅਉਗਣੁ ਕੋ ਨ ਚਿਤਾਰੇ ॥

Raag Soohee 5th Guru Shhantha |Mith Bolarraa Jee Har Sajan Suaamee Moraa |Ho Sanmal Thhakee Jee Ouhu Kadhae N Bolai Kouraa |Kourraa Bol N Jaanai Pooran Bhagavaanai Aougan Ko N Chithaarae |   Page-784

---

You alone are the only One, the only Lord; You alone are the King. O' God, it is by Your Grace that, I have found eternal peace.

---

ਰਾਮਕਲੀ ਮਹਲਾ ੫ ॥
ਏਕੈ ਏਕੈ ਏਕ ਤੂਹੀ ॥ਏਕੈ ਏਕੈ ਤੂ ਰਾਇਆ ॥ਤਉ ਕਿਰਪਾ ਤੇ ਸੁਖੁ ਪਾਇਆ ॥੧॥ ਰਹਾਉ ॥
Raamakalee 5th Guru |
Eaekai Eaekai Eaek Thoohee | Eaekai Eaekai Thoo Raaeiaa |
Tho Kirapaa Thae Sukh Paaeiaa |1| Rehaao | Page-884

---

Some pass their lives enjoying worldly pleasures, beauty and entertainments. Some pass their lives in the attachment with their mother, father and children, which is transitory. Only God is everlasting; this entire Creation is created by Him and He alone is the Master of All.

---

ਰਾਮਕਲੀ ਮਹਲਾ ੫ ॥
ਕਾਹੂ ਬਿਹਾਵੈ ਰੰਗ ਰਸ ਰੂਪ ॥ ਕਾਹੂ ਬਿਹਾਵੈ ਮਾਇ ਬਾਪ ਪੂਤ ॥
ਰਚਨਾ ਸਾਚੁ ਬਨੀ ॥ ਸਭ ਕਾ ਏਕੁ ਧਨੀ ॥੧॥ ਰਹਾਉ ॥
Raamakalee 5th Guru |
Kaahoo Bihaavai Rang Ras Roop | Kaahoo Bihaavai Maae Baap Pooth |
Rachanaa Saach Banee | Sabh Kaa Eaek Dhhanee |1| Rehaao | Page-914

O' brother, God is my dearest of dear Friends; He is my dear Companion and is always standing by my side. He is dearer to me than my Life and Soul; I have seen my Beloved Lord with my own eyes! I have seen that He, my very sweet and dear friend is present in All bodies, my Beloved is the sweetest Ambrosial Nectar. But the foolish do not enjoy the wonderful feeling of His presence and cannot find the Beloved Friend who is always with them. The foolish person is intoxicated with Maya, only indulges in little talk and cannot meet the eternal Friend. Says Nanak, without the Guru, one cannot understand the Lord, the Friend who is standing near everyone.

---

ਰਾਮਕਲੀ ਮਹਲਾ ੫ ਛੰਤ ॥
ਸਾਜਨੜਾ ਮੇਰਾ ਸਾਜਨੜਾ ਨਿਕਟਿ ਖਲੋਇਅੜਾ ਮੇਰਾ ਸਾਜਨੜਾ ॥ ਜਾਨੀਅੜਾ ਹਰਿ ਜਾਨੀਅੜਾ ਨੈਣ ਅਲੋਇਅੜਾ ਹਰਿ ਜਾਨੀਅੜਾ ॥ਨੈਣ ਅਲੋਇਆ ਘਟਿ ਘਟਿ ਸੋਇਆ ਅਤਿ ਅੰਮ੍ਰਿਤ ਪ੍ਰਿਅ ਗੂੜਾ ॥ ਨਾਲਿ ਹੋਵੰਦਾ ਲਹਿ ਨ ਸਕੰਦਾ ਸੁਆਉ ਨ ਜਾਣੈ ਮੂੜਾ ॥ਮਾਇਆ ਮਦਿ ਮਾਤਾ ਹੋਛੀ ਬਾਤਾ ਮਿਲਣੁ ਨ ਜਾਈ ਭਰਮ ਧੜਾ ॥ਕਹੁ ਨਾਨਕ ਗੁਰ ਬਿਨੁ ਨਾਹੀ ਸੂਝੈ ਹਰਿ ਸਾਜਨੁ ਸਭ ਕੈ ਨਿਕਟਿ ਖੜਾ ॥੧॥
Raamakalee Mehalaa 5 Shhantha |
Saajanarraa Maeraa Saajanarraa Nikatt Khaloeiarraa Maeraa Saajanarraa |
Jaaneearraa Har Jaaneearraa Nain Aloeiarraa Har Jaaneearraa |
Nain Aloeiaa Ghatt Ghatt Soeiaa Ath Anmrith Prdia Goorraa |Naal Hovandhaa Lehi N Sakandhaa Suaao N Jaanai Moorraa |Maaeiaa Madh Maathaa Hoshhee Baathaa Milan N Jaaee Bharam Dhharraa |Kahu Naanak Gur Bin Naahee Soojhai Har Saajan Sabh Kai Nikatt Kharraa |1|   Page-924

Within all hearts, the Lord speaks, the Lord speaks, no one else speaks other than the Lord. Like several types of utensils are cast from the same clay, same way from an elephant to the ant, in stationary life forms, moving beings, worms, moths, and within each, and every heart, the Lord lives. Remember the One, Infinite Lord and abandon all other hopes. Prays NaamDayv, whosoever contemplates on the Lord, becomes free of all attachments and their remains no difference between him and the Lord.

---

ਮਾਲੀ ਗਉੜਾ ਬਾਣੀ ਭਗਤ ਨਾਮਦੇਵ ਜੀ ਕੀ ॥
ਸਭੈ ਘਟ ਰਾਮੁ ਬੋਲੈ ਰਾਮਾ ਬੋਲੈ ॥ਰਾਮ ਬਿਨਾ ਕੋ ਬੋਲੈ ਰੇ ॥੧॥ ਰਹਾਉ ॥
ਏਕਲ ਮਾਟੀ ਕੁੰਜਰ ਚੀਟੀ ਭਾਜਨ ਹੈਂ ਬਹੁ ਨਾਨਾ ਰੇ ॥
ਅਸਥਾਵਰ ਜੰਗਮ ਕੀਟ ਪਤੰਗਮ ਘਟਿ ਘਟਿ ਰਾਮੁ ਸਮਾਨਾ ਰੇ ॥੧॥
ਏਕਲ ਚਿੰਤਾ ਰਾਖੁ ਅਨੰਤਾ ਅਉਰ ਤਜਹੁ ਸਭ ਆਸਾ ਰੇ ॥
ਪ੍ਰਣਵੈ ਨਾਮਾ ਭਏ ਨਿਹਕਾਮਾ ਕੋ ਠਾਕੁਰੁ ਕੋ ਦਾਸਾ ਰੇ ॥੨॥੩॥
Maalee Gourraa Baanee Bhagath Naamadhaev Jee Kee
Sabhai Ghatt Raam Bolai Raamaa Bolai | Raam Binaa Ko Bolai Rae |1|Pause |
Eaekal Maattee Kunjar Cheettee Bhaajan Hain Bahu Naanaa Rae |
Asathhaavar Jangam Keett Pathangam Ghatt Ghatt Raam Samaanaa Rae |1|
Eaekal Chinthaa Raakh Ananthaa Aour Thajahu Sabh Aasaa Rae |
Pranavai Naamaa Bheae Nihakaamaa Ko Thaakur Ko Dhaasaa Rae |2|3|
Page-988

The entire universe is made of the same clay.  The Potter has shaped it into all sorts of vessels.

---

ਰਾਗੁ ਭੈਰਉ ਮਹਲਾ ੩ ॥
ਮਾਟੀ ਏਕ ਸਗਲ ਸੰਸਾਰਾ ॥ ਬਹੁ ਬਿਧਿ ਭਾਂਡੇ ਘੜੈ ਕੁਮ੍ਹਾਰਾ ॥੩॥

Raag Bhairo Mehalaa 3 |
Maattee Eaek Sagal Sansaaraa | Bahu Bidhh Bhaanddae Gharrai Kumhaaraa |3|
Page-1128

Firstly, it is God's Light that has created the entire Creation. All forms of life have originated from God's Nature. The entire Universe has come into existence from the One Light, then why have misgivings of caste, religion, etc. and call people good or bad? O' people do not be deluded by doubt, the Creation is in the Creator and the Creator is in the Creation, and is All-Pervading. The everlasting True Lord abides in all and whatever is happening is by Divine Will. He is truly a man who realizes God's Will and cherishes only the One. Allah (Lord) is beyond any description and His praises cannot be sung enough. Says Kabeer, my Guru has given me the sweetness of His understanding, my anxieties and fear have disappeared, and I have seen the Maya (illusion) free God everywhere.

ਬਿਭਾਸ ਪ੍ਰਭਾਤੀ ਬਾਣੀ ਭਗਤ ਕਬੀਰ ਜੀ
ਅਵਲਿ ਅਲਹ ਨੂਰੁ ਉਪਾਇਆ ਕੁਦਰਤਿ ਕੇ ਸਭ ਬੰਦੇ ॥ ਏਕ ਨੂਰ ਤੇ ਸਭੁ ਜਗੁ ਉਪਜਿਆ ਕਉਨ ਭਲੇ ਕੋ ਮੰਦੇ ॥੧॥ਲੋਗਾ ਭਰਮਿ ਨ ਭੂਲਹੁ ਭਾਈ ॥ ਖਾਲਿਕੁ ਖਲਕ ਖਲਕ ਮਹਿ ਖਾਲਿਕੁ ਪੂਰਿ ਰਹਿਓ ਸ੍ਰਬ ਠਾਂਈ ॥੧॥ ॥ਸਭ ਮਹਿ ਸਚਾ ਏਕੋ ਸੋਈ ਤਿਸ ਕਾ ਕੀਆ ਸਭੁ ਕਛੁ ਹੋਈ ॥ ਹੁਕਮੁ ਪਛਾਨੈ ਸੁ ਏਕੋ ਜਾਨੈ ਬੰਦਾ ਕਹੀਐ ਸੋਈ ॥੩॥ਅਲਹੁ ਅਲਖੁ ਨ ਜਾਈ ਲਖਿਆ ਗੁਰਿ ਗੁੜੁ ਦੀਨਾ ਮੀਠਾ ॥ ਕਹਿ ਕਬੀਰ ਮੇਰੀ ਸੰਕਾ ਨਾਸੀ ਸਰਬ ਨਿਰੰਜਨ ਡੀਠਾ ॥੪॥੩॥
Bibhaas Prabhaathee Baanee Bhagath Kabeer Jee |Aval Aleh Noor Oupaaeiaa Kudharath Kae Sabh Bandhae |Eaek Noor Thae Sabh Jag Oupajiaa Koun Bhalae Ko Mandhae |1|Logaa Bharam N Bhoolahu Bhaaee |Khaalik Khalak Khalak Mehi Khaalik Poor Rehiou Srab Thaanee |1| Sabh Mehi Sachaa Eaeko Soee This Kaa Keeaa Sabh Kashh Hoee |Hukam Pashhaanai S Eaeko Jaanai Bandhaa Keheeai Soee |3|Alahu Alakh N Jaaee Lakhiaa Gur Gurr Dheenaa Meethaa |Kehi Kabeer Maeree Sankaa Naasee Sarab Niranjan Ddeethaa |4|3| Page-1349

Your devotees are totally fulfilled, throughout the ages; O Waah Guru, it is all You, forever. O Formless Lord God, You, are eternally intact; no one can say when You came into Existence. You created countless Brahmas and Vishnus; and their minds were intoxicated with arrogance. You created the millions of species of beings, and provided for their sustenance. Your devotees are totally fulfilled, throughout the ages; O' the Great Guru! It is all You, forever!

---

ਸਵਈਏ ਮਹਲੇ ਚਉਥੇ ਕੇ ੪ ਭਟ ਗਯੰਦ

ਸੇਵਕ ਕੈ ਭਰਪੂਰ ਜੁਗੁ ਜੁਗੁ ਵਾਹਗੁਰੂ ਤੇਰਾ ਸਭੁ ਸਦਕਾ ॥ ਨਿਰੰਕਾਰੁ ਪ੍ਰਭੁ ਸਦਾ ਸਲਾਮਤਿ ਕਹਿ ਨ ਸਕੈ ਕੋਊ ਤੂ ਕਦ ਕਾ ॥ ਬ੍ਰਹਮਾ ਬਿਸਨੁ ਸਿਰੇ ਤੈ ਅਗਨਤ ਤਿਨ ਕਉ ਮੋਹੁ ਭਯਾ ਮਨ ਮਦ ਕਾ ॥ ਚਵਰਾਸੀਹ ਲਖ ਜੋਨਿ ਉਪਾਈ ਰਿਜਕੁ ਦੀਆ ਸਭ ਹੂ ਕਉ ਤਦ ਕਾ ॥ ਸੇਵਕ ਕੈ ਭਰਪੂਰ ਜੁਗੁ ਜੁਗੁ ਵਾਹਗੁਰੂ ਤੇਰਾ ਸਭੁ ਸਦਕਾ ॥੧॥੧੧॥

Saveeeae Mehalae Chouthhae Kae 4 Bhatt Gayand
Saevak Kai Bharapoor Jug Jug Vaahaguroo Thaeraa Sabh Sadhakaa || Nirankaar Prabh Sadhaa Salaamath Kehi N Sakai Kooo Thoo Kadh Kaa || Brehamaa Bisan Sirae Thai Aganath Thin Ko Mohu Bhayaa Man Madh Kaa || Chavaraaseeh Lakh Jon Oupaaee Rijak Dheeaa Sabh Hoo Ko Thadh Kaa || Saevak Kai Bharapoor Jug Jug Vaahaguroo Thaeraa Sabh Sadhakaa ||1||11||   Page-1403

## Chapter-13  Pangs of Separation

Wealth, youth and flowers are guests for only a few days. Like the leaves of the water-lily, they wither, fade and finally die. Dear beloved, enjoy the bliss of God Awareness so long as your youth is fresh. But your days are few and your body will become old. My playful friends have gone to sleep in the graveyard; I cry in a feeble voice but do not realize in my double-mindedness that I shall have to go as well. Haven't you heard the call from beyond, O' my beautiful soul-bride? You must go to your in-laws; you cannot stay with your parents forever. Says Nanak, that she who carelessly sleeps in her parents' home without remembering God is plundered in broad daylight. She has lost her bouquet of merits; gathering a bundle of demerits, when she departs.

ਸਿਰੀਰਾਗੁ ਮਹਲਾ ੧ ॥

ਧਨੁ ਜੋਬਨੁ ਅਰੁ ਫੁਲੜਾ ਨਾਠੀਅੜੇ ਦਿਨ ਚਾਰਿ ॥ਪਬਣਿ ਕੇਰੇ ਪਤ ਜਿਉ ਢਲਿ ਢੁਲਿ ਜੁੰਮਣਹਾਰ ॥੧॥ ਰੰਗੁ ਮਾਣਿ ਲੈ ਪਿਆਰਿਆ ਜਾ ਜੋਬਨੁ ਨਉ ਹੁਲਾ ॥ਦਿਨ ਥੋੜੜੇ ਥਕੇ ਭਇਆ ਪੁਰਾਣਾ ਚੋਲਾ ॥੧॥ ਰਹਾਉ ॥ ਸਜਣ ਮੇਰੇ ਰੰਗੁਲੇ ਜਾਇ ਸੁਤੇ ਜੀਰਾਣਿ ॥ਹੰ ਭੀ ਵੰਞਾ ਡੁਮਣੀ ਰੋਵਾ ਝੀਣੀ ਬਾਣਿ ॥੨॥ ਕੀ ਨ ਸੁਣੇਹੀ ਗੋਰੀਏ ਆਪਣ ਕੰਨੀ ਸੋਇ ॥ਲਗੀ ਆਵਹਿ ਸਾਹੁਰੈ ਨਿਤ ਨ ਪੇਈਆ ਹੋਇ ॥੩॥ ਨਾਨਕ ਸੁਤੀ ਪੇਈਐ ਜਾਣੁ ਵਿਰਤੀ ਸੰਨਿ ॥ਗੁਣਾ ਗਵਾਈ ਗੰਠੜੀ ਅਵਗਣ ਚਲੀ ਬੰਨਿ ॥੪॥੨੪॥

Sireeraag Mehalaa 1 Ghar 2 |Dhhan Joban Ar Fularraa Naatheearrae Dhin Chaar |Paban Kaerae Path Jio Dtal Dtul Junmanehaar |1|Rang Maan Lai Piaariaa Jaa Joban No Hulaa |Dhin Thhorrarae Thhakae Bhaeiaa Puraanaa Cholaa |1|Pause |Sajan Maerae Rangulae Jaae Suthae Jeeraan |Han Bhee Vannjaa Ddumanee Rovaa Jheenee Baan |2|Kee N Sunaehee Goreeeae Aapan Kannee Soe |Lagee Aavehi Saahurai Nith N Paeeeaa Hoe |3|Naanak Suthee Paeeeai Jaan Virathee Sann |Gunaa Gavaaee Gantharree Avagan Chalee Bann |4|24|  Page-23

Arising each day, you cherish your body! Without understanding the purpose of life, it remains ignorant and foolish. The God who created it is never remembered and it is eventually cremated or covered under dust! O' man, still there is time, focus your consciousness on the Lord and enjoy true bliss forever and ever. O' mortal, you came here to earn the profit of Lord's Name, but the night of your life is coming to an end! What useless activities are you indulging in? The house you must abandon and vacate, you are attached to, but the place where you must go to dwell, you have not cared to even think about.

---

ਸਿਰੀਰਾਗੁ ਮਹਲਾ ੫ ॥

ਭਲਕੇ ਉਠਿ ਪਪੋਲੀਐ ਵਿਣੁ ਬੁਝੇ ਮੁਗਧ ਅਜਾਨਿ ॥ਸੋ ਪ੍ਰਭੁ ਚਿਤਿ ਨ ਆਇਓ ਛੁਟੈਗੀ ਬੇਬਾਨਿ ॥ ਸਤਿਗੁਰ ਸੇਤੀ ਚਿਤੁ ਲਾਇ ਸਦਾ ਸਦਾ ਰੰਗੁ ਮਾਨਿ ॥੧॥

ਪ੍ਰਾਣੀ ਤੂੰ ਆਇਆ ਲਾਹਾ ਲੈਨਿ ॥ਲਗਾ ਕਿਤੁ ਕੁਫਕੜੇ ਸਭ ਮੁਕਦੀ ਚਲੀ ਰੈਨਿ ॥੧॥ ਰਹਾਉ ॥ ਜੋ ਘਰੁ ਛਡਿ ਗਵਾਵਣਾ ਸੋ ਲਗਾ ਮਨ ਮਾਹਿ ॥ਜਿਥੈ ਜਾਇ ਤੁਧੁ ਵਰਤਣਾ ਤਿਸ ਕੀ ਚਿੰਤਾ ਨਾਹਿ ॥

Sireeraag 5th Guru |
Bhalakae Outh Papoleeai Vin Bujhae Mugadhh Ajaan |
So Prabh Chith N Aaeiou Shhuttaigee Baebaan |
Sathigur Saethee Chith Laae Sadhaa Sadhaa Rang Maan |1|
Praanee Thoon Aaeiaa Laahaa Lain |
Lagaa Kith Kufakarrae Sabh Mukadhee Chalee Rain |1| Pause |
Jo Ghar Shhadd Gavaavanaa So Lagaa Man Maahi |
Jithhai Jaae Thudhh Varathanaa This Kee Chinthaa Naahi |   Page-43

O' man, you are sitting on the collapsing bank of the death river, are you blind? You may die any moment! If pre-ordained through His Grace, you may contemplate on the Guru's Word and be saved. The Reaper does not look upon any as unripe, half-ripe or fully ripe crop. Picking up and wielding their sickles, the harvesters arrive. When the landlord gives the order, they measure and cut the crop. This way, when the Lord orders, death strikes at all, no matter young or old.

---

ਸਿਰੀਰਾਗੁ ਮਹਲਾ ੫ ॥

ਅੰਧੇ ਤੂੰ ਬੈਠਾ ਕੰਧੀ ਪਾਹਿ ॥ਜੇ ਹੋਵੀ ਪੂਰਬਿ ਲਿਖਿਆ ਤਾ ਗੁਰ ਕਾ ਬਚਨੁ ਕਮਾਹਿ ॥੧॥ ਰਹਾਉ ॥
ਹਰੀ ਨਾਹੀ ਨਹ ਡਡੁਰੀ ਪਕੀ ਵਢਣਹਾਰ ॥ਲੈ ਲੈ ਦਾਤ ਪਹੁਤਿਆ ਲਾਵੇ ਕਰਿ ਤਈਆਰੁ ॥
ਜਾ ਹੋਆ ਹੁਕਮੁ ਕਿਰਸਾਣ ਦਾ ਤਾ ਲੁਣਿ ਮਿਣਿਆ ਖੇਤਾਰੁ ॥੨॥

Sireeraag 5t Guru |

Andhhae Thoon Baithaa Kandhhee Paahi |

Jae Hovee Poorab Likhiaa Thaa Gur Kaa Bachan Kamaahi |1| Pause |

Haree Naahee Neh Ddadduree Pakee Vadtanehaar |

Lai Lai Dhaath Pahuthiaa Laavae Kar Theeaar |

Jaa Hoaa Hukam Kirasaan Dhaa Thaa Lun Miniaa Khaethaar |2|   Page-43

O' my Dear Beloved, meet me; without You, I am standing helpless. Sleep does not come to my eyes, and I have no wish for food or water. Food or water do not interest me, and I am dying from the pain of Your separation. Without my Husband Lord, how can I find peace?

O' my mother, the Husband Lord, Giver of all happiness and bliss, comes to whosoever He wishes and abides in their heart Himself. Says Nanak, such a soul-bride is blessed forever because her Husband Lord never dies and never leaves.

---

ਗਉੜੀ ਮਹਲਾ ੩ ॥
ਮਿਲੁ ਮੇਰੇ ਪ੍ਰੀਤਮਾ ਜੀਉ ਤੁਧੁ ਬਿਨੁ ਖਰੀ ਨਿਮਾਣੀ ॥
ਮੈ ਨੈਣੀ ਨੀਦ ਨ ਆਵੈ ਜੀਉ ਭਾਵੈ ਅੰਨੁ ਨ ਪਾਣੀ ॥
ਪਾਣੀ ਅੰਨੁ ਨ ਭਾਵੈ ਮਰੀਐ ਹਾਵੈ ਬਿਨੁ ਪਿਰ ਕਿਉ ਸੁਖੁ ਪਾਈਐ ॥
ਆਪੇ ਮੇਲਿ ਲਏ ਸੁਖਦਾਤਾ ਆਪਿ ਮਿਲਿਆ ਘਰਿ ਆਏ ॥
ਨਾਨਕ ਕਾਮਣਿ ਸਦਾ ਸੁਹਾਗਣਿ ਨਾ ਪਿਰੁ ਮਰੈ ਨ ਜਾਏ ॥੪॥੨॥
Gourree 3rd Guru |
Mil Maerae Preethamaa Jeeo Thudhh Bin Kharee Nimaanee |
Mai Nainee Needh N Aavai Jeeo Bhaavai Ann N Paanee |
Paanee Ann N Bhaavai Mareeai Haavai Bin Pir Kio Sukh Paaeeai |
Aapae Mael Leae Sukhadhaathaa Aap Miliaa Ghar Aaeae |
Naanak Kaaman Sadhaa Suhaagan Naa Pir Marai N Jaaeae |4|2|   Page-244

# Pangs of Separation (Birha)

Like those who have a festering boil within, alone know its pain; those who have the wound of separation from the Lord know its pain. Only they understand the love generated by this separation and I am forever a sacrifice to them.

---

ਸਲੋਕ ਮਹਲਾ ੪ ॥
ਜਿਨਾ ਅੰਦਰਿ ਉਮਰਥਲ ਸੇਈ ਜਾਣਨਿ ਸੂਲੀਆ ॥
ਹਰਿ ਜਾਣਹਿ ਸੇਈ ਬਿਰਹੁ ਹਉ ਤਿਨ ਵਿਟਹੁ ਸਦ ਘੁਮਿ ਘੋਲੀਆ ॥
Salok 4th Guru |
Jinaa Andhar Oumarathhal Saeee Jaanan Sooleeaa |
Har Jaanehi Saeee Birahu Ho Thin Vittahu Sadh Ghum Gholeeaa |  Page-311

---

Like in a deep well full of frogs; they do not know if there is another world outside the well. Similarly, my mind is so much engrossed in illusion (the visible world) that it cannot think of getting out. O Lord of all worlds: reveal to me, even for an instant, the Blessed Vision of Your Presence.

---

ਗਉੜੀ ਪੂਰਬੀ ਰਵਿਦਾਸ ਜੀਉ ॥
ਕੂਪੁ ਭਰਿਓ ਜੈਸੇ ਦਾਦਿਰਾ ਕਛੁ ਦੇਸੁ ਬਿਦੇਸੁ ਨ ਬੂਝ ॥
ਐਸੇ ਮੇਰਾ ਮਨੁ ਬਿਖਿਆ ਬਿਮੋਹਿਆ ਕਛੁ ਆਰਾ ਪਾਰੁ ਨ ਸੂਝ ॥੧॥
ਸਗਲ ਭਵਨ ਕੇ ਨਾਇਕਾ ਇਕੁ ਛਿਨੁ ਦਰਸੁ ਦਿਖਾਇ ਜੀ ॥੧॥ ਰਹਾਉ ॥
Gourree Poorabee Ravidhaas Jeeou |Koop Bhariou Jaisae Dhaadhiraa Kashh
Dhaes Bidhaes N Boojh |Aisae Maeraa Man Bikhiaa Bimohiaa Kashh Aaraa Paar
N Soojh |1|Sagal Bhavan Kae Naaeikaa Eik Shhin Dharas Dhikhaae Jee |1|
Rehaao |  Page-346

O' my mind, like the black deer, why are you so carelessly jumping around in the orchard of passion? The fruit of this orchard is poison, it only stays sweet for a short while, then it turns bitter. Without the Lord, there is no other protector, but you have forgotten Him. Nanak speaks the Truth. Reflect upon it; you shall die, O' black deer mind! The fish catches bait and leaves the water with tearful eyes, when caught. Similarly, man is caught in the illusion of visible world, but later repents for forsaking God. The streams once separated from the river may be united again with great fortune; same is true of man's separation from God. Nanak speaks the Truth; through the Wordless Word (*Shabad/Naam*), those long separated from the Lord, are united once again.

---

ਆਸਾ ਮਹਲਾ ੧ ॥

ਤੂੰ ਸੁਣਿ ਹਰਣਾ ਕਾਲਿਆ ਕੀ ਵਾੜੀਐ ਰਾਤਾ ਰਾਮ ॥ਬਿਖੁ ਫਲੁ ਮੀਠਾ ਚਾਰਿ ਦਿਨ ਫਿਰਿ ਹੋਵੈ ਤਾਤਾ ਰਾਮ ॥ ਹਰਿ ਬਾਝੁ ਰਾਖਾ ਕੋਇ ਨਾਹੀ ਸੋਇ ਤੁਝਹਿ ਬਿਸਾਰਿਆ ॥ਸਚੁ ਕਹੈ ਨਾਨਕੁ ਚੇਤਿ ਰੇ ਮਨ ਮਰਹਿ ਹਰਣਾ ਕਾਲਿਆ ॥੧॥ਮਛੁਲੀ ਵਿਛੁੰਨੀ ਨੈਣ ਰੁੰਨੀ ਜਾਲੁ ਬਧਿਕਿ ਪਾਇਆ ॥ ਨਦੀਆ ਵਾਹ ਵਿਛੁੰਨਿਆ ਮੇਲਾ ਸੰਜੋਗੀ ਰਾਮ ॥ਸਚੁ ਕਹੈ ਨਾਨਕੁ ਸਬਦਿ ਸਾਚੈ ਮੇਲਿ ਚਿਰੀ ਵਿਛੁੰਨਿਆ ॥੪॥੧॥੫॥

Aasaa 1ˢᵗ Guru |

Thoon Sun Haranaa Kaaliaa Kee Vaarreeai Raathaa Raam |Bikh Fal Meethaa Chaar Dhin Fir Hovai Thaathaa Raam |Har Baajh Raakhaa Koe Naahee Soe Thujhehi Bisaariaa |Sach Kehai Naanak Chaeth Rae Man Marehi Haranaa Kaaliaa |1|Mashhulee Vishhunnee Nain Runnee Jaal Badhhik Paaeiaa |Nadheeaa Vaah Vishhunniaa Maelaa Sanjogee Raam |Jug Jug Meethaa Vis Bharae Ko Jaanai Jogee Raam |Har Naam Bhagath N Ridhai Saachaa Sae Anth Dhhaahee Runniaa | Sach Kehai Naanak Sabadh Saachai Mael Chiree Vishhunniaa |4|1|5|  Page-438

Pangs of Separation (Birha)

Says Shaykh Fareed, O my dear friend, attach yourself to the
Lord. This body shall turn to dust, and its home shall be a
neglected grave. You can meet the Lord in this human life,
O' Shaykh Fareed, if you restrain your desire instincts which
keep your mind in turmoil. My dear mind, when you know
that you will die, and not return, then do not ruin yourself by
clinging to the world of falsehood.

---

ਆਸਾ ਸੇਖ ਫਰੀਦ ਜੀਉ ਕੀ ਬਾਣੀ ॥
ਬੋਲੈ ਸੇਖ ਫਰੀਦੁ ਪਿਆਰੇ ਅਲਹ ਲਗੇ ॥ ਇਹੁ ਤਨੁ ਹੋਸੀ ਖਾਕ ਨਿਮਾਣੀ ਗੋਰ ਘਰੇ ॥੧॥
ਆਜੁ ਮਿਲਾਵਾ ਸੇਖ ਫਰੀਦ ਟਾਕਿਮ ਕੂੰਜੜੀਆ ਮਨਹੁ ਮਚਿੰਦੜੀਆ ॥੧॥ ਰਹਾਉ ॥
ਜੇ ਜਾਣਾ ਮਰਿ ਜਾਈਐ ਘੁਮਿ ਨ ਆਈਐ ॥ ਝੂਠੀ ਦੁਨੀਆ ਲਗਿ ਨ ਆਪੁ ਵਞਾਈਐ ॥੨॥
Aasaa Saekh Fareedh Jeeo Kee Baanee |
Bolai Saekh Fareedh Piaarae Aleh Lagae |
Eihu Than Hosee Khaak Nimaanee Gor Gharae |1|
Aaj Milaavaa Saekh Fareedh Ttaakim Koonjarreeaa Manahu Machindharreeaa |1|
Rehaao |Jae Jaanaa Mar Jaaeeai Ghum N Aaeeai |
Jhoothee Dhuneeaa Lag N Aap Vanjaaeeai |2|    Page-488

You, the imbued in love of worldly objects are going on a path of pain and miseries. O' sinner, no one is or will be your friend to share your sins and you shall forever regret your actions. You did not sing with your tongue the Praises of the Sustainer of the World; when will, these days come again? The leaf, separated from the branch, shall not be joined with it again; all alone, it falls and so shall you be alone in death. Prays Nanak, without the Lord's Name, the soul wanders, forever suffering.

---

ਬਿਹਾਗੜਾ ਮਹਲਾ ੫ ॥

ਅਨ ਕਾਏ ਰਾਤੜਿਆ ਵਾਟ ਦੁਹੇਲੀ ਰਾਮ ॥ਪਾਪ ਕਮਾਵਦਿਆ ਤੇਰਾ ਕੋਇ ਨ ਬੇਲੀ ਰਾਮ ॥
ਕੋਏ ਨ ਬੇਲੀ ਹੋਇ ਤੇਰਾ ਸਦਾ ਪਛੋਤਾਵਹੇ ॥ਗੁਨ ਗੁਪਾਲ ਨ ਜਪਹਿ ਰਸਨਾ ਫਿਰਿ ਕਦਹੁ ਸੇ ਦਿਹ ਆਵਹੇ ॥
ਤਰਵਰ ਵਿਛੁੰਨੇ ਨਹ ਪਾਤ ਜੁੜਤੇ ਜਮ ਮਗਿ ਗਉਨੁ ਇਕੇਲੀ ॥
ਬਿਨਵੰਤ ਨਾਨਕ ਬਿਨੁ ਨਾਮ ਹਰਿ ਕੇ ਸਦਾ ਫਿਰਤ ਦੁਹੇਲੀ ॥੧॥

Bihaagarraa Mehalaa 5 |
An Kaaeae Raatharriaa Vaatt Dhuhaelee Raam |
Paap Kamaavadhiaa Thaeraa Koe N Baelee Raam |
Koeae N Baelee Hoe Thaeraa Sadhaa Pashhothaavehae |
Gun Gupaal N Japehi Rasanaa Fir Kadhahu Sae Dhih Aavehae |
Tharavar Vishhunnae Neh Paath Jurrathae Jam Mag Goun Eikaelee |
Binavanth Naanak Bin Naam Har Kae Sadhaa Firath Dhuhaelee |1| Page-546

O' sister; the rainy season "*Saawan*" has come, the peacocks are singing and dancing, and love is everywhere in the air! O' the innocent soul-bride, to meet your husband you are wearing full lenth bracelets and adorned with jewelry to look beautiful, but your Husband Lord is engrossed with someone else! So, smash your bracelets and break your arms by the sides of the bed! I have woven my hair into lovely braids, and saturated their partings with vermillion; but when I go before Him, I am not accepted, and I die, suffering in anguish. I weep; the whole world weeps; even the birds of the forest weep with me. In a dream, He came, and went away again; I cried so much. I can't come to You, O' my Beloved, and I can't send anyone to You. Come to me, O blessed sleep - perhaps I will see my Husband Lord again. Why haven't I died? Why hasn't my life just ended? My Husband Lord has become a stranger to me.

---

ਵਡਹੰਸੁ ਮਹਲਾ ੧ ॥

ਮੇਰੀ ਰੁਣ ਝੁਣ ਲਾਇਆ ਭੈਣੇ ਸਾਵਣੁ ਆਇਆ ॥

ਚੂੜਾ ਭੰਨੁ ਪਲੰਘ ਸਿਉ ਮੁੰਧੇ ਸਣੁ ਬਾਹੀ ਸਣੁ ਬਾਹਾ ॥ਏਤੇ ਵੇਸ ਕਰੇਦੀਏ ਮੁੰਧੇ ਸਹੁ ਰਾਤੋ ਅਵਰਾਹਾ ॥ ਮਾਠਿ ਗੁੰਦਾਈ. ਪਟੀਆ ਭਰੀਐ ਮਾਗ ਸੰਧੂਰੇ ॥ਅਗੈ ਗਈ ਨ ਮੰਨੀਆ ਮਰਉ ਵਿਸੂਰਿ ਵਿਸੂਰੇ ॥ ਮੈ ਰੋਵੰਦੀ ਸਭੁ ਜਗੁ ਰੁਨਾ ਰੁੰਨੜੇ ਵਣਹੁ ਪੰਖੇਰੂ ॥ ਸੁਪਨੈ ਆਇਆ ਭੀ ਗਇਆ ਮੈ ਜਲੁ ਭਰਿਆ ਰੋਇ ॥ਆਇ ਨ ਸਕਾ ਤੁਝ ਕਨਿ ਪਿਆਰੇ ਭੇਜਿ ਨ ਸਕਾ ਕੋਇ ॥ਆਉ ਸਭਾਗੀ ਨੀਦੜੀਏ ਮਤੁ ਸਹੁ ਦੇਖਾ ਸੋਇ ॥ ਕਿਉ ਨ ਮਰੀਜੈ ਜੀਅੜਾ ਨ ਦੀਜੈ ਜਾ ਸਹੁ ਭਇਆ ਵਿਡਾਣਾ ॥੧॥੩॥

Vaddehans 1st Guru |

Moree Run Jhun Laaeiaa Bhainae Saavan Aaeiaa |

Choorraa Bhann Palangh Sio Mundhhae San Baahee San Baahaa |

Eaethae Vaes Karaedheeeae Mundhhae Sahu Raatho Avaraahaa |Maath

Gundhaaeanaee Patteeaa Bhareeai Maag Sandhhoorae |

Agai Gee N Manneeaa Maro Visoor Visoorae |

Mai Rovandhee Sabh Jag Runaa Runnarrae Vanahu Pankhaeroo |

Pangs of Separation (Birha)

Eik N Runaa Maerae Than Kaa Birehaa Jin Ho Pirahu Vishhorree |
Supanai Aaeiaa Bhee Gaeiaa Mai Jal Bhariaa Roe |
Aae N Sakaa Thujh Kan Piaarae Bhaej N Sakaa Koe |
Aao Sabhaagee Needharreeeae Math Sahu Dhaekhaa Soe |
Kio N Mareejai Jeearraa N Dheejai Jaa Sahu Bhaeiaa Viddaanaa |1|3|  Page-557

---

Come, O' my companions - let us meet and dwell upon the
True Name. Let us remember again and again our separation
from the Lord and pray for its removal. Let us imbibe the
Lord in our hearts and remember the path that we all must go
through. To cry over anyone's death is useless, as the One
who created the life has taken it back; this is His Will. O'
people, do not decry death; death is also good if one can die
from "self" while living. This is only possible by
contemplating on the Lord's Name; then your path is
facilitated and you reap the fruits of coming into the Lord's
Presence, which is the ultimate bliss. Death would not be
called bad, O' people, if one knew how to truly die.

---

ਵਡਹੰਸੁ ਮਹਲਾ ੧ ॥
ਆਵਹੁ ਮਿਲਹੁ ਸਹੇਲੀਹੋ ਸਚੜਾ ਨਾਮੁ ਲਏਹਾਂ ॥ਰੋਵਹ ਬਿਰਹਾ ਤਨ ਕਾ ਆਪਣਾ ਸਾਹਿਬੁ ਸੰਮੁਹਾਲੇਹਾਂ ॥
ਸਾਹਿਬੁ ਸਮੁਹਾਲਿਹ ਪੰਥੁ ਨਿਹਾਲਿਹ ਅਸਾ ਭਿ ਓਥੈ ਜਾਣਾ ॥ਜਿਸ ਕਾ ਕੀਆ ਤਿਨ ਹੀ ਲੀਆ ਹੋਆ ਤਿਸੈ ਕਾ
ਭਾਣਾ ॥ਮਹਲੀ ਜਾਇ ਪਾਵਹੁ ਖਸਮੈ ਭਾਵਹੁ ਰੰਗ ਸਿਉ ਰਲੀਆ ਮਾਣੈ ॥ਮਰਣੁ ਨ ਮੰਦਾ ਲੋਕਾ ਆਖੀਐ ਜੇ ਕੋਈ
ਮਰਿ ਜਾਣੈ ॥੨॥
Vaddehans 1ˢᵗ Guru |
Aavahu Milahu Sehaeleeho Sacharraa Naam Leaehaan |Roveh Birehaa Than Kaa
Aapanaa Saahib Sanmhaalaehaan |Saahib Samhaalih Panthh Nihaalih Asaa Bh
Outhhai Jaanaa |Jis Kaa Keeaa Thin Hee Leeaa Hoaa Thisai Kaa Bhaanaa |
Mehalee Jaae Paavahu Khasamai Bhaavahu Rang Sio Raleeaa Maanai |Maran N
Mandhaa Lokaa Aakheeai Jae Koee Mar Jaanai |2|  Page-579

## Pangs of Separation (Birha)

Do not call them 'satee'*, who burn themselves along with their husbands' corpses. O Nanak, they alone are known as 'satee', who die from the shock of separation.

*Burning of the wife with her husband's body was called "satee", a custom now banned in India.

---

ਸਲੋਕੁ ਮਹਲਾ ੩ ॥
ਸਤੀਆ ਏਹਿ ਨ ਆਖੀਅਨਿ ਜੋ ਮੜਿਆ ਲਗਿ ਜਲੰਨ੍ਹਿ ॥
ਨਾਨਕ ਸਤੀਆ ਜਾਣੀਅਨ੍ਹਿ ਜਿ ਬਿਰਹੇ ਚੋਟ ਮਰੰਨ੍ਹਿ ॥
Salok 3rd Guru |
Satheeaa Eaehi N Aakheean Jo Marriaa Lag Jalannih |
Naanak Satheeaa Jaaneeanih J Birehae Chott Marannih |1|   Page-787

---

The soul-bride who has not experienced the pangs of separation, how can she understand the pain of those who live with it? The bridge over the fire of hell is difficult and treacherous. No one will accompany you there; you must go all alone. Suffering in pain, I have come to Your Door, O' Compassionate Lord. I am dying of the thirst to see You, but You do not answer!

---

ਰਾਗੁ ਸੂਹੀ ਬਾਣੀ ਸ੍ਰੀ ਰਵਿਦਾਸ ਜੀਉ ਕੀ ॥
ਸੋ ਕਤ ਜਾਨੈ ਪੀਰ ਪਰਾਈ ॥ ਜਾ ਕੈ ਅੰਤਰਿ ਦਰਦੁ ਨ ਪਾਈ ॥੧॥ ਰਹਾਉ ॥
ਪੁਰ ਸਲਾਤ ਕਾ ਪੰਥੁ ਦੁਹੇਲਾ ॥ਸੰਗਿ ਨ ਸਾਥੀ ਗਵਨੁ ਇਕੇਲਾ ॥੨॥
ਦੁਖੀਆ ਦਰਦਵੰਦੁ ਦਰਿ ਆਇਆ ॥ਬਹੁਤੁ ਪਿਆਸ ਜਬਾਬੁ ਨ ਪਾਇਆ ॥
Raag Soohee Baanee Sree Ravidhaas Jeeo Kee |
|So Kath Jaanai Peer Paraaee |Jaa Kai Anthar Dharadh N Paaee |1|Pause |
Pur Salaath Kaa Panthh Dhuhaelaa |Sang N Saathhee Gavan Eikaelaa |2|
Dhukheeaa Dharadhavandh Dhar Aaeiaa |Bahuth Piaas Jabaab N Paaeiaa |
Page-793

---

The day that dawns also sets, meaning life keeps reducing.
Everyone must leave here, no one can stay permanently. Our
companions are leaving and we must as well. We must travel
far away and death is hovering our heads. O' the ignorant
fool, why are you asleep? Wake up! You believe that life in
this world is true! Remember the Lord and renounce the me
and mine. Within your heart, contemplate on the Lord's
Name; this is the time!

ਰਾਗੁ ਸੂਹੀ ਬਾਣੀ ਸ੍ਰੀ ਰਵਿਦਾਸ ਜੀਉ ਕੀ
ਜੋ ਦਿਨ ਆਵਹਿ ਸੋ ਦਿਨ ਜਾਹੀ ॥ਕਰਨਾ ਕੂਚੁ ਰਹਨੁ ਥਿਰੁ ਨਾਹੀ ॥
ਸੰਗੁ ਚਲਤ ਹੈ ਹਮ ਭੀ ਚਲਨਾ ॥ਦੂਰਿ ਗਵਨੁ ਸਿਰ ਊਪਰਿ ਮਰਨਾ ॥੧॥
ਕਿਆ ਤੂ ਸੋਇਆ ਜਾਗੁ ਇਆਨਾ ॥ਤੈ ਜੀਵਨੁ ਜਗਿ ਸਚੁ ਕਰਿ ਜਾਨਾ ॥੧॥ ਰਹਾਉ ॥
ਕਰਿ ਬੰਦਿਗੀ ਛਾਡਿ ਮੈ ਮੇਰਾ ॥ਹਿਰਦੈ ਨਾਮੁ ਸਮੂਹਾਰਿ ਸਵੇਰਾ ॥੨॥
Raag Soohee Baanee Sree Ravidhaas Jeeo Kee |
Jo Dhin Aavehi So Dhin Jaahee | Karanaa Kooch Rehan Thhir Naahee |
Sang Chalath Hai Ham Bhee Chalanaa | Dhoor Gavan Sir Oopar Maranaa |1|
Kiaa Thoo Soeiaa Jaag Eiaanaa | Thai Jeevan Jag Sach Kar Jaanaa |1|Pause |
Kar Bandhigee Shhaadd Mai Maeraa | Hiradhai Naam Samhaar Savaeraa |2|
Page-793

In extreme misery, writhing in pain, I wring my hands. I have gone insane, seeking my Husband Lord. O my Lord, you are not happy with me; the fault is totally mine, and not Yours. O my Husband and Master, I never realized Your excellence and worth and having wasted my youth, I now regret and repent. O' black cuckoo, what qualities have made you black? She answers,"I have been burnt black by the separation from my Beloved!" O' brother, the path of our life is very dreadful. It is sharper than a double-edged sword, and very narrow. That is what we must go through. Says Shaykh Fareed, think of that path early on!

---

ਰਾਗੁ ਸੂਹੀ ਬਾਣੀ ਸੇਖ ਫਰੀਦ ਜੀ ਕੀ ॥
ਤਪਿ ਤਪਿ ਲੁਹਿ ਲੁਹਿ ਹਾਥ ਮਰੋਰਉ ॥ ਬਾਵਲਿ ਹੋਈ ਸੋ ਸਹੁ ਲੋਰਉ ॥
ਤੈ ਸਹਿ ਮਨ ਮਹਿ ਕੀਆ ਰੋਸੁ ॥ ਮੁਝੁ ਅਵਗਨ ਸਹ ਨਾਹੀ ਦੋਸੁ ॥੧॥
ਤੈ ਸਾਹਿਬ ਕੀ ਮੈ ਸਾਰ ਨ ਜਾਨੀ ॥ ਜੋਬਨੁ ਖੋਇ ਪਾਛੈ ਪਛੁਤਾਨੀ ॥੧॥ ਰਹਾਉ ॥
ਕਾਲੀ ਕੋਇਲ ਤੂ ਕਿਤ ਗੁਨ ਕਾਲੀ ॥ ਅਪਨੇ ਪ੍ਰੀਤਮ ਕੇ ਹਉ ਬਿਰਹੈ ਜਾਲੀ ॥
ਵਾਟ ਹਮਾਰੀ ਖਰੀ ਉਡੀਣੀ ॥ ਖੰਨਿਅਹੁ ਤਿਖੀ ਬਹੁਤੁ ਪਿਈਣੀ ॥
ਉਸੁ ਉਪਰਿ ਹੈ ਮਾਰਗੁ ਮੇਰਾ ॥ ਸੇਖ ਫਰੀਦਾ ਪੰਥੁ ਸਮੁਹਾਰਿ ਸਵੇਰਾ ॥੪॥੧॥
Raag Soohee Baanee Saekh Fareedh Jee Kee |Thap Thap Luhi Luhi Haathh Maroro | Baaval Hoee So Sahu Loro |Thai Sehi Man Mehi Keeaa Ros | Mujh Avagan Seh Naahee Dhos |1|Thai Saahib Kee Mai Saar N Jaanee | Joban Khoe Paashhai Pashhuthaanee |1| Rehaao |Kaalee Koeil Thoo Kith Gun Kaalee | Apanae Preetham Kae Ho Birehai Jaalee |Vaatt Hamaaree Kharee Ouddeenee | Khanniahu Thikhee Bahuth Pieenee |Ous Oopar Hai Maarag Maeraa | Saekh Fareedhaa Panthh Samhaar Savaeraa |4|1| Page-794

You were not able to build the raft of Lord's Name when you had the time. Now, when the worldly ocean is churning and over-flowing, it is very difficult for you to cross over. Do not touch the safflower with your hands; its color will fade away quickly.

Those who cling to the worldly illusion become weak and fall from the Husband Lord's Grace; like when the youth is wasted, milk will not return to the bossom. Says Fareed, O' my companions, when the Lord calls, sad at heart the soul must depart, and this body returns to dust!

---

ਰਾਗੁ ਸੂਹੀ ਬਾਣੀ ਸੇਖ ਫਰੀਦ ਜੀ ਕੀ ॥
ਬੇੜਾ ਬੰਧਿ ਨ ਸਕਿਓ ਬੰਧਨ ਕੀ ਵੇਲਾ ॥ਭਰਿ ਸਰਵਰੁ ਜਬ ਊਛਲੈ ਤਬ ਤਰਣੁ ਦੁਹੇਲਾ ॥੧॥
ਹਥੁ ਨ ਲਾਇ ਕਸੁੰਭੜੈ ਜਲਿ ਜਾਸੀ ਢੋਲਾ ॥੧॥ ਰਹਾਉ ॥
ਇਕ ਆਪੀਨੑੈ ਪਤਲੀ ਸਹ ਕੇਰੇ ਬੋਲਾ ॥ਦੁਧਾ ਥਣੀ ਨ ਆਵਈ ਫਿਰਿ ਹੋਇ ਨ ਮੇਲਾ ॥੨॥
ਕਹੈ ਫਰੀਦੁ ਸਹੇਲੀਹੋ ਸਹੁ ਅਲਾਏਸੀ ॥ਹੰਸੁ ਚਲਸੀ ਡੁੰਮਣਾ ਅਹਿ ਤਨੁ ਢੇਰੀ ਥੀਸੀ ॥੩॥੨॥
Raag Soohee Baanee Saekh Fareedh Jee Kee |
Baerraa Bandhh N Sakiou Bandhhan Kee Vaelaa |
Bhar Saravar Jab Ooshhalai Thab Tharan Dhuhaelaa |1|
Hathh N Laae Kasunbharrai Jal Jaasee Dtolaa |1| Pause |
Eik Aapeenhai Pathalee Seh Kaerae Bolaa |
Dhudhhaa Thhanee N Aavee Fir Hoe N Maelaa |2|
Kehai Fareedh Sehaeleeho Sahu Alaaeaesee |
Hans Chalasee Ddunmanaa Ahi Than Dtaeree Thheesee |3|2|   Page-794

My mind yearns so deeply for the Blessed Vision of the Lord, like the thirsty man without water. My heart is pierced through by the arrow of the Lord's Love. The Lord God knows my anguish, and the pain deep within my mind. Whosoever tells me the stories of my Beloved Lord is my brother and my friend. Come, and join, O' my companions; let's sing the Glorious Praises of my God, and follow the comforting advice of the True Guru. Please fulfill the hopes of servant Nanak, O' Lord; his body finds peace and tranquility in the Blessed Vision of the Lord.

---

ਗੋਂਡ ਮਹਲਾ ੪ ॥
ਹਰਿ ਦਰਸਨ ਕਉ ਮੇਰਾ ਮਨੁ ਬਹੁ ਤਪਤੈ ਜਿਉ ਤ੍ਰਿਖਾਵੰਤੁ ਬਿਨੁ ਨੀਰ ॥੧॥
ਮੇਰੈ ਮਨਿ ਪ੍ਰੇਮੁ ਲਗੋ ਹਰਿ ਤੀਰ ॥
ਹਮਰੀ ਬੇਦਨ ਹਰਿ ਪ੍ਰਭੁ ਜਾਨੈ ਮੇਰੇ ਮਨ ਅੰਤਰ ਕੀ ਪੀਰ ॥੧॥ ਰਹਾਉ ॥
ਮੇਰੇ ਹਰਿ ਪ੍ਰੀਤਮ ਕੀ ਕੋਈ ਬਾਤ ਸੁਨਾਵੈ ਸੋ ਭਾਈ ਸੋ ਮੇਰਾ ਬੀਰ ॥੨॥
ਮਿਲੁ ਮਿਲੁ ਸਖੀ ਗੁਣ ਕਹੁ ਮੇਰੇ ਪ੍ਰਭ ਕੇ ਲੇ ਸਤਿਗੁਰ ਕੀ ਮਤਿ ਧੀਰ ॥੩॥
ਜਨ ਨਾਨਕ ਕੀ ਹਰਿ ਆਸ ਪੁਜਾਵਹੁ ਹਰਿ ਦਰਸਨਿ ਸਾਂਤਿ ਸਰੀਰ ॥੪॥੬॥
Gonadd 4th Guru |
Har Dharasan Ko Maeraa Man Bahu Thapathai Jio Thrikhaavanth Bin Neer |1|
Maerai Man Praem Lago Har Theer |
Hamaree Baedhan Har Prabh Jaanai Maerae Man Anthar Kee Peer |1|Pause |
Maerae Har Preetham Kee Koee Baath Sunaavai So Bhaaee So Maeraa Beer |2|
Mil Mil Sakhee Gun Kahu Maerae Prabh Kae Lae Sathigur Kee Math Dhheer |3|
Jan Naanak Kee Har Aas Pujaavahu Har Dharasan Saanth Sareer |4|6|
Page-861

I have become sad, wondering where the soul comes from, and where it goes. The body is formed from the union of five elements (water, air, fire, sky, & earth); but where were the five elements created? You say that the soul is tied to its karma, but who gave karma to the body? The body is contained in the Lord, and the Lord is contained in the body. He is permeating within all. Says Kabeer, I shall not renounce the Lord's Name; I shall accept whatever happens calmly.

---

ਰਾਗੁ ਗੋਂਡ ਬਾਣੀ ਭਗਤਾ ਕੀ ॥ ਕਬੀਰ ਜੀ ॥
ਮੋਹਿ ਬੈਰਾਗੁ ਭਇਓ ॥ ਇਹੁ ਜੀਉ ਆਇ ਕਹਾ ਗਇਓ ॥੧॥ ਰਹਾਉ ॥
ਪੰਚ ਤਤੁ ਮਿਲਿ ਕਾਇਆ ਕੀਨ੍ਹੀ ਤਤੁ ਕਹਾ ਤੇ ਕੀਨੁ ਰੇ ॥
ਕਰਮ ਬਧ ਤੁਮ ਜੀਉ ਕਹਤ ਹੌ ਕਰਮਹਿ ਕਿਨਿ ਜੀਉ ਦੀਨੁ ਰੇ ॥੨॥
ਹਰਿ ਮਹਿ ਤਨੁ ਹੈ ਤਨ ਮਹਿ ਹਰਿ ਹੈ ਸਰਬ ਨਿਰੰਤਰਿ ਸੋਇ ਰੇ ॥
ਕਹਿ ਕਬੀਰ ਰਾਮ ਨਾਮੁ ਨ ਛੋਡਉ ਸਹਜੇ ਹੋਇ ਸੁ ਹੋਇ ਰੇ ॥੩॥੩॥
Raag Gonadd Baanee Bhagathaa Kee | Kabeer Jee |
Mohi Bairaag Bhaeiou |Eihu Jeeo Aae Kehaa Gaeiou |1| Pause|
Panch Thath Mil Kaaeiaa Keenhee Thath Kehaa Thae Keen Rae |
Karam Badhh Thum Jeeo Kehath Ha Karamehi Kin Jeeo Dheen Rae |2|
Har Mehi Than Hai Than Mehi Har Hai Sarab Niranthar Soe Rae |
Kehi Kabeer Raam Naam N Shhoddo Sehajae Hoe S Hoe Rae |3|3|   Page-870

# Pangs of Separation (Birha)

In "*Saawan*" (July), the clouds have burst with rains; O' my mind be happy!  In such a weather, the one whose husband has gone away is torn by the separation in the depths of her love.  She sobs, saying, "my husband is not home, I am dying of deep sighs and the lightening bursts are scaring me.  My lonely bed is giving me extreme pain and I am suffering in agony.  O' my mother, I am dying!"

The soul-bride who is full of love for her Husband Lord; the pangs of separation do not let her, sleep, feel hungry, or enjoy bodily comforts.  O' Nanak, she alone is a happy soul-bride, who merges in the Being of her Beloved Husband Lord.

---

ਤੁਖਾਰੀ ਛੰਤ ਮਹਲਾ ੧ ॥

ਸਾਵਣਿ ਸਰਸ ਮਨਾ ਘਣ ਵਰਸਹਿ ਰੁਤਿ ਆਏ ॥ ਮੈ ਮਨਿ ਤਨਿ ਸਹੁ ਭਾਵੈ ਪਿਰ ਪਰਦੇਸਿ ਸਿਧਾਏ ॥

ਪਿਰੁ ਘਰਿ ਨਹੀ ਆਵੈ ਮਰੀਐ ਹਾਵੈ ਦਾਮਨਿ ਚਮਕਿ ਡਰਾਏ ॥

ਸੇਜ ਇਕੇਲੀ ਖਰੀ ਦੁਹੇਲੀ ਮਰਣੁ ਭਇਆ ਦੁਖੁ ਮਾਏ ॥

ਹਰਿ ਬਿਨੁ ਨੀਦ ਭੂਖ ਕਹੁ ਕੈਸੀ ਕਾਪੜੁ ਤਨਿ ਨ ਸੁਖਾਵਏ ॥

ਨਾਨਕ ਸਾ ਸੋਹਾਗਣਿ ਕੰਤੀ ਪਿਰ ਕੈ ਅੰਕਿ ਸਮਾਵਏ ॥੯॥

Thukhaaree Shhanth 1ˢᵗ Guru |

Saavan Saras Manaa Ghan Varasehi Ruth Aaeae |

Mai Man Than Sahu Bhaavai Pir Paradhaes Sidhhaaeae |

Pir Ghar Nehee Aavai Mareeai Haavai Dhaaman Chamak Ddaraaeae |

Saej Eikaelee Kharee Dhuhaelee Maran Bhaeiaa Dhukh Maaeae |

Har Bin Needh Bhookh Kahu Kaisee Kaaparr Than N Sukhaaveae |

Naanak Saa Sohaagan Kanthee Pir Kai Ank Samaaveae |9|   Page-1108

---

The soul-bride suffering from the pangs of separation from the Lord thinks, He has gone to a distant land (although He is within her). Due to being overtaken by pain, she sends to Him messages of her helplessness. Her eyes are filled with tears and she dwells upon His Glorious Vitues, wondering, "how can I meet my Beloved, I do not know the treacherous path to reach You; how can I find You and cross over the worldly ocean?"

---

ਤੁਖਾਰੀ ਮਹਲਾ ੧ ॥

ਸਾਜਨ ਦੇਸਿ ਵਿਦੇਸੀਅੜੇ ਸਾਨੇਹੜੇ ਦੇਦੀ ॥ਸਾਰਿ ਸਮਾਲੇ ਤਿਨ ਸਜਣਾ ਮੁੰਧ ਨੈਣ ਭਰੇਦੀ ॥

ਮੁੰਧ ਨੈਣ ਭਰੇਦੀ ਗੁਣ ਸਾਰੇਦੀ ਕਿਉ ਪ੍ਰਭ ਮਿਲਾ ਪਿਆਰੇ ॥

ਮਾਰਗੁ ਪੰਥੁ ਨ ਜਾਣਉ ਵਿਖੜਾ ਕਿਉ ਪਾਈਐ ਪਿਰੁ ਪਾਰੇ ॥

Thukhaaree 1st Guru |

Saajan Dhaes Vidhaeseearrae Saanaeharrae Dhaedhee |

Saar Samaalae Thin Sajanaa Mundhh Nain Bharaedhee |

Mundhh Nain Bharaedhee Gun Saaraedhee Kio Prabh Milaa Piaarae |

Maarag Panthh N Jaano Vikharraa Kio Paaeeai Pir Paarae |    Page-1111

O' my Husband Lord, if I had known that my robe tie to You would come loose, I would have tied a tighter knot. I have looked and searched all over the world, but have found none as great a companion as You.

---

ਸਲੋਕ ਸੇਖ ਫਰੀਦ ਕੇ ॥
ਜੇ ਜਾਣਾ ਲੜੁ ਛਿਜਣਾ ਪੀੜੀ ਪਾਈਂ ਗੰਢਿ ॥ਤੈ ਜੇਵਡੁ ਮੈ ਨਾਹਿ ਕੋ ਸਭੁ ਜਗੁ ਡਿਠਾ ਹੰਢਿ ॥੫॥
Salok Saekh Fareedh Kae |
Jae Jaanaa Larr Shhijanaa Peeddee Paaeen Gandt |
Thai Jaevadd Mai Naahi Ko Sabh Jag Ddithaa Handt |5|    Page-1378

---

Says, Fareed, I am worried that my turban might become dirty with a spec of dust. But, my foolish self does not realize that one-day dust will consume my head as well.

---

ਸਲੋਕ ਸੇਖ ਫਰੀਦ ਕੇ ॥
ਫਰੀਦਾ ਮੈ ਭੋਲਾਵਾ ਪਗ ਦਾ ਮਤੁ ਮੈਲੀ ਹੋਇ ਜਾਇ ॥ਗਹਿਲਾ ਰੂਹੁ ਨ ਜਾਣਈ ਸਿਰੁ ਭੀ ਮਿਟੀ ਖਾਇ ॥੨੬॥
Salok Saekh Fareedh Kae |
Fareedhaa Mai Bholaavaa Pag Dhaa Math Mailee Hoe Jaae |
Gehilaa Roohu N Jaanee Sir Bhee Mittee Khaae |26|    Page-1379

---

If my love for the Husband Lord is not broken, then I am not afraid of the passing away of my youth. O'Fareed, devoid of the Lord's love, so many youths have dried and withered away. Everyone says separation is bad; but, O'separation, you are the king and I salute to you. Says Fareed, the body which has not experienced the pangs of separation from the Lord, is akin to a cremation ground! Fareed, the hours of the day are lost wandering around, and the hours of the night are lost in sleep. God will call for an account, and ask you," why you came into this world?"

---

ਸਲੋਕ ਸੇਖ ਫਰੀਦ ਕੇ ॥
ਜੋਬਨ ਜਾਂਦੇ ਨਾ ਡਰਾਂ ਜੇ ਸਹ ਪ੍ਰੀਤਿ ਨ ਜਾਇ ॥
ਫਰੀਦਾ ਕਿਤੀ. ਜੋਬਨ ਪ੍ਰੀਤਿ ਬਿਨੁ ਸੁਕਿ ਗਏ ਕੁਮਲਾਇ ॥੩੪॥
ਬਿਰਹਾ ਬਿਰਹਾ ਆਖੀਐ ਬਿਰਹਾ ਤੂ ਸੁਲਤਾਨੁ ॥ਫਰੀਦਾ ਜਿਤੁ ਤਨਿ ਬਿਰਹੁ ਨ ਊਪਜੈ ਸੋ ਤਨੁ ਜਾਣੁ ਮਸਾਨੁ ॥੩੬॥
ਫਰੀਦਾ ਚਾਰਿ ਗਵਾਇਆ ਹੰਢਿ ਕੈ ਚਾਰਿ ਗਵਾਇਆ ਸੰਮਿ ॥ਲੇਖਾ ਰਬੁ ਮੰਗੇਸੀਆ ਤੂ ਆਂਹੋ ਕੇਰ੍ਹੇ ਕੰਮਿ ॥੩੮॥
Salok Saekh Fareedh Kae |
Joban Jaandhae Naa Ddaraan Jae Seh Preeth N Jaae |
Fareedhaa Kithanaee Joban Preeth Bin Suk Geae Kumalaae |34|
Birehaa Birehaa Aakheeai Birehaa Thoo Sulathaan |
Fareedhaa Jith Than Birahu N Oopajai So Than Jaan Masaan |36|
Fareedhaa Chaar Gavaaeiaa Handt Kai Chaar Gavaaeiaa Sanm |
Laekhaa Rab Mangaeseeaa Thoo Aaanho Kaerhae Kanm |38|  Page-1379

Pangs of Separation (Birha)

O'Fareed, have you gone to the Lord's Temple Door and seen the gong being struck with a mellet. This blameless object is being beaten - imagine what is in store for us the sinners! Each, and every hour, it is beaten; it is punished every day. This beautiful body is like the gong; it spent the entire life chasing illusion and now passes the night in pain.

---

ਸਲੋਕ ਸੇਖ ਫਰੀਦ ਕੇ ॥
ਫਰੀਦਾ ਦਰਿ ਦਰਵਾਜੈ ਜਾਇ ਕੈ ਕਿਉ ਡਿਠੋ ਘੜੀਆਲੁ ॥
ਏਹੁ ਨਿਦੋਸਾਂ ਮਾਰੀਐ ਹਮ ਦੋਸਾਂ ਦਾ ਕਿਆ ਹਾਲੁ ॥੩੯॥
ਘੜੀਏ ਘੜੀਏ ਮਾਰੀਐ ਪਹਰੀ ਲਹੈ ਸਜਾਇ ॥
ਸੋ ਹੇੜਾ ਘੜੀਆਲ ਜਿਉ ਡੁਖੀ ਰੈਣਿ ਵਿਹਾਇ ॥੪੦॥

Salok Saekh Fareedh Kae |
Fareedhaa Dhar Dharavaajai Jaae Kai Kio Dditho Gharreeaal |
Eaehu Nidhosaan Maareeai Ham Dhosaan Dhaa Kiaa Haal |39|
Gharreeeae Gharreeeae Maareeai Peharee Lehai Sajaae |
So Haerraa Gharreeaal Jio Ddukhee Rain Vihaae |40|   Page-1379

O'Fareed, my withered body has become a skeleton; the crows are pecking at my palms (I am still clinging to greed). Even now, God has not come! Behold, this fate of the human mortal! The crows have scorched my skeleton, and eaten away my flesh (sins and evil deeds are still strong). God willing, let no evil touch my eyes as they still long to see the Beloved Lord. Right before my eyes I have seen a great many leave; fallen a prey to death. Says Fareed, everyone is worried about their own fate, and I am also worried about mine!

---

ਸਲੋਕ ਸੇਖ ਫਰੀਦ ਕੇ ॥
ਫਰੀਦਾ ਤਨੁ ਸੁਕਾ ਪਿੰਜਰੁ ਥੀਆ ਤਲੀਆਂ ਖੂੰਡਹਿ ਕਾਗ ॥ਅਜੈ ਸੁ ਰਬੁ ਨ ਬਾਹੁੜਿਓ ਦੇਖੁ ਬੰਦੇ ਕੇ ਭਾਗ ॥੯੦॥
ਕਾਗਾ ਕਰੰਗ ਢੰਢੋਲਿਆ ਸਗਲਾ ਖਾਇਆ ਮਾਸੁ ॥
ਏ ਦੁਇ ਨੈਨਾ ਮਤਿ ਛੁਹਉ ਪਿਰ ਦੇਖਨ ਕੀ ਆਸ ॥੯੧॥
ਏਨੀ ਲੋਇਣੀ ਦੇਖਦਿਆ ਕੇਤੀ ਚਲਿ ਗਈ ॥ਫਰੀਦਾ ਲੋਕਾਂ ਆਪੋ ਆਪਣੀ ਮੈ ਆਪਣੀ ਪਈ ॥੯੪॥
Salok Saekh Fareedh Kae |
Fareedhaa Than Sukaa Pinjar Thheeaa Thaleeaaan Khoonddehi Kaag |
Ajai S Rab N Baahurriou Dhaekh Bandhae Kae Bhaag |90|
Kaagaa Karang Dtandtoliaa Sagalaa Khaaeiaa Maas |
Eae Dhue Nainaa Math Shhuho Pir Dhaekhan Kee Aas |91|
Eaenee Loeinee Dhaekhadhiaa Kaethee Chal Gee |
Fareedhaa Lokaan Aapo Aapanee Mai Aapanee Pee |94|   Page-1382

## Chapter-14  Saint/God & Holy Company (Saadh Sangat)

O' Lord You, are me, and I am You; what kind of difference there is? Just the same as between gold and the gold bracelet, or as between water and the waves. O' Infinite Lord, if we humans did not commit sins, then how could You be called the 'Redeemer of sinners'?

ਸਿਰੀਰਾਗੁ ॥ਬਾਣੀ ਭਗਤ ਰਵਿਦਾਸ ਜੀਉ ਕੀ ॥
ਤੋਹੀ ਮੋਹੀ ਮੋਹੀ ਤੋਹੀ ਅੰਤਰੁ ਕੈਸਾ ॥ਕਨਕ ਕਟਿਕ ਜਲ ਤਰੰਗ ਜੈਸਾ ॥੧॥
ਜਉ ਪੈ ਹਮ ਨ ਪਾਪ ਕਰੰਤਾ ਅਹੇ ਅਨੰਤਾ ॥ਪਤਿਤ ਪਾਵਨ ਨਾਮੁ ਕੈਸੇ ਹੁੰਤਾ ॥੧॥ ਰਹਾਉ ॥
Sireeraag | Baanee Bhagath Ravidhaas Jeeo Kee |
Thohee Mohee Mohee Thohee Anthar Kaisaa |Kanak Kattik Jal Tharang Jaisaa |1|Jo
Pai Ham N Paap Karanthaa Ahae Ananthaa |Pathith Paavan Naam Kaisae Hunthaa
|1| Pause |  Page-93

Only those are handsome and lead beautiful lives, who participate in the Company of the Holy; *Saadh Sangat*. Those who have gathered the treasure of the Lord's Name, become extremely composed and calm.

ਮਾਝ ਮਹਲਾ ੫ ॥ਸੋਈ ਸੁੰਦਰ ਸੋਹਨੇ ॥ ਸਾਧਸੰਗਿ ਜਿਨ ਬੈਹਨੇ ॥ ਹਰਿ ਧਨੁ ਜਿਨੀ ਸੰਜਿਆ ਸੇਈ
ਗੰਭੀਰ ਅਪਾਰ ਜੀਉ ॥੩॥
Maajh 5th Guru |
Saeee Sundhar Sohanae | Saadhhasang Jin Baihanae |Har Dhhan Jinee Sanjiaa
Saeee Ganbhleer Apaar Jeeo |3|  Page-132

O' Lord, you are the sandalwood tree, and I am the poor castor oil plant; with Your Mercy, I can dwell near You. Your exquisite fragrance has permeated me and now I have become exalted from a lowly plant. O' Lord, I seek the Sanctuary of the Company of the Holy; *Saadh Sangat*. Please do not separate me from it; I am full of demerits, and You are so benevolent.

---

ਆਸਾ ਬਾਣੀ ਸ੍ਰੀ ਰਵਿਦਾਸ ਜੀਉ ਕੀ ॥
ਤੁਮ ਚੰਦਨ ਹਮ ਇਰੰਡ ਬਾਪੁਰੇ ਸੰਗਿ ਤੁਮਾਰੇ ਬਾਸਾ ॥
ਨੀਚ ਰੂਖ ਤੇ ਊਚ ਭਏ ਹੈ ਗੰਧ ਸੁਗੰਧ ਨਿਵਾਸਾ ॥੧॥
ਮਾਧਉ ਸਤਸੰਗਤਿ ਸਰਨਿ ਤੁਮ੍ਹਾਰੀ ॥ ਹਮ ਅਉਗਨ ਤੁਮ੍ਹ ਉਪਕਾਰੀ ॥੧॥ ਰਹਾਉ ॥
Aasaa Baanee Sree Ravidhaas Jeeo Kee |
Thum Chandhan Ham Eirandd Baapurae Sang Thumaarae Baasaa |
Neech Rookh Thae Ooch Bheae Hai Gandhh Sugandhh Nivaasaa |1|
Maadhho Sathasangath Saran Thumhaaree |
Ham Aougan Thumh Oupakaaree |1| Pause |   Page-486

O' brother, me the foolish have not understood even one Virtue of the Lord. He is the Master of millions of universes, is the Giver to all, nourishes and always takes care of all. To save an ignorant fool like me is no big thing for Him, who has saved millions of sinners. Those who have heard Guru Nanak's message and seen Guru Nanak, become free of the life and death cycle.

---

ਸੋਰਠਿ ਮਹਲਾ ੫ ॥
ਕੋਟਿ ਬ੍ਰਹਮੰਡ ਕੋ ਠਾਕੁਰੁ ਸੁਆਮੀ ਸਰਬ ਜੀਆ ਕਾ ਦਾਤਾ ਰੇ ॥
ਪ੍ਰਤਿਪਾਲੈ ਨਿਤ ਸਾਰਿ ਸਮਾਲੈ ਇਕੁ ਗੁਨੁ ਨਹੀ ਮੂਰਖਿ ਜਾਤਾ ਰੇ ॥੧॥
ਮੈ ਮੂਰਖ ਕੀ ਕੇਤਕ ਬਾਤ ਹੈ ਕੋਟਿ ਪਰਾਧੀ ਤਰਿਆ ਰੇ ॥
ਗੁਰੁ ਨਾਨਕੁ ਜਿਨ ਸੁਣਿਆ ਪੇਖਿਆ ਸੇ ਫਿਰਿ ਗਰਭਾਸਿ ਨ ਪਰਿਆ ਰੇ ॥੪॥੨॥੧੩॥
Sorath 5th Guru |
Kott Brehamandd Ko Thaakur Suaamee Sarab Jeeaa Kaa Dhaathaa Rae |
Prathipaalai Nith Saar Samaalai Eik Gun Nehee Moorakh Jaathaa Rae |1|
Mai Moorakh Kee Kaethak Baath Hai Kott Paraadhhee Thariaa Rae |
Gur Naanak Jin Suniaa Paekhiaa Sae Fir Garabhaas N Pariaa Rae |4|2|13|
Page-612

They read scriptures, and contemplate the Vedas; they practice
the inner cleansing techniques of Yoga, and control of the
breath. But they cannot escape from the five passions (sex,
anger, greed, attachment, pride); and are increasingly bound to
the ego.

O' my friend, this is not the way to meet the Lord; I have
performed such rituals many times. Ultimately, I am
exhausted and fallen at the Door of the Lord Master! I pray
that He may grant me a discerning intellect.

Singing the Lord's Praises in the *Saadh Sangat*, the Company
of the Holy, is the highest of all actions. Says Nanak, he alone
obtains it, who is pre-ordained to receive it.

---

ਸੋਰਠਿ ਮਹਲਾ ੫ ਅਸਟਪਦੀਆ ॥
ਪਾਠੁ ਪੜਿਓ ਅਰੁ ਬੇਦੁ ਬੀਚਾਰਿਓ ਨਿਵਲਿ ਭੁਅੰਗਮ ਸਾਧੇ ॥
ਪੰਚ ਜਨਾ ਸਿਉ ਸੰਗੁ ਨ ਛੁਟਕਿਓ ਅਧਿਕ ਅਹੰਬੁਧਿ ਬਾਧੇ ॥੧॥
ਪਿਆਰੇ ਇਨ ਬਿਧਿ ਮਿਲਣੁ ਨ ਜਾਈ ਮੈ ਕੀਏ ਕਰਮ ਅਨੇਕਾ ॥
ਹਾਰਿ ਪਰਿਓ ਸੁਆਮੀ ਕੈ ਦੁਆਰੈ ਦੀਜੈ ਬੁਧਿ ਬਿਬੇਕਾ ॥ ਰਹਾਉ ॥
ਹਰਿ ਕੀਰਤਿ ਸਾਧਸੰਗਤਿ ਹੈ ਸਿਰਿ ਕਰਮਨ ਕੈ ਕਰਮਾ ॥
ਕਹੁ ਨਾਨਕ ਤਿਸੁ ਭਇਓ ਪਰਾਪਤਿ ਜਿਸੁ ਪੁਰਬ ਲਿਖੇ ਕਾ ਲਹਨਾ ॥੮॥
Sorath 5th Guru Asattapadheeaa |
Paath Parriou Ar Baedh Beechaariou Nival Bhuangam Saadhhae |
Panch Janaa Sio Sang N Shhuttakiou Adhhik Ahanbudhh Baadhhae |1|
Piaarae Ein Bidhh Milan N Jaaee Mai Keeeae Karam Anaekaa |
Haar Pariou Suaamee Kai Dhuaarai Dheejai Budhh Bibaekaa | Pause |
Har Keerath Saadhhasangath Hai Sir Karaman Kai Karamaa |
Kahu Naanak This Bhaeiou Paraapath Jis Purab Likhae Kaa Lehanaa |8|
Page-641

The woman next door asked Naam Dayv, "Who built your house? I shall pay him double the wages. Tell me, who is your carpenter?" O sister, this carpenter cannot be given just like this! Behold, my carpenter is pervading everywhere. My carpenter is the Support of the breath of life; He demands the wages of love, if someone wants Him to build their house. Listen to the virtues of this carpenter, O" sister; He stopped the oceans, and established Dhroo as the pole star. Naam Dayv's Lord Master brought Sita* back, and gave Sri Lanka to Bhabheekhan.

*Ramayana is an Indian epic, which is the story of Lord Rama; his wife Sita was abducted by Raavnaa, the then king of Sri Lanka. Lord Rama rescued her and killed Raavnaa to establish the victory of good over evil.

---

ਰਾਗੁ ਸੋਰਠਿ ਬਾਣੀ ਭਗਤ ਨਾਮਦੇਵ ਜੀ ਕੀ ॥
ਪਾੜ ਪੜੋਸਣਿ ਪੂਛਿ ਲੇ ਨਾਮਾ ਕਾ ਪਹਿ ਛਾਨਿ ਛਵਾਈ ਹੋ ॥
ਤੋ ਪਹਿ ਦੁਗਣੀ ਮਜੂਰੀ ਦੈਹਉ ਮੋ ਕਉ ਬੇਢੀ ਦੇਹੁ ਬਤਾਈ ਹੋ ॥੧॥
ਰੀ ਬਾਈ ਬੇਢੀ ਦੇਨੁ ਨ ਜਾਈ ॥ਦੇਖੁ ਬੇਢੀ ਰਹਿਓ ਸਮਾਈ ॥ਹਮਾਰੈ ਬੇਢੀ ਪ੍ਰਾਨ ਅਧਾਰਾ ॥੧॥ ਰਹਾਉ ॥
ਬੇਢੀ ਪ੍ਰੀਤਿ ਮਜੂਰੀ ਮਾਂਗੈ ਜਉ ਕੋਉ ਛਾਨਿ ਛਵਾਵੈ ਹੋ ॥ ਬੇਢੀ ਕੇ ਗੁਣ ਸੁਨਿ ਰੀ ਬਾਈ ਜਲਧਿ ਬਾਂਧਿ ਧ੍ਰੂ ਥਾਪਿਓ ਹੋ
॥ਨਾਮੇ ਕੇ ਸੁਆਮੀ ਸੀਅ ਬਹੋਰੀ ਲੰਕ ਭਭੀਖਣ ਆਪਿਓ ਹੋ ॥੪॥੨॥
Raag Sorath Baanee Bhagath Naamadhae Jee Kee |
Paarr Parrosan Pooshh Lae Naamaa Kaa Pehi Shhaan Shhavaaee Ho |
Tho Pehi Dhuganee Majooree Dhaiho Mo Ko Baedtee Dhaehu Bathaaee Ho |1|
Ree Baaee Baedtee Dhaen N Jaaee |Dhaekh Baedtee Rehiou Samaaee |
Hamaarai Baedtee Praan Adhhaaraa |1| Pause |Baedtee Preeth Majooree Maangai Jo
Kooo Shhaan Shhavaavai Ho | Baedtee Kae Gun Sun Ree Baaee Jaladhh Baandhh
Dhhroo Thhaapiou Ho |Naamae Kae Suaamee Seea Behoree Lank Bhabheekhan
Aapiou Ho |4|2|Page-656

Those who serve the Lord; whatever they ask, He gives them in plenty. Says Nanak, whatever the Lord's devotee utters from his mouth, is proven to be true here and hereafter!

---

ਧਨਾਸਰੀ ਮਹਲਾ ੫ ॥
ਜੋ ਮਾਗਹਿ ਠਾਕੁਰ ਅਪੁਨੇ ਤੇ ਸੋਈ ਸੋਈ ਦੇਵੈ ॥
ਨਾਨਕ ਦਾਸੁ ਮੁਖ ਤੇ ਜੋ ਬੋਲੈ ਈਹਾ ਊਹਾ ਸਚੁ ਹੋਵੈ ॥੨॥੧੪॥੪੫॥
Dhhanaasaree 5th Guru |
Jo Maagehi Thaakur Apunae Thae Soee Soee Dhaevai |
Naanak Dhaas Mukh Thae Jo Bolai Eehaa Oohaa Sach Hovai |2|14|45|
Page-681

---

O' brother, always Contemplate on the Name of the Lord. This Awareness of the Lord of the Universe gives you happiness in this world and the world hereafter. The sins of many past lives can be erased in the *Saadh Sangat,* the Company of the Holy, wherein new life can be infused in the internally dead!

---

ਧਨਾਸਰੀ ਮਹਲਾ ੫ ॥
ਹਲਤਿ ਸੁਖ ਪਲਤਿ ਸੁਖ ਨਿਤ ਸੁਖ ਸਿਮਰਨੋ ਨਾਮੁ ਗੋਬਿੰਦ ਕਾ ਸਦਾ ਲੀਜੈ ॥
ਮਿਟਹਿ ਕਮਾਣੇ ਪਾਪ ਚਿਰਾਣੇ ਸਾਧਸੰਗਤਿ ਮਿਲਿ ਮੁਆ ਜੀਜੈ ॥੧॥ ਰਹਾਉ ॥
Dhhanaasaree 5th Guru |
Halath Sukh Palath Sukh Nith Sukh Simarano Naam Gobindh Kaa Sadhaa Leejai
|Mittehi Kamaanae Paap Chiraanae Saadhhasangath Mil Muaa Jeejai |1| Pause |
Page-683

---

O' Lord, we humans after wandering through many incarnations, have come to Your Sanctuary. Please save us from the dark dungeons of the worldly illusion (Maya) and keep us attached to Your Feet. I do not know anything about spiritual wisdom, meditation or karma. My mind does not stay attuned to You and I do not know how to perform good deeds. Please attach me to the hem of the robe of the *Saadh Sangat*, the Company of the Holy; so, that I may cross over the terrible world ocean.

---

ਜੈਤਸਰੀ ਮਹਲਾ ੫ ॥
ਆਏ ਅਨਿਕ ਜਨਮ ਭ੍ਰਮਿ ਸਰਣੀ ॥ ਉਧਰੁ ਦੇਹ ਅੰਧ ਕੂਪ ਤੇ ਲਾਵਹੁ ਅਪੁਨੀ ਚਰਣੀ ॥੧॥ ਰਹਾਉ ॥
ਗਿਆਨੁ ਧਿਆਨੁ ਕਿਛੁ ਕਰਮੁ ਨ ਜਾਨਾ ਨਾਹਿਨ ਨਿਰਮਲ ਕਰਣੀ ॥
ਸਾਧਸੰਗਤਿ ਕੈ ਅੰਚਲਿ ਲਾਵਹੁ ਬਿਖਮ ਨਦੀ ਜਾਇ ਤਰਣੀ ॥੧॥
Jaithasaree 5th Guru |
Aaeae Anik Janam Bhram Saranee |
Oudhhar Dhaeh Andhh Koop Thae Laavahu Apunee Charanee |1| Rehaao |
Giaan Dhhiaan Kishh Karam N Jaanaa Naahin Niramal Karanee |
Saadhhasangath Kai Anchal Laavahu Bikham Nadhee Jaae Tharanee |1|
Page-702

O' Lord, Your Saints are extremely fortunate as Your Name abides in their hearts. Their coming into this world is Your blessing and they lead successful lives. My Lord, I am a sacrifice to these Saints. I will make my hair into a fan to wave over them and apply the dust of their feet to my face. The Saints are above the cycle of life and death and come here for the good of others. They show the path of a spiritual life, inculcate Awareness of God and ultimately connect you with God.

---

ਸੂਹੀ ਮਹਲਾ ੫ ॥
ਭਾਗਠੜੇ ਹਰਿ ਸੰਤ ਤੁਮ੍ਹਾਰੇ ਜਿਨ੍ਹ ਘਰਿ ਧਨੁ ਹਰਿ ਨਾਮਾ ॥
ਪਰਵਾਣੁ ਗਣੀ ਸੇਈ ਇਹ ਆਏ ਸਫਲ ਤਿਨਾ ਕੇ ਕਾਮਾ ॥੧॥
ਮੇਰੇ ਰਾਮ ਹਰਿ ਜਨ ਕੈ ਹਉ ਬਲਿ ਜਾਈ ॥
ਕੇਸਾ ਕਾ ਕਰਿ ਚਵਰੁ ਢੁਲਾਵਾ ਚਰਣ ਧੂਰਿ ਮੁਖਿ ਲਾਈ ॥੧॥ ਰਹਾਉ ॥
ਜਨਮ ਮਰਣ ਦੁਹਹੂ ਮਹਿ ਨਾਹੀ ਜਨ ਪਰਉਪਕਾਰੀ ਆਏ ॥
ਜੀਅ ਦਾਨੁ ਦੇ ਭਗਤੀ ਲਾਇਨਿ ਹਰਿ ਸਿਉ ਲੈਨਿ ਮਿਲਾਏ ॥੨॥
Soohee 5th Guru |
Bhaagatharrae Har Santh Thumhaarae Jinh Ghar Dhhan Har Naamaa |
Paravaan Ganee Saeee Eih Aaeae Safal Thinaa Kae Kaamaa |1|
Maerae Raam Har Jan Kai Ho Bal Jaaee |
Kaesaa Kaa Kar Chavar Dtulaavaa Charan Dhhoorr Mukh Laaee |1| Pause |
Janam Maran Dhuhehoo Mehi Naahee Jan Paroupakaaree Aaeae |
Jeea Dhaan Dhae Bhagathee Laaein Har Sio Lain Milaaeae |2| Page-749

Says Kabeer, they bundled me up, and threw me before an elephant. The elephant driver struck him on the head to run over me, but the elephant ran away screaming! I am a sacrifice to this image of the Lord; Oh my Master, this is Your strength! The Mullah yelled out, "O driver, I shall cut you into pieces; hit him, and drive him on!" But the elephant did not move and became silent! He heard the Lord say, "What sin has this Saint committed, that he is bundled up and thrown before the elephant?" Lifting the bundle, the elephant bows down before it! The Mullah could not understand; he was blind. Three times, he tried to do it; even then his hardened mind was not satisfied. Says Kabeer, such is my Lord and Master; the soul of His humble servant dwells in Him.

ਰਾਗੁ ਗਾਂਡੀ ਕਬੀਰ ਜੀਉ ਕੀ ॥
ਭੁਜਾ ਬਾਂਧਿ ਭਿਲਾ ਕਰਿ ਡਾਰਿਓ ॥ ਹਸਤੀ ਕ੍ਰੋਪਿ ਮੂੰਡ ਮਹਿ ਮਾਰਿਓ ॥
ਹਸਤਿ ਭਾਗਿ ਕੈ ਚੀਸਾ ਮਾਰੈ ॥ ਇਆ ਮੂਰਤਿ ਕੈ ਹਉ ਬਲਿਹਾਰੈ ॥੧॥
ਆਹਿ ਮੇਰੇ ਠਾਕੁਰ ਤੁਮਰਾ ਜੋਰੁ ॥ ਕਾਜੀ ਬਕਿਬੋ ਹਸਤੀ ਤੋਰੁ ॥੧॥ ਰਹਾਉ ॥
ਰੇ ਮਹਾਵਤ ਤੁਝੁ ਡਾਰਉ ਕਾਟਿ ॥ ਇਸਹਿ ਤੁਰਾਵਹੁ ਘਾਲਹੁ ਸਾਟਿ ॥
ਹਸਤਿ ਨ ਤੋਰੈ ਧਰੈ ਧਿਆਨੁ ॥ ਵਾ ਕੈ ਰਿਦੈ ਬਸੈ ਭਗਵਾਨੁ ॥੨॥
ਕਿਆ ਅਪਰਾਧੁ ਸੰਤ ਹੈ ਕੀਨਹਾ ॥ ਬਾਂਧਿ ਪੋਟ ਕੁੰਚਰ ਕਉ ਦੀਨਹਾ ॥
ਕੁੰਚਰੁ ਪੋਟ ਲੈ ਲੈ ਨਮਸਕਾਰੈ ॥ ਬੂਝੀ ਨਹੀ ਕਾਜੀ ਅੰਧਿਆਰੈ ॥੩॥
ਤੀਨਿ ਬਾਰ ਪਤੀਆ ਭਰਿ ਲੀਨਾ ॥ ਮਨ ਕਠੋਰੁ ਅਜਹੂ ਨ ਪਤੀਨਾ ॥
ਕਹਿ ਕਬੀਰ ਹਮਰਾ ਗੋਬਿੰਦੁ ॥ ਚਉਥੇ ਪਦ ਮਹਿ ਜਨ ਕੀ ਜਿੰਦੁ ॥੪॥੧॥੪॥

Raag Gonadd Baanee Kabeer Jeeo Kee |
Bhujaa Baandhh Bhilaa Kar Ddaariou |Hasathee Krop Moondd Mehi Maariou |
Hasath Bhaag Kai Cheesaa Maarai |Eiaa Moorath Kai Ho Balihaarai |1|
Aahi Maerae Thaakur Thumaraa Jor |Kaajee Bakibo Hasathee Thor |1| Pause |
Rae Mehaavath Thujh Ddaaro Kaatt |Eisehi Thuraavahu Ghaalahu Saatt |
Hasath N Thorai Dhharai Dhhiaan |Vaa Kai Ridhai Basai Bhagavaan |2|
Kiaa Aparaadhh Santh Hai Keenhaa |Baandhh Pott Kunchar Ko Dheenhaa |

Kunchar Pott Lai Lai Namasakaarai |Boojhee Nehee Kaajee Andhhiaarai |3|
Theen Baar Patheeaa Bhar Leenaa |Man Kathor Ajehoo N Patheenaa |
Kehi Kabeer Hamaraa Gobindh |Chouthhae Padh Mehi Jan Kee Jindh |4|1|4|
Page-870

---

Meditate on the Lord of the Universe, the Beloved Lord of the World. Meditating in remembrance on the Lord's Name, you shall live a high spiritual life, and the mighty Death shall never consume your true self ever again. Through millions of incarnations, you have come, wandering, wandering, and wandering. By the greatest fortune, you have found the *Saadh Sangat*, the Company of the Holy. After deep reflection, Elderly Nanak says to you the bottom line, "without submitting to the Perfect Guru, you cannot be saved."

---

ਰਾਮਕਲੀ ਮਹਲਾ ੫ ॥
ਜਪਿ ਗੋਬਿੰਦੁ ਗੋਪਾਲ ਲਾਲੁ ॥ ਰਾਮ ਨਾਮ ਸਿਮਰਿ ਤੂ ਜੀਵਹਿ ਫਿਰਿ ਨ ਖਾਈ ਮਹਾ ਕਾਲੁ ॥੧॥ ਰਹਾਉ ॥
ਕੋਟਿ ਜਨਮ ਭ੍ਰਮਿ ਭ੍ਰਮਿ ਭ੍ਰਮਿ ਆਇਓ ॥ ਬਡੈ ਭਾਗਿ ਸਾਧਸੰਗੁ ਪਾਇਓ ॥੧॥
ਬਿਨੁ ਗੁਰ ਪੂਰੇ ਨਾਹੀ ਉਧਾਰੁ ॥ ਬਾਬਾ ਨਾਨਕੁ ਆਖੈ ਏਹੁ ਬੀਚਾਰੁ ॥੨॥੧੧॥
Raamakalee 5th Guru |
Jap Gobindh Gopaal Laal |
Raam Naam Simar Thoo Jeevehi Fir N Khaaee Mehaa Kaal |1|Pause |
Kott Janam Bhram Bhram Bhram Aaeiou |
Baddai Bhaag Saadhhasang Paaeiou |1|
Bin Gur Poorae Naahee Oudhhaar |
Baabaa Naanak Aakhai Eaehu Beechaar |2|11|   Page-885

If being God Oriented is going astray; a stream flowing near the sacred river Ganges goes astray and ends up merging with the holy Ganges! Just so, for God's sake, Kabeer has gone astray and merged with the Lord and is now totally calm. Encountering the philosophers' stone, copper is transformed into gold. In the Holy Company of the Saints, *Saadh Sangat*, Kabeer is transformed; and has ended up becoming One with the Lord.

---

ਭੈਰਉ ਬਾਣੀ ਭਗਤਾ ਕੀ ॥ ਕਬੀਰ ਜੀਉ ॥
ਗੰਗਾ ਕੈ ਸੰਗਿ ਸਲਿਤਾ ਬਿਗਰੀ ॥ਸੋ ਸਲਿਤਾ ਗੰਗਾ ਹੋਇ ਨਿਬਰੀ ॥੧॥
ਬਿਗਰਿਓ ਕਬੀਰਾ ਰਾਮ ਦੁਹਾਈ ॥ਸਾਚੁ ਭਇਓ ਅਨ ਕਤਹਿ ਨ ਜਾਈ ॥੧॥ ਰਹਾਉ ॥
ਪਾਰਸ ਕੈ ਸੰਗਿ ਤਾਂਬਾ ਬਿਗਰਿਓ ॥ਸੋ ਤਾਂਬਾ ਕੰਚਨੁ ਹੋਇ ਨਿਬਰਿਓ ॥੩॥
ਸੰਤਨ ਸੰਗਿ ਕਬੀਰਾ ਬਿਗਰਿਓ ॥ਸੋ ਕਬੀਰੁ ਰਾਮੈ ਹੋਇ ਨਿਬਰਿਓ ॥੪॥੫॥
Bhairo Baanee Bhagathaa Kee | Kabeer Jeeo |
Gangaa Kai Sang Salithaa Bigaree | So Salithaa Gangaa Hoe Nibaree |1|
Bigariou Kabeeraa Raam Dhuhaaee |
Saach Bhaeiou An Kathehi N Jaaee |1|Pause |
|Paaras Kai Sang Thaanbaa Bigariou | So Thaanbaa Kanchan Hoe Nibariou |3|
Santhan Sang Kabeeraa Bigariou | So Kabeer Raamai Hoe Nibariou |4|5|
Page-1158

They tied me up (Kabeer) in chains and took me to the profoundly deep river Ganges (which they call Mother), to throw me in and kill me. O' brother, the man who is attuned to the Lord's lotus feet, his mind is never shaken, there is no use in scaring his body!

But, instead of drowning, the waves of the Ganges broke my chains and I started floating as though I am sitting on a deer skin! Says Kabeer, there is no friend or companion who can save you; it is only the Lord of the Universe who is our protector on land and water.

---

ਭੈਰਉ ਬਾਣੀ ਭਗਤਾ ਕੀ ॥ ਕਬੀਰ ਜੀਉ ॥

ਗੰਗ ਗੁਸਾਇਨਿ ਗਹਿਰ ਗੰਭੀਰ ॥ ਜੰਜੀਰ ਬਾਂਧਿ ਕਰਿ ਖਰੇ ਕਬੀਰ ॥੧॥

ਮਨੁ ਨ ਡਿਗੈ ਤਨੁ ਕਾਹੇ ਕਉ ਡਰਾਇ ॥ ਚਰਨ ਕਮਲ ਚਿਤੁ ਰਹਿਓ ਸਮਾਇ ॥ ਰਹਾਉ ॥

ਗੰਗਾ ਕੀ ਲਹਰਿ ਮੇਰੀ ਟੂਟੀ ਜੰਜੀਰ ॥ ਮ੍ਰਿਗਛਾਲਾ ਪਰ ਬੈਠੇ ਕਬੀਰ ॥੨॥

ਕਹਿ ਕੰਬੀਰ ਕੋਉ ਸੰਗ ਨ ਸਾਥ ॥ ਜਲ ਥਲ ਰਾਖਨ ਹੈ ਰਘੁਨਾਥ ॥੩॥੧੦॥੧੮॥

Bhairo Baanee Bhagathaa Kee | Kabeer Jeeo |
Gang Gusaaein Gehir Ganbheer | Janjeer Baandhh Kar Kharae Kabeer |1|
Man N Ddigai Than Kaahae Ko Ddaraae |
Charan Kamal Chith Rehiou Samaae |Pause |
Gangaa Kee Lehar Maeree Ttuttee Janjeer |
Mrigashhaalaa Par Baithae Kabeer |2|
Kehi Kanbeer Kooo Sang N Saathh |
Jal Thhal Raakhan Hai Raghunaathh |3|10|18|  Page-1162

O, brother, if you long for eternal peace, then join the *Saadh Sangat*, the Company of the Holy; this is the Guru's advice. There, only the Name of the Lord, is contemplated; in the Company of the Holy, *Saadh Sangat*, you can cross the worldly ocean.

ਬਸੰਤੁ ਮਹਲਾ ੫ ॥
ਜੇ ਲੋੜਹਿ ਸਦਾ ਸੁਖੁ ਭਾਈ ॥ ਸਾਧੂ ਸੰਗਤਿ ਗੁਰਹਿ ਬਤਾਈ ॥
ਉਹਾ ਜਪੀਐ ਕੇਵਲ ਨਾਮ ॥ ਸਾਧੂ ਸੰਗਤਿ ਪਾਰਗਰਾਮ ॥੩॥
Basanth 5<sup>th</sup> Guru |
Jae Lorrehi Sadhaa Sukh Bhaaee | Saadhhoo Sangath Gurehi Bathaaee |
Oohaa Japeeai Kaeval Naam | Saadhhoo Sangath Paaragaraam |3|
Page-1182

O' my Beautiful Lord, please do not forget me; please do not forget; please do not forget me. The temple priests say, they are of the higher caste; they call me the untouchable, have beaten me up and thrown me out of the temple! What should I do, O' Beloved Father? If You give me salvation after death no one will know of this liberation; these priests call me low caste and hence tarnish Your Honor. Can your devotee stay low caste?

You are called kind, compassionate, the embodiment of Grace, and then Infinitely Powerful. Upon listening to the prayer, the Lord turned the temple around* to face Naam Dayv; and turned His back on the priests!

*This temple near Bombay, India with its face turned behind the street front still exists and is a landmark to visit.

---

ਰਾਗੁ ਮਲਾਰ ਬਾਣੀ ਭਗਤ ਨਾਮਦੇਵ ਜੀਉ ਕੀ ॥ਮੋ ਕਉ ਤੂੰ ਨ ਬਿਸਾਰਿ ਤੂ ਨ ਬਿਸਾਰਿ ॥ਤੂ ਨ ਬਿਸਾਰੇ ਰਾਮਈਆ ॥੧॥ ਰਹਾਉ ॥ਆਲਾਵੰਤੀ ਇਹੁ ਭ੍ਰਮੁ ਜੋ ਹੈ ਮੁਝ ਉਪਰਿ ਸਭ ਕੋਪਿਲਾ ॥ਸੂਦੁ ਸੂਦੁ ਕਰਿ ਮਾਰਿ ਉਠਾਇਓ ਕਹਾ ਕਰਉ ਬਾਪ ਬੀਠੁਲਾ ॥੧॥ਮੂਏ ਹੂਏ ਜਉ ਮੁਕਤਿ ਦੇਹੁਗੇ ਮੁਕਤਿ ਨ ਜਾਨੈ ਕੋਇਲਾ ॥ਏ ਪੰਡੀਆ ਮੋ ਕਉ ਢੇਢ ਕਹਤ ਤੇਰੀ ਪੈਜ ਪਿਛੰਉਡੀ ਹੋਇਲਾ ॥੨॥ਤੂ ਜੁ ਦਇਆਲੁ ਕ੍ਰਿਪਾਲੁ ਕਹੀਅਤੁ ਹੈਂ ਅਤਿਭੁਜ ਭਇਓ ਅਪਾਰਲਾ ॥ਫੇਰਿ ਦੀਆ ਦੇਹੁਰਾ ਨਾਮੇ ਕਉ ਪੰਡੀਅਨ ਕਉ ਪਿਛਵਾਰਲਾ ॥੩॥੨॥

Raag Malaar Baanee Bhagath Naamadhaev Jeeo Kee |Mo Ko Thoon N Bisaar Thoo N Bisaar |Thoo N Bisaarae Raameeaa |1| Rehaao |
Aalaavanthee Eihu Bhram Jo Hai Mujh Oopar Sabh Kopilaa |Soodh Soodh Kar Maar Outhaaeiou Kehaa Karo Baap Beethulaa |1|Mooeae Hooeae Jo Mukath Dhaehugae Mukath N Jaanai Koeilaa |Eae Panddeeaa Mo Ko Dtaedt Kehath Thaeree Paij Pishhanouddee Hoeilaa |2|Thoo J Dhaeiaal Kirapaal Keheeath Hain Athibhuj Bhaeiou Apaaralaa |Faer Dheeaa Dhaehuraa Naamae Ko Panddeean Ko Pishhavaaralaa |3|2| Page-1292

Saint/God & Holy Company (Saadh Sangat)

I have totally overcome my jealousy of others, Since I found the *Saadh Sangat*, the Company of the Holy. No one is my enemy, and no one is a stranger. I get along equally with everyone. Whatever God does, I accept that as good. This is the sublime wisdom I have obtained from the Holy. The One God is pervading in all. Gazing upon Him, beholding Him, Nanak blossoms forth in happiness.

---

ਕਾਨੜਾ ਮਹਲਾ ੫ ॥
ਬਿਸਰਿ ਗਈ ਸਭ ਤਾਤਿ ਪਰਾਈ ॥ ਜਬ ਤੇ ਸਾਧਸੰਗਤਿ ਮੋਹਿ ਪਾਈ ॥੧॥ ਰਹਾਉ ॥
ਨਾ ਕੋ ਬੈਰੀ ਨਹੀ ਬਿਗਾਨਾ ਸਗਲ ਸੰਗਿ ਹਮ ਕਉ ਬਨਿ ਆਈ ॥੧॥
ਜੋ ਪ੍ਰਭ ਕੀਨੋ ਸੋ ਭਲ ਮਾਨਿਓ ਏਹ ਸੁਮਤਿ ਸਾਧੂ ਤੇ ਪਾਈ ॥੨॥
ਸਭ ਮਹਿ ਰਵਿ ਰਹਿਆ ਪ੍ਰਭੁ ਏਕੈ ਪੇਖਿ ਪੇਖਿ ਨਾਨਕ ਬਿਗਸਾਈ ॥੩॥੮॥
Kaanarraa 5th Guru |
Bisar Gee Sabh Thaath Paraaee | Jab Thae Saadhhasangath Mohi Paaee |1|Pause |
Naa Ko Bairee Nehee Bigaanaa Sagal Sang Ham Ko Ban Aaee |1|
Jo Prabh Keeno So Bhal Maaniou Eaeh Sumath Saadhhoo Thae Paaee |2|
Sabh Mehi Rav Rehiaa Prabh Eaekai Paekh Paekh Naanak Bigasaaee |3|8|
Page-1299

Spiritual Gems    220

Kabeer, my mind has become immaculate, like the holy waters of the Ganges. The Lord now walks behind me; saying, "Kabeer! Kabeer!"

ਸਲੋਕ ਭਗਤ ਕਬੀਰ ਜੀਉ ਕੇ ॥
ਕਬੀਰ ਮਨੁ ਨਿਰਮਲੁ ਭਇਆ ਜੈਸਾ ਗੰਗਾ ਨੀਰੁ ਪਾਛੈ ਲਾਗੋ ਹਰਿ ਫਿਰੈ ਕਹਤ ਕਬੀਰ ਕਬੀਰ ॥੫੫॥
Salok Bhagath Kabeer Jeeo Kae |
Kabeer Man Niramal Bhaeiaa Jaisaa Gangaa Neer |
Paashhai Laago Har Firai Kehath Kabeer Kabeer |55|  Page-1367

Kabeer, never leave the track of the Saints; keep walking upon this Path. Seeing them you are purified and meeting them, you begin to contemplate on the Lord's Name.

ਸਲੋਕ ਭਗਤ ਕਬੀਰ ਜੀਉ ਕੇ ॥
ਕਬੀਰ ਸੰਤ ਕੀ ਗੈਲ ਨ ਛੋਡੀਐ ਮਾਰਗਿ ਲਾਗਾ ਜਾਉ ॥
ਪੇਖਤ ਹੀ ਪੁੰਨੀਤ ਹੋਇ ਭੇਟਤ ਜਪੀਐ ਨਾਉ ॥੧੩੦॥
Salok Bhagath Kabeer Jeeo Kae |
Kabeer Santh Kee Gail N Shhoddeeai Maarag Laagaa Jaao |
Paekhath Hee Punneeth Hoe Bhaettath Japeeai Naao |130|  Page-1371

Kabeer, it is good to perform selfless service for both the Saint and the Lord. The Lord is the Giver of liberation, and the Saint inspires us to contemplate on the Lord's Name.

---

ਸਲੋਕ ਭਗਤ ਕਬੀਰ ਜੀਉ ਕੇ ॥
ਕਬੀਰ ਸੇਵਾ ਕਉ ਦੁਇ ਭਲੇ ਏਕੁ ਸੰਤੁ ਇਕੁ ਰਾਮੁ ॥
ਰਾਮੁ ਜੁ ਦਾਤਾ ਮੁਕਤਿ ਕੋ ਸੰਤੁ ਜਪਾਵੈ ਨਾਮੁ ॥੧੬੪॥
Salok Bhagath Kabeer Jeeo Kae |
Kabeer Saevaa Ko Dhue Bhalae Eaek Santh Eik Raam ||
Raam J Dhaathaa Mukath Ko Santh Japaavai Naam |164|   Page-1373

---

Says Nanak, please bless me, O' God. Have Mercy upon me, and give me the Company of the Holy, the *Saadh Sangat*.

---

ਸੂਹੀ ਮਹਲਾ ੫ ॥
ਕਹੁ ਨਾਨਕ ਪ੍ਰਭ ਬਖਸ ਕਰੀਜੈ ॥ ਕਰਿ ਕਿਰਪਾ ਮੋਹਿ ਸਾਧਸੰਗੁ ਦੀਜੈ ॥੪॥
Soohee 5th Guru |
Kahu Naanak Prabh Bakhas Kareejai |
Kar Kirapaa Mohi Saadhhasang Dheejai |4|   Page-738

Says Kabeer, I was going on a pilgrimage to Mecca, and God met me on the way. He scolded me and asked, "Who told you that I live only there?"
Says Kabeer, repeating, ""You, You"", I have become You; nothing of me remains in myself. When the difference between myself and others is removed, then wherever I look, I see only You!

---

ਸਲੋਕ ਭਗਤ ਕਬੀਰ ਜੀਉ ਕੇ ॥
ਕਬੀਰ ਹਜ ਕਾਬੇ ਹਉ ਜਾਇ ਥਾ ਆਗੈ ਮਿਲਿਆ ਖੁਦਾਇ ॥
ਸਾਂਈ ਮੁਝ ਸਿਉ ਲਰਿ ਪਰਿਆ ਤੁਝੈ ਕਿਨ੍ਹਿ ਫੁਰਮਾਈ ਗਾਇ ॥੧੯੭॥
ਕਬੀਰ ਤੂੰ ਤੂੰ ਕਰਤਾ ਤੂ ਹੂਆ ਮੁਝ ਮਹਿ ਰਹਾ ਨ ਹੂੰ ॥
ਜਬ ਆਪਾ ਪਰ ਕਾ ਮਿਟਿ ਗਇਆ ਜਤ ਦੇਖਉ ਤਤ ਤੂ ॥੨੦੪॥
Salok Bhagath Kabeer Jeeo Kae |
Kabeer Haj Kaabae Ho Jaae Thhaa Aagai Miliaa Khudhaae |
Saanee Mujh Sio Lar Pariaa Thujhai Kinih Furamaaee Gaae |197|
Kabeer Thoon Thoon Karathaa Thoo Hooaa Mujh Mehi Rehaa N Hoon |
Jab Aapaa Par Kaa Mitt Gaeiaa Jath Dhaekho Thath Thoo |204|   Page-1375

## Chapter-15   Coming Face to Face with God

O' my sister friends, my deepest desire has been fulfilled; My Husband Lord has come to abide in my heart! Now, rejoice and sing the auspicious songs of happiness at this union of the Husband and wife. Singing the songs of joyful praise and love to Him, the soul-bride's mind is thrilled and delighted. With clasped hands, the soul-bride prays, that she may remain immersed in the Love of her Husband, day and night. Says Nanak, my deepest desire has been fulfilled, the Husband Lord and the soul-bride revel together in bliss!

ਰਾਗੁ ਗਉੜੀ ਪੂਰਬੀ ਛੰਤ ਮਹਲਾ ੧ ॥
ਮੇਰੀ ਇਛ ਪੁਨੀ ਜੀਉ ਹਮ ਘਰਿ ਸਾਜਨੁ ਆਇਆ ॥ ਮਿਲਿ ਵਰੁ ਨਾਰੀ ਮੰਗਲੁ ਗਾਇਆ ॥
ਗੁਣ ਗਾਇ ਮੰਗਲੁ ਪ੍ਰੇਮਿ ਰਹਸੀ ਮੁੰਧ ਮਨਿ ਓਮਾਹਓ ॥  ਕਰ ਜੋੜਿ ਸਾ ਧਨ ਕਰੈ ਬਿਨਤੀ ਰੈਣਿ ਦਿਨੁ ਰਸਿ
ਭਿੰਨੀਆ ॥ ਨਾਨਕ ਪਿਰੁ ਧਨ ਕਰਹਿ ਰਲੀਆ ਇਛ ਮੇਰੀ ਪੁੰਨੀਆ ॥੪॥੧॥
Raag Gourree Poorabee Shhanth 1st Guru |
Maeree Eishh Punee Jeeo Ham Ghar Saajan Aaeiaa |
Mil Var Naaree Mangal Gaaeiaa |
Gun Gaae Mangal Praem Rehasee Mundhh Man Oumaahou |
Kar Jorr Saa Dhhan Karai Binathee Rain Dhin Ras Bhinneeaa |
Naanak Pir Dhhan Karehi Raleeaa Eishh Maeree Punneeaa |4||1|        Page-242

O' sister, tell me how your face is glowing red? With what make-up, have you acquired this profoundly beautiful look? You look so pretty in the red dress you are wearing! It seems that the Husband Lord loves you; that is why you have also captivated my mind! You are looking extremely beautiful, indeed your Husband Lord by great fortune has come to abide in you!

---

ਰਾਗੁ ਆਸਾ ਮਹਲਾ ੫ ॥
ਲਾਲੁ ਚੋਲਨਾ ਤੈ ਤਨਿ ਸੋਹਿਆ ॥ ਸੁਰਿਜਨ ਭਾਨੀ ਤਾਂ ਮਨੁ ਮੋਹਿਆ ॥੧॥
ਕਵਨ ਬਨੀ ਰੀ ਤੇਰੀ ਲਾਲੀ ॥ ਕਵਨ ਰੰਗਿ ਤੂੰ ਭਈ ਗੁਲਾਲੀ ॥੧॥ ਰਹਾਉ ॥
ਤੁਮ ਹੀ ਸੁੰਦਰਿ ਤੁਮਹਿ ਸੁਹਾਗੁ ॥ ਤੁਮ ਘਰਿ ਲਾਲਨੁ ਤੁਮ ਘਰਿ ਭਾਗੁ ॥੨॥
Raag Aasaa 5<sup>th</sup> Guru |
Laal Cholanaa Thai Than Sohiaa | Surijan Bhaanee Thaan Man Mohiaa |1|
Kavan Banee Ree Thaeree Laalee |
Kavan Rang Thoon Bhee Gulaalee |1| Pause |
Thum Hee Sundhar Thumehi Suhaag | Thum Ghar Laalan Thum Ghar Bhaag |2|
Page-384

He is "beyond description" of the Vedas (Hindu), and the religious books of the Muslim, Christian and Jewish faiths. The Supreme Lord/King of Nanak is clearly seen manifest everywhere.

Note: Meaning, He cannot be "described" including in any Holy Scripture, but can be realized thru His Grace.

---

ਆਸਾ ਮਹਲਾ ੫ ॥
ਬੇਦ ਕਤੇਬ ਸੰਸਾਰ ਹਭਾ ਹੂੰ ਬਾਹਰਾ ॥ਨਾਨਕ ਕਾ ਪਾਤਿਸਾਹੁ ਦਿਸੈ ਜਾਹਰਾ ॥੪॥੩॥੧੦੫॥
Aasaa 5th Guru | Baedh Kathaeb Sansaar Habhaa Hoon Baaharaa |
Naanak Kaa Paathisaahu Dhisai Jaaharaa |4|3|105|  Page-397

---

O' brother, I am full of joy and bliss, because I have come face to face with the Lord! I have tasted the Ambrosial Nectar of God's Name. Says Nanak, now my mind is immersed in the Lord as I have seen the Lord with my eyes!

---

ਰਾਗੁ ਆਸਾ ਮਹਲਾ ੫ ॥
ਅਨਦੋ ਅਨਦੁ ਘਣਾ ਮੈ ਸੋ ਪ੍ਰਭੁ ਡੀਠਾ ਰਾਮ ॥ ਚਾਖਿਅੜਾ ਚਾਖਿਅੜਾ ਮੈ ਹਰਿ ਰਸੁ ਮੀਠਾ ਰਾਮ ॥
ਕਹੁ ਨਾਨਕ ਹਰਿ ਸਿਉ ਮਨੁ ਮਾਨਿਆ ਸੋ ਪ੍ਰਭੁ ਨੈਣੀ ਡੀਠਾ ॥੧॥
Raag Aasaa 5th Guru |
Anadho Anadh Ghanaa Mai So Prabh Ddeethaa Raam |
Chaakhiarraa Chaakhiarraa Mai Har Ras Meethaa Raam |
Kahu Naanak Har Sio Man Maaniaa So Prabh Nainee Ddeethaa |1|  Page-452

O' my sister friend, when I heard the Lord coming towards me, my mind was overtaken by bliss and my inner self was adorned in splendor! Meeting God, the Lord/Master, I have entered the realm of peace; I am filled with joy and delight. He is joined to me, in my very fiber; my sorrows have departed, and my body, mind, and soul are all rejuvenated. My sister friends ask me, "please tell us a sign of recognizing the Husband Lord?" I am overflowing with His Love and Bliss, but I cannot utter a single word!

---

ਆਸਾ ਮਹਲਾ ੫ ਛੰਤ ॥
ਮੇਰੀ ਸੇਜੜੀਐ ਆਡੰਬਰੁ ਬਣਿਆ ॥ ਮਨਿ ਅਨਦੁ ਭਇਆ ਪ੍ਰਭੁ ਆਵਤ ਸੁਣਿਆ ॥
ਪ੍ਰਭ ਮਿਲੇ ਸੁਆਮੀ ਸੁਖਹ ਗਾਮੀ ਚਾਵ ਮੰਗਲ ਰਸ ਭਰੇ ॥
ਅੰਗ ਸੰਗਿ ਲਾਗੇ ਦੂਖ ਭਾਗੇ ਪ੍ਰਾਣ ਮਨ ਤਨ ਸਭਿ ਹਰੇ ॥
ਮਿਲਿ ਸਖੀਆ ਪੁਛਹਿ ਕਹੁ ਕੰਤ ਨੀਸਾਣੀ ॥ ਰਸਿ ਪ੍ਰੇਮ ਭਰੀ ਕਛੁ ਬੋਲਿ ਨ ਜਾਣੀ ॥
Aasaa 5th Guru Shhanth |
Maeree Saejarreeai Aaddanbar Baniaa |
Man Anadh Bhaeiaa Prabh Aavath Suniaa |
Prabh Milae Suaamee Sukheh Gaamee Chaav Mangal Ras Bharae |
Ang Sang Laagae Dhookh Bhaagae Praan Man Than Sabh Harae |
Mil Sakheeaa Pushhehi Kahu Kanth Neesaanee |
Ras Praem Bharee Kashh Bol N Jaanee |  Page-459

O' the newly wed brides, sing again and again the sweet songs of the Husband Lord, because the Lord Master has come to live within me! Within the lotus of my heart, I have made my bridal pavilion, and have spoken the Truth. I am now the bride of my Bridegroom, Husband Lord! Such is my great fortune. The angles, holy men, silent sages, and the 33 million deities have come in their heavenly chariots to see this spectacle! Says Kabeer, the One Supreme Lord has married me and is taking me away!

---

ਆਸਾ ਸ੍ਰੀ ਕਬੀਰ ਜੀਉ ॥
ਗਾਉ ਗਾਉ ਰੀ ਦੁਲਹਨੀ ਮੰਗਲਚਾਰਾ ॥ ਮੇਰੇ ਗ੍ਰਿਹ ਆਏ ਰਾਜਾ ਰਾਮ ਭਤਾਰਾ ॥੧॥ ਰਹਾਉ ॥
ਨਾਭਿ ਕਮਲ ਮਹਿ ਬੇਦੀ ਰਚਿ ਲੇ ਬ੍ਰਹਮ ਗਿਆਨ ਉਚਾਰਾ ॥
ਰਾਮ ਰਾਇ ਸੋ ਦੂਲਹੁ ਪਾਇਓ ਅਸ ਬਡਭਾਗ ਹਮਾਰਾ ॥੨॥
ਸੁਰਿ ਨਰ ਮੁਨਿ ਜਨ ਕਉਤਕ ਆਏ ਕੋਟਿ ਤੇਤੀਸ ਉਜਾਨਾਂ ॥
ਕਹਿ ਕਬੀਰ ਮੋਹਿ ਬਿਆਹਿ ਚਲੇ ਹੈ ਪੁਰਖ ਏਕ ਭਗਵਾਨਾ ॥੩॥੨॥੨੪॥
Aasaa Sree Kabeer Jeeo |
Gaao Gaao Ree Dhulehanee Mangalachaaraa |
Maerae Grih Aaeae Raajaa Raam Bhathaaraa |1|Pause |
Naabh Kamal Mehi Baedhee Rach Lae Breham Giaan Ouchaaraa |
Raam Raae So Dhoolahu Paaeiou As Baddabhaag Hamaaraa |2|
Sur Nar Mun Jan Kouthak Aaeae Kott Thaethees Oujaanaan |
Kehi Kabeer Mohi Biaahi Chalae Hai Purakh Eaek Bhagavaanaa |3|2|24|
Page-482

---

First, there was only the Primal Being.  From that Primal Being, Maya (Illusion) was created.  Then with the coming together of the Lord and Illusion, this beautiful garden (world) was created; which is revolving like the pots in the Persian wheel.  There is no one other than the Lord; don't dispute this and don't doubt this.  O' Lord, like the pots in the Persian wheel, wandering and roaming, I have at last come and fallen at Your Door. "Who are you?" "I am Sir, Naamaa"; Yes, Sir!".  O Lord, please save me from Maya Illusion, the cause of death.

ਧਨਾਸਰੀ ਬਾਣੀ ਭਗਤ ਨਾਮਦੇਵ ਜੀ ਕੀ ॥
ਪਹਿਲ ਪੁਰਸਾਬਿਰਾ ॥ ਅਥੋਨ ਪੁਰਸਾਦਮਰਾ ॥ ਅਸਗਾ ਅਸ ਉਸਗਾ ॥ ਹਰਿ ਕਾ ਬਾਗਰਾ ਨਾਚੈ ਪਿੰਧੀ ਮਹਿ ਸਾਗਰਾ ॥੧॥ ਰਹਾਉ ॥
ਨਈਆ ਤੇ ਬੈਰੇ ਕੰਨਾ ॥ ਤਰਕੁ ਨ ਚਾ ॥ ਭੂਮੀਆ ਚਾ ॥
ਪਿੰਧੀ ਉਭਕਲੇ ਸੰਸਾਰਾ ॥ ਭ੍ਰਮਿ ਭ੍ਰਮਿ ਆਏ ਤੁਮ ਚੇ ਦੁਆਰਾ ॥
ਤੂ ਕੁਨੁ ਰੇ ॥ਮੈ ਜੀ ॥ ਨਾਮਾ ॥ ਹੋ ਜੀ ॥ਆਲਾ ਤੇ ਨਿਵਾਰਣਾ ਜਮ ਕਾਰਣਾ ॥੩॥੪॥
Dhhanaasaree Baanee Bhagath Naamadhaev Jee Kee |
Pehil Purasaabiraa |Athhon Purasaadhamaraa | Asagaa As Ousagaa | Har Kaa
Baagaraa Naachai Pindhhee Mehi Saagaraa |1| Rehaao |
Neeaa Thae Bairae Kannaa | Tharak N Chaa | Bhrameeaa Chaa |
Pindhhee Oubhakalae Sansaaraa |Bhram Bhram Aaeae Thum Chae Dhuaaraa |
Thoo Kun Rae |Mai Jee |Naamaa |Ho Jee |
Aalaa Thae Nivaaranaa Jam Kaaranaa |3|4|    Page-693

O' my dear friend, please listen to my prayer! I am searching the mind enticing sweet Beloved. Please tell me His whereabouts; I will sever my head and place it before Him to have the Divine Vision even for a moment. My eyes are drenched with the Love of my Beloved; without Him, I do not have even a moment's peace.

All the dear sisters are in the company of the Beloved Lord, but I am not pretty like them. They are all beautiful, one more than the other, how can anyone remember me?

The Lord Master has also grabbed my arm and made me His Companion without looking at my merits or demerits!

---

ਜੈਤਸਰੀ ਮਹਲਾ ੫ ॥
ਸੁਣਿ ਯਾਰ ਹਮਾਰੇ ਸਜਣ ਇਕ ਕਰਉ ਬੇਨੰਤੀਆ ॥
ਤਿਸੁ ਮੋਹਨ ਲਾਲ ਪਿਆਰੇ ਹਉ ਫਿਰਉ ਖੋਜੰਤੀਆ ॥
ਤਿਸੁ ਦਸਿ ਪਿਆਰੇ ਸਿਰੁ ਧਰੀ ਉਤਾਰੇ ਇਕ ਭੋਰੀ ਦਰਸਨੁ ਦੀਜੈ ॥
ਨੈਨ ਹਮਾਰੇ ਪ੍ਰਿਅ ਰੰਗ ਰੰਗਾਰੇ ਇਕੁ ਤਿਲੁ ਭੀ ਨਾ ਧੀਰੀਜੈ ॥
ਯਾਰ ਵੇ ਪ੍ਰਿਅ ਹਭੇ ਸਖੀਆ ਮੂ ਕਹੀ ਨ ਜੇਹੀਆ ॥
ਯਾਰ ਵੇ ਹਿਕ ਡੂੰ ਹਿਕਿ ਚਾੜੈ ਹਉ ਕਿਸੁ ਚਿਤੇਹੀਆ
ਬਾਂਹ ਪਕਰਿ ਠਾਕੁਰਿ ਹਉ ਘਿਧੀ ਗੁਣ ਅਵਗਣ ਨ ਪਛਾਣੇ ॥
Jaithasaree 5th Guru |
Sun Yaar Hamaarae Sajan Eik Karo Baenantheeaa |
This Mohan Laal Piaarae Ho Firo Khojantheeaa |
This Dhas Piaarae Sir Dhharee Outhaarae Eik Bhoree Dharasan Dheejai |
Nain Hamaarae Pria Rang Rangaarae Eik Thil Bhee Naa Dhheereejai |
Yaar Vae Pria Habhae Sakheeaa Moo Kehee N Jaeheeaa |
Yaar Vae Hik Ddoon Hik Chaarrai Ho Kis Chithaeheeaa |
Baanh Pakarr Thaakur Ho Ghidhhee Gun Avagan N Pashhaanae |     Page-703

---

My Friend, Lord has come into my heart! The True Lord has united me with Him! The Lord has ushered me into everlasting bliss and now I am in Love with the Lord. The five senses in lieu of indulging in perversions have come together in this bliss. I have obtained which my mind so desired; now day and night I am remembering the Lord's Name and my "inner self" has purified. The Five Primal Sounds, "Celestial Music" is playing; my Friend, Lord has come into my heart!

---

ਰਾਗੁ ਸੂਹੀ ਮਹਲਾ ੧॥
ਹਮ ਘਰਿ ਸਾਜਨ ਆਏ ॥ਸਾਚੈ ਮੇਲਿ ਮਿਲਾਏ ॥
ਸਹਜਿ ਮਿਲਾਏ ਹਰਿ ਮਨਿ ਭਾਏ ਪੰਚ ਮਿਲੇ ਸੁਖੁ ਪਾਇਆ ॥
ਸਾਈ ਵਸਤੁ ਪਰਾਪਤਿ ਹੋਈ ਜਿਸੁ ਸੇਤੀ ਮਨੁ ਲਾਇਆ ॥
ਅਨਦਿਨੁ ਮੇਲੁ ਭਇਆ ਮਨੁ ਮਾਨਿਆ ਘਰ ਮੰਦਰ ਸੋਹਾਏ ॥
ਪੰਚ ਸਬਦ ਧੁਨਿ ਅਨਹਦ ਵਾਜੇ ਹਮ ਘਰਿ ਸਾਜਨ ਆਏ ॥੧॥
Raag Soohee 1ˢᵗ Guru |
Ham Ghar Saajan Aaeae | Saachai Mael Milaaeae |
Sehaj Milaaeae Har Man Bhaaeae Panch Milae Sukh Paaeiaa |
Saaee Vasath Paraapath Hoee Jis Saethee Man Laaeiaa |
Anadhin Mael Bhaeiaa Man Maaniaa Ghar Mandhar Sohaaeae |
Panch Sabadh Dhhun Anehadh Vaajae Ham Ghar Saajan Aaeae |1|  Page-764

O' Lord, my Friend come! So, that I may behold Your
Blessed Vision. I stand in my doorway patiently, watching
for You; my mind is filled with such a great yearning!
Upon coming Face to Face with You, I have become desire
less; and my pain of birth and death is ended. Your Light is
in everyone; From that Light, You, are known. Through love,
You, are easily met with. Says Nanak, I am a sacrifice to my
Lord Friend; thru Truth He comes to live within you!

---

ਰਾਗੁ ਸੂਹੀ ਮਹਲਾ ੧॥
ਆਵਹੁ ਸਜਣਾ ਹਉ ਦੇਖਾ ਦਰਸਨੁ ਤੇਰਾ ਰਾਮ ॥ ਘਰਿ ਆਪਨੜੈ ਖੜੀ ਤਕਾ ਮੈ ਮਨਿ ਚਾਉ ਘਨੇਰਾ ਰਾਮ ॥
ਦਰਸਨੁ ਦੇਖਿ ਭਈ ਨਿਹਕੇਵਲ ਜਨਮ ਮਰਣ ਦੁਖ ਨਾਸਾ ॥
ਸਗਲੀ ਜੋਤਿ ਜਾਤਾ ਤੂ ਸੋਈ ਮਿਲਿਆ ਭਾਇ ਸੁਭਾਏ ॥
ਨਾਨਕ ਸਾਜਨ ਕਉ ਬਲਿ ਜਾਈਐ ਸਾਚਿ ਮਿਲੇ ਘਰਿ ਆਏ ॥੧॥
Raag Soohee 1ˢᵗ Guru |
Aavahu Sajanaa Ho Dhaekhaa Dharasan Thaeraa Raam |
Ghar Aapanarrai Kharree Thakaa Mai Man Chaao Ghanaeraa Raam |
Dharasan Dhaekh Bhee Nihakaeval Janam Maran Dhukh Naasaa |
Sagalee Joth Jaathaa Thoo Soee Miliaa Bhaae Subhaaeae |
Naanak Saajan Ko Bal Jaaeeai Saach Milae Ghar Aaeae |1|   Page-764

The Lord, my Friend has come to dwell within my heart!
Singing the glorious praises of the Lord, I am satisfied and
fulfilled. Says Nanak, He Himself joins and separates us;
there is no one other than the Lord. The Lord, my Friend has
come to dwell within my heart!

---

ਰਾਗੁ ਸੂਹੀ ਛੰਤ ਮਹਲਾ ੩ ॥
ਸਾਜਨ ਆਇ ਵੁਠੇ ਘਰ ਮਾਹੀ ॥ ਹਰਿ ਗੁਣ ਗਾਵਹਿ ਤ੍ਰਿਪਤਿ ਅਘਾਹੀ ॥
ਨਾਨਕ ਹਰਿ ਆਪੇ ਜੋੜਿ ਵਿਛੋੜੇ ਹਰਿ ਬਿਨੁ ਕੋ ਦੂਜਾ ਨਾਹੀ ॥
ਸਾਜਨ ਆਇ ਵੁਠੇ ਘਰ ਮਾਹੀ ॥੪॥੧॥
Raag Soohee Shhanth 3rd Guru |
Saajan Aae Vuthae Ghar Maahee |Har Gun Gaavehi Thripath Aghaahee |
Naanak Har Aapae Jorr Vishhorrae Har Bin Ko Dhoojaa Naahee |
Saajan Aae Vuthae Ghar Maahee |4|1|    Page-768

Coming Face to Face with God

Hearing the Guru's Word, the thirst to see God has welled up deep within me; I feel as though my heart is pierced by the arrow of separation from the Lord! The pain of my mind is known to my mind alone; who else can know the pain of another?
The Beloved Guru God, has filled my mind with His Love. Upon coming Face to Face with Him, I lost all my senses and have been thrown upside down!

---

ਬਿਲਾਵਲੁ ਮਹਲਾ ੪ ॥
ਅੰਤਰਿ ਪਿਆਸ ਉਠੀ ਪ੍ਰਭ ਕੇਰੀ ਸੁਣਿ ਗੁਰ ਬਚਨ ਮਨਿ ਤੀਰ ਲਗਾਈਆ ॥
ਮਨ ਕੀ ਬਿਰਥਾ ਮਨ ਹੀ ਜਾਣੈ ਅਵਰੁ ਕਿ ਜਾਣੈ ਕੋ ਪੀਰ ਪਰਾਈਆ ॥੧॥
ਰਾਮ ਗੁਰਿ ਮੋਹਨਿ ਮੋਹਿ ਮਨੁ ਲਈਆ ॥
ਹਉ ਆਕਲ ਬਿਕਲ ਭਈ ਗੁਰ ਦੇਖੇ ਹਉ ਲੋਟ ਪੋਟ ਹੋਇ ਪਈਆ ॥੧॥ ਰਹਾਉ ॥
Bilaaval 4th Guru |
Anthar Piaas Outhee Prabh Kaeree Sun Gur Bachan Man Theer Lageeaa |
Man Kee Birathhaa Man Hee Jaanai Avar K Jaanai Ko Peer Pareeaa |1|
Raam Gur Mohan Mohi Man Leeaa |
Ho Aakal Bikal Bhee Gur Dhaekhae Ho Lott Pott Hoe Peeaa |1| Pause |
Page-835

O' Lord, by Your Grace, the ballad singer may sing Your
Praises at Your Door. You are the Ever Stable; while others
come, and go. I beg the Lord Master to quench my hunger
for desires; O' Lord let me have Your Blessed Vision so that
I may be satisfied and fulfilled.

The Lord heard the prayer and called the ballad singer to His
Mansion! Coming Face to Face with the Lord, the hunger
and miseries disappeared and the ballad singer forgot to beg
for anything!

Coming into His Benevolent Presence all the desires were
fulfilled. The Primal Lord by His Grace pardoned the
humble unmeritorious ballad singer!

---

ਮਹਲਾ ੫ ॥ਪਉੜੀ ॥

ਹਉ ਢਾਢੀ ਹਰਿ ਗੁਣ ਗਾਵਦਾ ਜੇ ਹਰਿ ਪ੍ਰਭ ਭਾਵੈ ॥ ਪ੍ਰਭ ਮੇਰਾ ਥਿਰ ਥਾਵਰੀ ਹੋਰ ਆਵੈ ਜਾਵੈ ॥
ਸੋ ਮੰਗਾ ਦਾਨੁ ਗੁਸਾਈਆ ਜਿਤੁ ਭੁਖ ਲਹਿ ਜਾਵੈ ॥
ਪ੍ਰਭ ਜੀਉ ਦੇਵਹੁ ਦਰਸਨੁ ਆਪਣਾ ਜਿਤੁ ਢਾਢੀ ਤ੍ਰਿਪਤਾਵੈ ॥
ਅਰਦਾਸਿ ਸੁਣੀ ਦਾਤਾਰਿ ਪ੍ਰਭਿ ਢਾਢੀ ਕਉ ਮਹਲਿ ਬੁਲਾਵੈ ॥ਪ੍ਰਭ ਦੇਖਦਿਆ ਦੁਖ ਭੁਖ ਗਈ ਢਾਢੀ ਕਉ ਮੰਗਣੁ
ਚਿਤਿ ਨ ਆਵੈ ॥
ਸਭੇ ਇਛਾ ਪੂਰੀਆ ਲਗਿ ਪ੍ਰਭ ਕੈ ਪਾਵੈ ॥ਹਉ ਨਿਰਗੁਣੁ ਢਾਢੀ ਬਖਸਿਓਨੁ ਪ੍ਰਭਿ ਪੁਰਖਿ ਵੇਦਾਵੈ ॥੯॥

5ᵗʰ Guru | Pourree |
Ho Dtaadtee Dhar Gun Gaavadhaa Jae Har Prabh Bhaavai |
Prabh Maeraa Thhir Thhaavaree Hor Aavai Jaavai |
So Mangaa Dhaan Guosaaeeaa Jith Bhukh Lehi Jaavai |
Prabh Jeeo Dhaevahu Dharasan Aapanaa Jith Dtaadtee Thripathaavai |
Aradhaas Sunee Dhaathaar Prabh Dtaadtee Ko Mehal Bulaavai |
Prabh Dhaekhadhiaa Dhukh Bhukh Gee Dtaadtee Ko Mangan Chith N Aavai |
Sabhae Eishhaa Pooreeaa Lag Prabh Kai Paavai |
Ho Niragun Dtaadtee Bakhasioun Prabh Purakh Vaedhaavai |9|    Page-1097

Like the drops of water merge and become one with the
ocean; like waves in the stream merge and become one with
the stream and like the air merges with air, my mind is
completely calm and has merged with the Lord; I now see
Him everywhere!
Why should I come again and again into the life and death
cycle? The coming and going happen under His Will; I have
realized this and merged into Him!

---

ਰਾਗੁ ਮਾਰੂ ਬਾਣੀ ਕਬੀਰ ਜੀਉ ਕੀ ॥
ਉਦਕ ਸਮੁੰਦ ਸਲਲ ਕੀ ਸਾਖਿਆ ਨਦੀ ਤਰੰਗ ਸਮਾਵਹਿਗੇ ॥
ਸੁੰਨਹਿ ਸੁੰਨ ਮਿਲਿਆ ਸਮਦਰਸੀ ਪਵਨ ਰੂਪ ਹੋਇ ਜਾਵਹਿਗੇ ॥੧॥
ਬਹੁਰਿ ਹਮ ਕਾਹੇ ਆਵਹਿਗੇ ॥ ਆਵਨ ਜਾਨਾ ਹੁਕਮੁ ਤਿਸੈ ਕਾ ਹੁਕਮੈ ਬੁਝਿ ਸਮਾਵਹਿਗੇ ॥੧॥ ਰਹਾਉ ॥
Raag Maaroo Baanee Kabeer Jeeo Kee |
Oudhak Samundh Salal Kee Saakhiaa Nadhee Tharang Samaavehigae |
Sunnehi Sunn Miliaa Samadharasee Pavan Roop Hoe Jaavehigae |1|
Bahur Ham Kaahae Aavehigae |
Aavan Jaanaa Hukam Thisai Kaa Hukamai Bujh Samaavehigae |1| Pause |
Page-1103

O' my sister friend, the clouds are bursting with rain; the Lord Guest has come to my home! I am meek; my Lord and Master is the Ocean of Mercy; I am absorbed in the nine treasures of the Lord's Name. I have prepared all sorts of foods in various ways, and all sorts of sweet desserts. I have made my kitchen pure and sacred. Now, O' my Sovereign Lord King, please sample my food! When my Playful Beloved came into my household, then I found total peace and happiness!

ਰਾਗੁ ਮਲਾਰ ਮਹਲਾ ੫ ॥
ਬਰਸੈ ਮੇਘੁ ਸਖੀ ਘਰਿ ਪਾਹੁਨ ਆਏ ॥
ਮੋਹਿ ਦੀਨ ਕ੍ਰਿਪਾ ਨਿਧਿ ਠਾਕੁਰ ਨਵ ਨਿਧਿ ਨਾਮਿ ਸਮਾਏ ॥੧॥ ਰਹਾਉ ॥
ਅਨਿਕ ਪ੍ਰਕਾਰ ਭੋਜਨ ਬਹੁ ਕੀਏ ਬਹੁ ਬਿੰਜਨ ਮਿਸਟਾਏ ॥
ਕਰੀ ਪਾਕਸਾਲ ਸੋਚ ਪਵਿਤ੍ਰਾ ਹੁਣਿ ਲਾਵਹੁ ਭੋਗੁ ਹਰਿ ਰਾਏ ॥੨॥
ਜਉ ਗ੍ਰਿਹਿ ਲਾਲੁ ਰੰਗੀਓ ਆਇਆ ਤਉ ਮੈ ਸਭਿ ਸੁਖ ਪਾਏ ॥੩॥
Raag Malaar Mehalaa 5 |
Barasai Maegh Sakhee Ghar Paahun Aaeae |
Mohi Dheen Kirapaa Nidhh Thaakur Nav Nidhh Naam Samaaeae |1| Pause |
Anik Prakaar Bhojan Bahu Keeeae Bahu Binjan Misattaaeae |
Karee Paakasaal Soch Pavithraa Hun Laavahu Bhog Har Raaeae |2|
|Jo Grihi Laal Rangeeou Aaeiaa Tho Mai Sabh Sukh Paaeae |3|    Page-1266

Says Kabeer, the True Guru (Lord), the Spiritual Warrior, has shot me with His Arrow. As soon as it struck me, I fell to the ground, with a hole in my heart!

ਸਲੋਕ ਭਗਤ ਕਬੀਰ ਜੀਉ ਕੇ
ਕਬੀਰ ਸਤਿਗੁਰ ਸੂਰਮੇ ਬਾਹਿਆ ਬਾਨੁ ਜੁ ਏਕੁ ॥
ਲਾਗਤ ਹੀ ਭੁਇ ਗਿਰਿ ਪਰਿਆ ਪਰਾ ਕਰੇਜੇ ਛੇਕੁ ॥੧੯੪॥

Salok Bhagath Kabeer Jeeo Kae |
Kabeer Sathigur Sooramae Baahiaa Baan J Eaek |
Laagath Hee Bhue Gir Pariaa Paraa Karaejae Shhaek |194| Page-1374

O' brother, the one who has tasted the Lord's Name, only he knows the taste; it is like the dumb man tasting sweet candy, but cannot describe! If someone is blessed with the Gem of Lord's Name and tries to hide it, he can't; because it becomes visible from his looks!

ਸੋਰਠਿ ਮਹਲਾ ੪ ॥
ਜਿਨਿ ਇਹ ਚਾਖੀ ਸੋਈ ਜਾਨੈ ਗੂੰਗੇ ਕੀ ਮਿਠਿਆਈ ॥
ਰਤਨੁ ਲੁਕਾਇਆ ਲੂਕੈ ਨਾਹੀ ਜੇ ਕੋ ਰਖੈ ਲੁਕਾਈ ॥੪॥

Sorath 4th Guru |
Jin Eih Chaakhee Soee Jaanai Goongae Kee Mithiaaee |
Rathan Lukaaeiaa Lookai Naahee Jae Ko Rakhai Lukaaee |4| Page-607

A glimpse of the True Guru (Lord) left me bereft of all my consciousness, senses, intelligence, cleverness and all other considered wisdom of the world. I lost my awareness, attachment of mind with insignificant matters, desires to acquire base or futile ego inflating knowledge, and other worldly predicaments.

---

ਬਾਣੀ ਭਾਈ ਗੁਰਦਾਸ ।
ਦਰਸਨ ਦੇਖਤ ਹੀ ਸੁਧਿ ਕੀ ਨ ਸੁਧਿ ਰਹੀ ਬੁਧਿ ਕੀ ਨ ਬੁਧਿ ਰਹੀ ਮਤਿ ਮੈ ਨ ਮਤਿ ਹੈ ।
ਸੁਰਤਿ ਮੈ ਨ ਸੁਰਤਿ ਅਉ ਧਿਆਨ ਮੈ ਨ ਧਿਆਨੁ ਰਹਿਓ ਗਿਆਨ ਮੈ ਨ ਗਿਆਨ ਰਹਿਓ ਗਤਿ ਮੈ ਨ ਗਤਿ ਹੈ ।
ਕਬਿਤ 9

Baani Bhai Gurdas |
Darasan Daykhat Hee Sudhi Kee N Sudhi Rahee , Budhi Kee N Budhi Rahee
Mati Mai N Mati Hai |
Surati Mai N Surati Au Dhiaan Mai N Dhiaanu Rahiao , Giaan Mai N Giaan
Rahiao Gati Mai N Gati Hai |

References

## References

Guru Granth Sahib (The Holy Scripture), 1432 Pages. Punjabi Translation of GGS by Prof. Sahib Singh, 10 Volumes.

Website: SearchGurbani.com

GGS Punjabi and English Translation by SGPC, the Sikh Gurdwara Prabandhak Committee, 8 Volumes.

Gurbani Vichars (GGS Contemplations), 132 writings by Revered Bauji (Jaswant Singh).

Bandagi Naama and Ardaas, S. Raghbir Singh Bir.

Waheguru Darshan by S. Sher Singh.

Puratan Janamsakhi and other books by Bhai Vir Singh.

Prakasina and other books by Prof, Puran Singh.

Mahan Kosh, Encyclopedia of Sikh Literature, by Bhai Kahn Singh Nabha.

The Punjabi to English Dictionary by Bhai Maya Singh.

Made in the USA
Monee, IL
15 July 2021